The field of criminology has always foct  the power*less*. There is overwhelming evi ated with the crimes of the power*ful*. Thi first textbook that systematically addresses the crimes of the powerful. The authors are long-standing and highly-regarded criminological students of the crimes of the powerful. They have here produced a comprehensive survey of what contemporary criminology and criminal justice students need to know about such crimes. All reputable criminology and criminal justice programs should offer a course on crimes of the powerful, if they do not already do so. Instructors of such a course make a wise choice if they choose to assign this accessible, provocative textbook. It addresses the most consequential types of crimes, and initiatives to control such crimes.

David O. Friedrichs, *Distinguished Professor, Department of Sociology, Criminal Justice and Criminology, University of Scranton, USA*

Confronting the powerful is confronting—especially when the crimes, harms, threats and risks produced by the powerful are seen as simply a "natural" part of everyday life. This book challenges this status quo by exposing the crimes of the powerful to systematic critical scrutiny, thereby demonstrating that these elite activities far outweigh conventional crimes in their damaging social, economic and ecological impacts. The entrenchment of general misery is socially constructed by the powerful, in the interests of the powerful. This book explains why this is the case, and what can be done about it. A must read.

Rob White, *Professor of Criminology, University of Tasmania, Australia*

Theoretically astute, empirically rich, global in scope and always student-oriented, this passionate yet considered text is a significant contribution for those who seek to mainstream the crimes of the powerful in the teaching and learning of criminology. This is not just a superb book about power and the powerful—but represents a thoroughgoing challenge to them.

Steve Tombs, *Professor, Head of Social Policy and Criminology at the Open University and Director of the International Centre for Comparative Criminological Research, UK*

This outstanding book shines a bright light into the dark area of the crimes of the powerful, a darkness that too few criminology and criminal justice students ever get to explore. Rothe and Kauzlarich do an excellent job of introducing students to the study of the criminal acts of the powerful, illuminating a form of criminality that inflicts the most harm and fills the world with death and devastation, misery, and want.

Ronald C. Kramer, *Professor of Sociology, Western Michigan University, USA*

Rothe and Kauzlarich provide a thorough and meticulous guide to the "Crimes of the Powerful." Unlike many textbooks this is an impassioned and engaging introduction. A "must have" text for any criminology student!

Simon Pemberton, *Birmingham Fellow, School of Social Policy, University of Birmingham, UK*

Crimes of the Powerful

As politicians and the media perpetuate the stereotype of the "common criminal," crimes committed by the powerful remain for the most part invisible, or are reframed as a "bad decision" or a "rare mistake." This is a topic that remains marginalized within the field of criminology and criminal justice, yet crimes of the powerful cause more harm, perpetuate more inequalities, and result in more victimization than street crimes.

Crimes of the Powerful: An introduction is the first textbook to bring together and show the symbiotic relationships between the related fields of state crime, white-collar crime, corporate crime, financial crime, organized crime, and environmental crime. Dawn L. Rothe and David Kauzlarich introduce the many types of crimes, methodological issues associated with research, theoretical relevance, and issues surrounding regulations and social controls for crimes of the powerful. Themes covered include:

- media, culture, and the Hollywoodization of crimes of the powerful;
- theoretical understanding and the study of the crimes of the powerful;
- a typology of crimes of the powerful with examples and case studies;
- victims of the crimes of the powerful;
- the regulation and resistance of elite crime.

An ideal introductory text for both undergraduate and postgraduate students taking modules on the crimes of the powerful, white-collar crime, state crime, and green criminology, this text includes chapter summaries, activities and discussion questions, and lists of additional resources including films, websites, and additional readings.

Dawn L. Rothe is Professor of Criminology at Old Dominion University, USA, the Director of the International State Crime Research Center, and of the PhD in Criminology Program at Old Dominion University. She is the author or co-author of eight books and over seven dozen peer-reviewed articles and book chapters, some of which have been reproduced and translated into Italian, Spanish, and Chinese. She has formerly served as Chair of the American Society of Criminology Division of Critical Criminology.

David Kauzlarich is Professor of Sociology at Southern Illinois University Edwardsville, USA, and Editor-in-Chief of *Critical Criminology: An International Journal*. He is widely published in the areas of state crime, criminological theory, and resistance to crimes of the powerful.

Global Issues in Crime and Justice

Crimes of the Powerful

An introduction

Dawn L. Rothe and David Kauzlarich

Routledge
Taylor & Francis Group
LONDON AND NEW YORK

First published 2016
by Routledge
2 Park Square, Milton Park, Abingdon, Oxon OX14 4RN

and by Routledge
711 Third Avenue, New York, NY 10017

Routledge is an imprint of the Taylor & Francis Group, an informa business

© 2016 Dawn L. Rothe and David Kauzlarich

British Library Cataloguing in Publication Data
A catalogue record for this book is available from the British Library

Library of Congress Cataloguing in Publication Data
Rothe, Dawn, 1961– author. | Kauzlarich, David, author.
Title: Crimes of the powerful: an introduction / Dawn L. Rothe and David Kauzlarich.
Description: Abingdon, Oxon; New York, NY: Routledge, 2016. |
Series: Global issues in crime and justice; 5 | Includes bibliographical
references and index. Identifiers: LCCN 2015041076 |
ISBN 9781138797932 (hardback) | ISBN 9781138797949 (pbk.) |
ISBN 9781315756776 (ebook) Subjects: LCSH: State crimes. |
Commercial crimes. | Criminology–Political aspects.
Classification: LCC HV6251.6.R67 2016 | DDC 364.1–dc23
LC record available at http://lccn.loc.gov/2015041076

ISBN: 978-1-138-79793-2 (hbk)
ISBN: 978-1-138-79794-9 (pbk)
ISBN: 978-1-315-75677-6 (ebk)

Typeset in Times New Roman
by Out of House Publishing

Contents

PART III
The master's tools and beyond   181

Illustrations

Figures

Images

Every effort has been made to identify, and make an appropriate citation to, the original sources. If there have been any accidental errors, or omissions, we apologize to those concerned.

Tables

A reflexive preamble

We are often asked what brings our passion and academic pursuit to crimes of the powerful and so we decided it was time for a full disclosure, to break the chains of academic correctness. Neither of us is a fan or believer, if you will, in the dogmatic doctrine of positivist epistemology, where the researcher offers a presumably value-free and objective analysis. Contrary to this, we choose to commit positivistic blasphemy: to reject our science's delusional notions that we can somehow objectively understand phenomena by leaving behind our own life experiences, knowledge, biases, values, and worldviews. We also reject the notion that private should not be public, as it is only by being honest and open about our own oppression, challenges, joys, and pains that we can cast off our self-imposed chains of silence and conformity by resisting and rejecting an oppressive system of self-censorship. As such, we are proud of who we are and where we come from.

Studying crimes of the powerful is, to us, an outcome of living within the lower stratus of a system of unequal power relations, domination, and subjugation where dominant "knowledge" and "truths" dictate our self-definitions and attempt to define our life trajectories. "Get a job, get married, work hard, be satisfied of being nothing." We are a proud part of the lower working class, having watched both of our dads struggle to make a living and provide for us by working swing shifts in a steel mill and a glass factory in the Midwest, as their bodies endured the havoc of the corporate entity that exploited their labor, health, and overall well-being for profit. Dawn's father bears the scars of hundreds of pieces of steel shrapnel to this day, his skin bleeding upon touch. He has lived through experiences of the steel mill furnaces exploding, casting rockets of molten steel in every direction and injuring his foot, though he continued to work through the rest of his shift, only then going to a hospital and undergoing massive skin grafting. Dave's father lost three fingers and much of his hearing at work. His great-grandfather fell to the ongoing threat of black lung disease that so many miners across the globe continue to experience and, as a result of which, their families continue to deal with their loss.

Upon "adulthood" (defined loosely), we ventured out into this same world of our parents, holding our pride, willingly giving our labor, tears, and bodies to the powerful. Between us both, we have worked as a waitress, bartender, bouncer, and factory and warehouse laborer, sometimes holding down two or three jobs at a time and not as a means to get us through school, but to provide for ourselves and our children. Yet, we dreamed of more with an insatiable appetite to understand life, the meaning of being in this "game," and thinking there had to be more to living than working to live. We are lucky today, we sit in privileged positions. However, we cannot ever let go of where we come from, of our struggles, our pain, our joy, and our tears, nor assimilate fully into this academic tower, and nor would we want to. As such, we have dedicated years to studying, exposing, and teaching about the crimes of the powerful, continuing the practice of our mentors and theirs by pushing the boundaries of "acceptable" criminological inquiry.

After all, the "truth" and "knowledge" of the working class is reified within the broader system from education to politics; moreover, it continues to be used, misused, and abused, as if the term "working class" is now some acceptable cliché. Moreover, this is reproduced even within criminology, reinforcing our belief in bringing a critical perspective to our research as well as leaving behind the orthodox tradition of seeing crime, criminals, and victimization linked to the lower classes. After all, how many studies can predict the likelihood of someone committing some form of street crime on the basis of their education, class, or sex, while generally going by abstract, imputed statistics? This myopic view not only reduces human agency and value, but serves to legitimize and valorize the dysfunctional system that facilitates and authorizes the violence and harms of the powerful.

We are also tired of being told that our stories are inspiring, of people wanting to hold up our lives as examples. We are not symbols or tools to be used to legitimate a system that reifies the very power relations and domination that we grew up with and lived with for many years in our adult lives. We do not want to be a part of the "chess board" or be a poster child for the hyper-individualized lifestyle within this neoliberal capitalistic system that is dysfunctional for the many. We refuse to be a part of, or be used to promote, the dogma of the "American ethos," to tell people "you too can bring yourself out of the gutter, the impoverished, the lower working class; just work hard and go to school." No, we believe in humanism, if we have to accept any label. We are all but one, and what others feel and experience in this system of oppression and exploitation we feel and experience too. We are not worse than, nor better, we simply are. As such, we now try to give our voice, passion, and energy to unmasking the charade of the system, the symbiotic relations and pathways that continue to harm and wreak violence across the globe.

Preface

Many undergraduate criminology and criminal justice students assume that topics addressed in core courses such as Introduction to Criminal Justice, Criminology, Juvenile Delinquency, Policing, Courts, Corrections, and so forth, represent the core of crime and criminal justice, and that traditional street crimes such as robbery and assault place individuals at the most risk and harm. This text will take a different route by introducing you to a topic that continues to remain marginalized within the field of criminology and criminal justice, yet causes more harm, costs more to society and individuals, perpetuates more inequalities, and results in more victimization than street crimes. We call these "crimes of the powerful." Many commentators—especially in recent years—have noted the parochialism of much mainstream criminology. We would like to think that this text makes one modest contribution to the larger project of transcending such parochialism, and that students of crime and criminal justice at all levels will derive some benefit from such endeavors.

We are not deriding, wholesale, the value of mainstream criminological scholarship and research. Conventional crime, broadly defined, is real and clearly has multiple harmful consequences, disproportionately visited upon the disadvantaged and underprivileged. But we also claim here that mainstream criminological and criminal justice research serves unfairly the interests of the powerful and privileged classes, and either intentionally or unintentionally contributes to the perpetuation of many forms of oppression and injustice against the powerless and the underprivileged classes. Furthermore, we would suggest that at least some types of conventional crime and the control of such crimes have been over-studied by now, with diminishing returns in terms of achieving socially useful outcomes (Rothe and Friedrichs 2014).

Crimes of the powerful have surely been under-studied to date, and we like to think that promotion of greater attention to such phenomena is as, if not more, important than the overwhelming focus on street crime. You may be asking why, if our assertion is correct, would crimes that cause more damage, harm, and victims be relegated to the back burner while issues such as juvenile delinquency, homicide, or drug use are a mainstay of traditional criminology and criminal justice textbooks?

There are a host of issues that have kept crimes of the powerful from becoming a main topic within criminology and criminal justice texts, courses, and the field more broadly, many of which will be touched upon in the following chapters. One of the largest obstacles has to do with challenging and changing the "criminal" stereotype. After all, politicians love to tell us about the dangers we face due to "rampant street crime": from gun violence to gangs, drugs, and home-grown terrorists, all of which necessitate a "tough on crime" agenda. Likewise, the media further perpetuates the stereotype of the "common criminal": young black males and the impoverished class. Crimes committed by the powerful, for the most part, remain invisible from political discourse or media coverage. Indeed, the rare cases that receive exposure are more often than not reframed as a "mistake," "accident," "bad choice," or "bad apple." Most cases are reframed to legitimate the violence perpetuated by the powerful. Further, as we will suggest in the later chapters of this book, most if not all crimes of the powerful are part and parcel of the broader political and economic structures that maintain such criminality and, in other cases, it is through the casuistry of law that crimes of the powerful come to be normalized and accepted. In the end, however, crimes of the powerful remain hidden, as do their victims, much like the "pink elephant" in the room.

Another barrier to the "mainstreaming" of crimes of the powerful within the criminology and criminal justice curriculum, research, and general focus of students is the belief that any criminological attention to crimes of the powerful and their control is not to be analyzed within the dominant positivistic perspective—rendering it to "less than scientific" scrutiny. We do not accept this position; rather, we note that overemphasis on a specific method misses the complexities of humans. Additionally, it is often claimed that a criminology of crimes of the powerful is highly unlikely to have a measurable influence on those who make and implement crime-related policies. As one author has stated recently in relation to crimes of globalization, we have no illusions about the resistance of policymakers and practitioners to engaging in any way with such scholarship, for multiple reasons, and most especially if it explicitly or implicitly challenges their interests and agendas (Rothe and Friedrichs 2014). But has mainstream criminological scholarship been constructively influential with those policymakers and practitioners? Arguably, in some limited areas it has been, but often only when it is in synch with their political agendas.

We do not have any illusions. Altogether, we like to think that it is worthwhile to produce criminological scholarship that reveals the direct and indirect harms and crimes committed by the powerful and that dissects situations that are demonstrably harmful and perpetuate the conditions that facilitate these types of crimes as well as produce especially pervasive forms of social injustice. One of our objectives for this book, then, is to help render visible a hitherto largely invisible and marginalized type of crime, in the hope that it will over time become the focus of a significant volume of criminological inquiry and a common discussion amongst students of criminology and criminal justice.

The following chapters explore many of the pieces that comprise our overall understanding of crimes of the powerful. In Part I, we set out to define and conceptualize the crimes of the powerful, discussing their presentation in the media, how they are researched and measured, and how to theoretically and philosophically understand the causes and correlates of the crimes. Part II is devoted to an examination of specific forms of crimes of the powerful, including state, corporate, state-corporate, and others. We review dozens of cases of these forms of crime to provide readers with a good grasp of the behavioral elements of the crimes. The third and last part of the book is devoted to regulating and resisting elite crime. In this section, we raise questions about both traditional and novel ways of addressing the immense problems created by crimes of the powerful. All told, we hope to provide students with a rich but broad overview of a class of crimes that urgently requires more public and scholarly attention.

Reference

Rothe, D. L., and Friedrichs, D. O. (2014). *Crimes of Globalization*. London: Routledge.

Part I

The foundations

Chapter 1

An introduction to crimes
of the powerful

Any endeavor to expand criminological inquiry to crimes of the powerful should first begin by addressing what most students of criminology and criminal justice take for granted: the definition of crime. The concept of crime has had quite diverse meanings throughout the long history of its use and, as we will discuss, a certain understanding has been the dominant and accepted one, namely that a crime is an act prohibited by the law. Yet, as Michalowski (2013: 1) states, "criminology is a subject matter more than an academic discipline …[it] occupies the contradictory position of being a framework for intellectual inquiry into matters of crime and justice while simultaneously operating as an extension of the political state." It is the state, not criminologists' agendas, "that determines what behaviors are legal, which are illegal, and among those that are illegal, which will be nominated as serious crimes, which will be lesser offenses or minor infractions, and which will be treated as non-criminal administrative matters." A recent anthology—Mary Bosworth and Carolyn Hoyle's *What is Criminology?* (2011)—recognizes that there are vastly different conceptions of what criminology is and ought to be, and accordingly of how crime is best defined. There is, in fact, a long-standing tradition of critique of conventional conceptions of crime that have been advanced by self-described radical or critical criminologists (for example, see DeKeseredy and Dragiewicz 2012; Tifft and Sullivan 1980; Watts *et al.* 2008). Furthermore, orthodox criminology generally self-identifies as a scientific endeavor and is inherently biased in favor of definitions of crime that lend themselves easily to quantitative analysis. It has been suggested that this bias inevitably privileges attention to the conventional forms of crime that by their very natures lend themselves more readily to operationalization. In one sense, then, criminologists' focus on street crime reinforces individual, rational, and even moral explanations of criminality, in so doing impeding any persistent critique of existing social arrangements. The dominant focus on state definitions of crime has resulted in an inverted criminology where the gravest social harms receive the least attention (Michalowski 2013). David Friedrichs suggests that there is "an *inverse relationship* between the level of harms caused by some human (individual or organizational) activity and the level of criminological concern" (Friedrichs 2009: 1).

Altogether, the critical analyses of the definition of crime promote attention to the crimes of the powerful rather than the crimes of the powerless. Our approach here is more closely aligned with a zemiological approach, while still recognizing some value to using state-produced definitions of crime, to include those harms that are not recognized by the state for a variety of reasons that we will discuss in more detail in subsequent chapters (Friedrichs and Schwartz 2007; Hillyard *et al.* 2004). This includes the harms of the existing social structure that facilitates crimes of the powerful, from hyper-commodification to unequal social formations. After all, most people are concerned with reducing harm and victimization in society, not necessarily what legislators decide is against the law.

The next point that needs some brief attention, when talking about crimes of the powerful, is what we really mean when we talk about "power" and the "powerful." After all, conceptualizations of power vary greatly within the social sciences and in sociology and criminology in particular. Definitions range from having the capacity to direct or influence others or the course of events or resources; having political or social authority or control over others; or having authority that is given or delegated to someone or to a group (namely, government or police). It is generally accepted that power is tied to authority and trust. For example, Sutherland (1939), when defining white-collar crime, suggested that it involves individuals of respectability and high social status, and that the crime includes a violation of delegated or implied trust. Both of these generally involve legitimate authority to exercise control over others and resources. With these positions, there is trust. We have politicians in positions of authority (power), whom we trust to represent and protect us; we trust heads of corporations not to endanger the environment or to produce products that will result in physical harm. In other words, we, through trust and granted authority, give power to individuals in positions where they exercise control over us and/or our resources.

While we do not wish to spend a great time on the debate over what is power and who are the powerful (as this will also be discussed further in Chapter 4), it is important to recognize that power exists only through social relationships and is historically and culturally specific, as well as always being present throughout time. It is not an identifiable object; rather, it is produced and reproduced within social structures: power subjugates. Power is exercised, obtained, legitimated, and maintained through capital accumulation of varying types from the economic, military, and political, to social status, discourse, and knowledge. Perhaps the easiest way to determine power and the powerful, then, is to contest those relations by resisting the state definitions of crime, recognizing and claiming the harms of those with power as crimes.

Figure 1.1 The two main types of white-collar crime

Crimes of the powerful as a contested topic

Crimes of the powerful, as a subject matter, have been critiqued for problems of inclusion and exclusion of "crimes." This extends beyond being marginalized within the field of criminology, and continues to remain a contested topic even within the various fields that fall under the umbrella of crimes of the powerful. Of course, in part this is due to the debate over the expansion of the term "crime" beyond the traditionally accepted state-provided definition. But, it is also a matter of which harms and crimes should be considered. Are crimes of the powerful the same as what are called "white-collar crimes?" We suggest crimes of the powerful are far more expansive. However, we should first discuss what falls under the definition of white-collar crime. Returning again to Sutherland's call for criminology (at that time, sociology) to expand the study of crimes to include regulatory violations committed by individuals of high social status during the course of their occupations, the expansion of "crime" was still limited to state-produced definitions of law and regulations. Additionally, his definition was vague and ambiguous, leading to controversy—given that he defined white-collar crimes as those committed by individuals during their occupations—yet much of his research examined corporations. As a result, the field of white-collar crime has examined what we call occupational and organizational crimes (see Figure 1.1), both based on two different understandings of Sutherland's definition.

Here, the distinction is that occupational crimes are committed by individuals during the course of their occupations for their own self-interests (for example, a bank teller stealing $10,000), while organizational crimes are committed by individuals during the course of their occupations for their organization's interests (for example, cooking the audit books to increase stock value and sales). Occupational crimes are committed generally by lower level employees, or what is often referred to as middle- and upper-lower-class crimes. They generally involve those who are powerless more than powerful. We should also note here that corporations or organizations do not commit crimes, it is the individuals acting within them, even though we often refer to a company as an "entity" (for example, "I called Comcast today" or "McDonald's ripped me off of my cheeseburger"). In a legal sense, however, corporations have

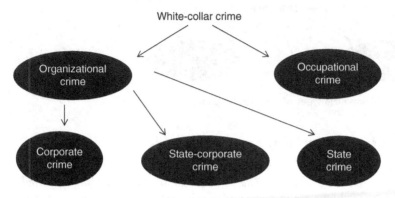

Figure 1.2 Varieties of white-collar crime

gained the legitimate status of individuals, which will be further discussed in later chapters.

Since the late 1970s and early 1980s, research on organizational crime has produced other fields of inquiry that now stand as recognized areas and are at least briefly touched upon in nearly all introductory criminology and criminal justice textbooks. There are many different terms used to describe these types of crime including suite crime, elite deviance, political crime, corporate crime, state-corporate crime, state-organized crime, government crime, and state crime. In some instances, some of the terms are referring to the same type of crime (state crime or government crime). We prefer to use the terms corporate crime, state-corporate crime, and state crime (see Figure 1.2).

State-corporate crime, first conceptualized by Kramer and Michalowski (1990: 4), is defined as "illegal or socially injurious actions that occur when *one* or more institutions or political governance pursue a goal in direct cooperation with one or more institutions of economic production and distribution." State-corporate crime increasingly came to be seen as taking two forms, although these often interact with each other. Accordingly, a distinction has emerged between state-facilitated and state-initiated crimes, and earlier works proposed and explored a "framework for examining how corporations and governments intersect to produce social harm" (Kramer *et al.* 2000: 263). Such intersections can work in a myriad of fashions: states can create laws that facilitate corporate wrongdoing and crimes (for example, the infamous savings and loan debacle in the United States), and regulatory and advisement agencies can simply fail to do their appointed tasks (for example, OSHA's failure to provide remedies for safety violations at an Imperial Chicken plant in Hamlet, North Carolina [Aulette and Michalowski 1993]; the FAA's failure to ground ValuJet [Matthews and Kauzlarich 2000], and NHTSA's failure to investigate tire malfunctions and roll-over incidents on Ford Explorers [Mullins 2006]). States and state actors can also directly collude and conspire with private corporations to violate laws, as in the case of Halliburton's war profiteering since the "war on terror" or Blackwater's killing of innocent civilians (Rothe 2006). With the increasingly international nature of corporate operations, capital accumulation, and dispersement, these types of crimes take on an increasingly international flavor and situation (Friedrichs and Friedrichs 2002; Rothe *et al.* 2006).

The field of state crime is one of the newer areas of research, beginning in 1989 with Chambliss' presidential speech at the American Society of Criminology conference, where he made a call to criminologists to pay attention to state-organized crime. Chambliss defined state crime as "acts defined by law as criminal and committed by state officials in pursuit of their jobs as representatives of the state" (1989: 184). Kramer and Michalowski (1990) quickly followed with the definition of state-facilitated crime: those activities of the state which fail to constrain criminal and dangerous behaviors. Since Chambliss' speech, the field of state crime has grown significantly and with that, the definition of state crime has also expanded. This includes acts that are harmful but not criminalized by the state (for example, torture) or by the international political community through international treaties (for example, crimes of aggression), as well as acts of omission (for example, failing to respond to a natural disaster or prevent one that could have been prevented through upgraded infrastructure). In recognizing the power of states' agents, a zemiological approach is necessary; given it is highly unlikely that a state is going to criminalize an act that serves its interests, the same is true for those holding these positions of power. This approach also avoids the limitations on state crime, often referred to as "international crime" or "supranational crime" where the focus is on violations of international criminal law (for example, war crimes, genocide, and crimes against humanity).

More recently, crimes of the powerful has expanded beyond the types noted above to include harms caused by international financial institutions: the World Bank and the International Monetary Fund. This new area of research has been coined "crimes of globalization" (Friedrichs and Friedrichs 2002; Rothe and Friedrichs 2014). They are the demonstrably harmful policies and practices of institutions and entities that are specifically a product of the forces of globalization, and that by their very nature operate within a global context.

To minimize the interplay of all of these institutions would be a mistake. The relationship between corporations, states, and international financial institutions is complex and it would be myopic to think that one operates independently of the others. As such, it is necessary to view these types of crimes (corporate, state-corporate, state, and international financial institutions: crimes of globalization) beyond their independent fields, bringing them together and recognizing the relations of power (see Figure 1.3).

The crimes of international financial institutions have a generic relationship to state-corporate crimes insofar as they are cooperative ventures involving public sector and private sector entities, and in some respects are hybrid public–private sector entities. In the recent era, Western states as well as corporations have promoted neoliberalism or a supposed "free market" model

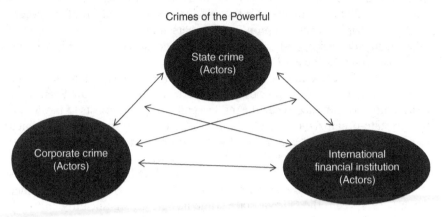

Figure 1.3 State, corporate, and international relationships

for the global political economy. Within such an environment the crimes of international financial institutions are intertwined with crimes of states and of corporations. The policies and practices of the international financial institutions are largely driven by the global agenda of powerful developed states such as the United States. These states in turn are strongly oriented toward supporting the interests of corporations.

While such inclusion may seem complete, we would be short-sighted if we limited crimes of the powerful to only those noted above. Consider the many crimes and harms committed by elite or powerful people who do not operate within a corporation, state, or international financial organization. What about organized crime syndicates, especially given their more often than not connections with corporations and/or states? What about the militia or insurgency groups that can exercise vast power and violence (for example, Joseph Kony and the Lord's Resistance Army)? What about various forms of transnational crimes that require immense resources and power, such as arms trafficking (for example, Viktor Bout)? These too need to be included in any discussion of crimes of the powerful. As such, we suggest that the various divisions—white-collar crime, corporate crime, state-corporate crime, state crime, crimes of globalization, organized crime, and even environmental crimes—be considered under one umbrella: crimes of the powerful. Otherwise, with the divisions and typologies that keep these various fields separate, one misses the broader symbiotic nature and relationship they have with each other, leading to the systematic, routine production and reproduction of crime and harm that are situated within the broader global neoliberal agenda (see Figure 1.4; see also Chapter 5 for more discussion on these relationships).

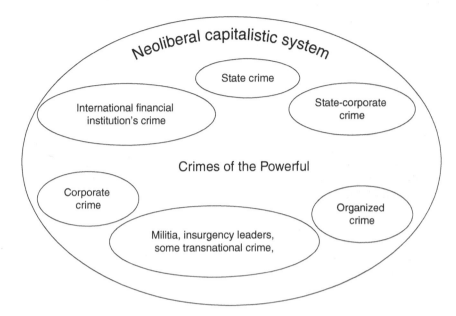

Figure 1.4 Neoliberal capitalism and crimes of the powerful

Of course, we can be criticized ourselves for our attention to crimes of the powerful. One could argue that a call for attention to crimes of the powerful and subsequent focus is not any different from traditional or orthodox criminology and its obsession with traditional street crime, save for the type of "crime" or "criminal," in that we are partaking in the same process of legitimating the broader social structure and system, perpetuating the status quo of power relations and subsequent harms. Yet, we suggest that it is through enhancing and expanding our conceptual, theoretical understandings of crimes of the powerful that a stronger push to resist them and the structures that produce and reproduce them will occur.

Having laid out in brief the various fields or subfields that examine crimes of the powerful, the following section provides more context for the scope of crimes committed by the powerful.

Scope of crimes of the powerful

The scope of crimes of the powerful is vast and by far outnumbers "street crime," yet, as we have noted, criminologists and students of criminology and criminal justice, as well as politicians and the media, overall neglect to give any sustained attention to crimes of power and the powerful. Here we provide a bit more of an overview of the scope of crimes of the powerful, their harms, and the likely costs.

Consider the following acts:

- Bribery
- Corruption
- Coups
- Covert war
- Crimes against humanity
- Cyber warfare
- Deforestation
- Defrauding citizens
- Denial of basic human rights
- Displacement of indigenous peoples
- Economic crisis/collapse
- Electoral fraud
- Faulty products
- "Forced" debt
- Forced disappearances
- Genocide
- Illegal detention
- Illegal mining
- Mandated structural adjustment policies
- Market domination
- Mass imprisonment
- Monopolies
- Nuclear production and threat to use
- Open pit mining
- Price fixing
- Price gouging
- Production and dumping of toxic waste
- State oppression
- Surveillance
- Systematic rape
- Targeted assassinations
- Torture
- Unfair labor practices
- Unsafe products
- Unsafe working conditions.

The list could go on, as many cases in later chapters will demonstrate. Within the past year there has been an abundance of crimes committed by the powerful. For example, consider the cases of Insull, Enron, Freddie Mac, Bank of America, Capital One, and other financial institutions and their role in the economic crisis as well as ongoing unethical practices. From fracking in the United States to oil extraction in Nigeria, consider the harms that result from these practices. When talking about states, a glance at the past two years tells a tale of corruption, electoral fraud, aggressive cyber warfare, surveillance of citizens' private information and behavior, assassinations, coups, political and physical oppression, displacement, torture, mass murder, crimes against humanity, denial of basic subsistence, illegal occupation of territories, forced land removal, and a host of cases of collusion between states, multinational corporations, organized crime syndicates, and international financial institutions, to mention only a few.

Consider that in one week of this writing (June 2–8, 2014), the headlines talk of many crimes of the powerful: "Indian police use water cannons to disperse women's rights protesters after gang-rape and murder" (Buncome 2014); "The Supreme Court refuses to support appeal and hold lower court's decision to not force James Risen to testify and disclose his source—a blow to journalists, free speech and whistleblowers" (Berman 2014); "Russia, China block Syria from facing International Criminal Court" (CNN 2014); "Boko Haram attack villages in Nigeria" (News 24 2014); "Russian indicted in cyber attack on Erie business" (Thompson 2014); "General Motors will pay a $35 million civil penalty to settle allegations brought by the Department of Transportation that the auto maker failed to report a safety defect in the Chevrolet Cobalt in a timely manner" (Corporate Crime Reporter 2014); "Former Homes & Land CEO charged with grand theft" (Rossman 2014); and "Report: Former Charlotte mayor to plead guilty to corruption charge" (MyFox8 2014). Israel continues to defy international public opinion and increases settlement construction in the West Bank and East Jerusalem "as retaliation against the new Palestinian consensus government backed by Hamas" (Kershner and Rudoren 2014).

Costs of the crimes of the powerful

The costs associated with these crimes are enormous. Costs are generally thought of in terms of monetary costs; however, the costs associated with crimes of the powerful are not limited to economic costs, whether direct or indirect. There are significant social, cultural, political, environmental, physical, and mental costs, none of which can be assigned random price tags or given a fixed dollar amount.

Financial costs

The financial costs of white-collar crime far exceed those resulting from traditional crimes. This reflects the greater frequency with which white-collar crimes are committed and also the fact that a single offense can result in losses running into millions of dollars. Estimates place direct financial losses resulting from traditional street crimes such as burglary, murder, and robbery at less than $30 billion per year (Federal Bureau of Investigation 2015). By contrast, losses attributed to occupational fraud alone (which is only a very small sliver of white-collar crime) have been estimated at hundreds of billions per year (Association of Certified Fraud Examiners 2013). Other white-collar crimes cost the public billions more: financial fraud by the Enron Corporation cost investors and employees $25–50 billion (Greider 2001); the savings and loan disaster of the late 1980s ended up costing more than $500 billion (Chambliss 1999: 152); and price fixing costs at least $60 billion a year (Friedrichs 2009). Although the overall financial costs of white-collar crime cannot be estimated with confidence—there are simply too many types and no systematic data collection for most of them—they are huge relative to street crimes. A conservative estimate puts the costs of street crime at only 6 percent of the costs of white-collar crime (Rosoff *et al.* 2010).

Damage to institutions and moral climate

Deception, fraud, price fixing, bribery, kickbacks, and violations of trust undermine principles of honesty and fair play. They also foster a moral climate in which lawlessness provokes little indignation, especially when its victims are vague entities such as "the public," "the consumer," "the corporation," and "the government," and occurs largely free from any sense of guilt on the part of offenders. This results in the erosion of economic and political institutions. Looking out for number one, beating the system, getting something for nothing, or doing a favor for a price become accepted and expected practices for all social strata. When there is pervasive and unpunished thievery and corruption among leaders in business, the professions, and government, street criminals can easily rationalize their own illegal conduct as no different from that of their "betters" (Kauzlarich *et al.* 2001; Rothe and Kauzlarich 2014).

More broadly, in terms of political, social, and cultural effects, consider that when the wealthy and privileged take advantage of the power they have over others, and when those who control state and corporate institutions refuse to reorganize their operations to meet human needs, society suffers socially and culturally. A culture of narcissism and selfishness breeds cruelty and thoughtlessness and a sense of hopelessness and cynicism for change on the part of the publics. Prioritizing making money or organizational goals over treating people with respect chips away at political and economic democracy, produces cover-ups that are sometimes worse than the initial offense (as in the Watergate case), alienates people from the political process, and continues to deposit more resources into the very systems of corruption and wealth that help produce white-collar crime in the first place. In Illinois, for example, two successive governors in recent years—Blagojevich and Ryan—have been imprisoned for corruption. The result is that few Illinoisans trust their government to do the right thing and likely expect that political dealings will be at least unethical on a regular basis, if not criminal.

Personal health and safety

Another of the greatest losses as a result of crimes of the powerful involves personal health and safety. The following are a few examples of the most commonly recognized types of harm:

- companies violating safety standards for their products (cars, tires, electrical appliances, toys, nightclothes, Christmas tree lights, and many others) expose their customers to possible injury or death;
- physicians who do unnecessary surgery expose their patients to the risk of surgical complications;
- pharmaceutical companies conspiring to fix high prices threaten the well-being of those who need but cannot afford their products;
- mine and factory bosses who violate health and safety regulations expose their workers to injury, disease, and death;
- companies manufacturing or selling contaminated food products or mislabeled drugs expose their customers to unnecessary health hazards.

Now consider how state crime may produce physical injury and death:

- illegal wars, invasions, and genocides have easily cost the lives of tens of millions of people in the twentieth and early twenty-first century;
- US governmental projects such as the manufacture and production of nuclear weapons have resulted in hundreds of thousands of deaths and perhaps millions of health problems;
- illegal radiation experiments and nuclear weapons testing have claimed the lives of thousands of US veterans and civilians. Thousands more have had their health compromised by such state actions;
- poor treatment of immigrants including those deemed "illegal immigrants";
- states' use of power for general oppression;
- the denial of basic rights across the globe within criminal justice systems as well as in everyday life;
- poor treatment of the impoverished including the homeless;
- state regulatory agencies that ignore their mandate to protect workers, airplane passengers, and the environment have directly and indirectly led to death and injury.

There can be little doubt that when the health and safety of the population as a whole are considered, the threats posed by crimes of the powerful are far greater than those posed by traditional crimes. This is not to minimize the dangers associated with violence, rape, and robbery, but, rather, to place the two broad categories of crime in perspective. It is easy to overlook the dangers posed by crimes of the powerful because these are often less visible, less direct, and appear less concrete than those of street crimes. They are also commonly committed by people or groups in positions of considerable power. Yet these crimes are extensive. Take, for instance, the physical dangers associated with environmental pollution in the air, water, soil, workplace, and home. Millions of workers are exposed every day to known carcinogens and other potentially lethal substances, often because corporations and businesses fail to meet environmental standards or find legal ways to circumvent them, including taking their practices to countries where they can operate with impunity, so exposing workers while exploiting their labor (Ruggiero and South 2013; Stretesky and Lynch 2014).

Many thousands of industrial workers will become ill or die because they work under conditions that needlessly expose them to carcinogens and severe respiratory ailments. Those in the rubber, steel, asbestos, coal, and chemical industries are especially vulnerable to such diseases. The December 1984 gas leak at the Union Carbide pesticide plant in Bhopal, India, one of the most costly industrial disasters of all time, has been tied to "unlawful, willful, malicious, and wanton" disregard for human safety and claimed at least 3,800 lives and injured hundreds and thousands more (Taylor, 2014). The Indian government eventually charged Union Carbide with moral responsibility and legal liability for the leak. For its part, the company accepted some responsibility, but denied any criminal negligence.

As with most forms of crime, the risks and costs of being victimized by crimes of the powerful are not borne equally. The young, poor, and elderly are especially vulnerable to environmental crimes and to frauds of all sorts; moreover, the impact is by far geopolitically split where the Global South does and will continue to bear the worst impact of environmental harms. As the population ages, we can expect to see more and more victimization of the elderly not only by fast talking salespeople, but by corporate marketers who capitalize on their fear of change, their susceptibility to illness, their fear of having inadequate insurance, and their loneliness.

Environmental damage is mostly caused by crimes of the powerful, not everyday people who drive their cars to work or use plastic bags at the grocery store. Rather, from climate change and global warming—what some feel to be the largest issue human beings have ever faced—all the way to fracking and other forms of pollution, these are largely the products of the normal operations of corporations that are facilitated by states and international financial institutions.

Summary

Crimes of the powerful involve a range of activities and harms from the economic to the physical and psychological. The costs of elite crime easily outweigh the costs of traditional street crimes such as robbery, burglary, and theft. Some crimes are committed for the gain of individuals, whereas others are motivated by corporate or government goals; in many cases, these are not so easily distinguishable. The latter are known as organizational crimes, while the former are usually referred to as occupational crimes. Criminologists have offered many different definitions of white-collar crime and the crimes of the powerful. This book uses the broadest definition of crime: that something is specifically against a written law is less important than if the action in question is socially harmful and just like an illegality, except for the name applied to the act or omission by a political authority.

Activities and discussion questions

1. How does political and economic power shape what we think and know about crime? What is the media's role in influencing views?
2. Ask friends or family for examples of white-collar crime or crimes of the powerful and determine how well they are at distinguishing them from traditional street crimes.
3. Many think crimes by corporations are only economic in nature. Do an Internet search for corporate violence and see what events, if any, are returned by your search.

References

Association of Certified Fraud Examiners (2013). Report to the Nations on Occupational Fraud and Abuse. Available at: www.acfe.com/rttn.aspx (accessed on July 14, 2015).

Aulette, J., and Michalowski, R. (1993). Fire in Hamlet: A Case Study of a State-Corporate Crime. In K. Tunnell (ed.), *Political Crime in Contemporary America: A Critical Approach*, 171–206. New York: Garland.

Berman, M. (2014). The Supreme Court Won't Intervene in the James Risen Case. What's Next? *The Washington Post*, June 2. Available at: www.washingtonpost.com/news/post-nation/wp/2014/06/02/the-supreme-court-wont-intervene-in-the-james-risen-case-whats-next/ (accessed on June 2, 2014).

Bosworth, M., and Hoyle, C. (2011). *What is Criminology?* Oxford: Oxford University Press.

Buncome, A (2014). Indian Police Use Water Cannons to Disperse Women's Rights Protesters after Gang-Rape and Murder. *The Independent*, June 2. Available at: www.independent.co.uk/news/world/indian-police-use-water-cannons-to-disperse-womens-rights-protesters-after-gangrape-and-murder-9474305.html (accessed on June 2, 2014).

Chambliss, W. J. (1989). State-Organized Crime: The American Society of Criminology, 1988 Presidential Address. *Criminology*, 27(2): 183–207.

Chambliss, William J. (1999). *Power, Politics and Crime*. Boulder, CO: Westview.

CNN (2014). Russia, China Block Syria from Facing International Criminal Court. May 22. Available at: www.cnn.com/2014/05/22/world/syria-un/ (accessed on June 5, 2014).

Corporate Crime Reporter (2014). Auto Safety Group Calls for Criminal Prosecution of GM Execs. May 16. Available at: www.corporatecrimereporter.com/news/200/auto-safety-group-calls-for-criminal-prosecution-of-gm-execs/ (accessed on June 5, 2014).

DeKeseredy, W., and Dragiewicz, M. (2012). *Routledge Handbook of Critical Criminology*. London: Routledge.

Federal Bureau of Investigation (2015). Uniform Crime Reports. Available at: www.fbi.gov/about-us/cjis/ucr/crime-in-the-u.s/2014 (accessed on July 15, 2015).

Friedrichs, D. (2009). *Trusted Criminals: White Collar Crime in Contemporary Society*. Belmont, CA: Wadsworth.

Friedrichs, D. O., and Friedrichs, J. (2002). The World Bank and Crimes of Globalization: A Case Study. *Social Justice*, 29(1/2): 1–12.

Friedrichs, D., and Schwartz, M. (2007). Editors' Introduction: On Social Harm and a Twenty-First Century Criminology. *Crime, Law & Social Change*, 48(1/2): 1–7.

Greider, W. (2001). Enron's Rise and Fall. *The Nation*, December 24: 5–6.

Hillyard, P., Pantazis, C., Tombs, S., and Gordon, D. (eds.) (2004). *Beyond Criminology: Taking Harm Seriously*. London: Pluto Press.

Kauzlarich, D., Matthews, R. A., and Miller, W. J. (2001). Toward a Victimology of State Crime. *Critical Criminology: An International Journal*, 10(3): 173–194.

Kershner, I., and Rudoren, J. (2014). Israel Expands Settlements to Rebuke Palestinians. *New York Times*, June 5. Available at: www.nytimes.com/2014/06/06/world/middleeast/new-israeli-settlement-plans-draw-swift-condemnation.html?partner=rss&emc=rss&_r=2 (accessed on June 8, 2014).

Kramer, R., and Michalowski, R. (1990). Toward an Integrated Theory of State-Corporate Crime. Paper presented at the American Society of Criminology, Baltimore, MD, November.

Kramer, R., Michalowski, R., and Kauzlarich, D. (2000). The Origins and Development of the Concept and Theory of State-Corporate Crime. *Crime and Delinquency*, 48(2): 263–282.

Matthews, R. A., and Kauzlarich, D. (2000). The Crash of ValuJet Flight 592: A Case Study in State-Corporate Crime. *Sociological Focus*, 33(3): 281–298.

Michalowski, R. (2013). What is Crime? Why is Criminology? Paper presented at the American Society of Criminology, Chicago, IL, November.

Mullins, C. W. (2006). Bridgestone/Firestone, Ford, and the NHTSA. In R. Kramer and R. Michalowski (eds.), *State-Corporate Crime: Wrongdoing at the Intersection of Business and Government*, 134–148. Piscataway, NJ: Rutgers University Press.

MyFox8 (2014). Report: Former Charlotte Mayor to Plead Guilty to Corruption Charge. June 2. Available at: http://myfox8.com/2014/06/02/report-former-charlotte-mayor-to-plead-guilty-to-corruption-charge/ (accessed on June 4, 2014).

News24 (2014). Boko Haram Attack Villages in Nigeria. June 1. Available at: www.news24.com/Africa/News/Boko-Haram-attack-villages-in-Nigeria-20140601 (accessed on June 4, 2014).

Rossman, S. (2014). Former Homes & Land CEO Charged with Grand Theft. Tallahassee Democrat, June 2. Available at: www.tallahassee.com/story/news/local/2014/06/02/former-homes-land-ceo-charged-with-grand-theft/9861197/ (accessed on June 7, 2014).

Rosoff, S., Pontell, H., and Tillman, R. (2010). *Profit Without Honor: White Collar Crime and the Looting of America*. 5th edition. Upper Saddle River, NJ: Prentice Hall.

Rothe, D. (2006). Iraq and Halliburton. In R. Kramer and R. Michalowski (eds.), *State-Corporate Crime: Wrongdoing at the Intersection of Business and Government*, 215–238. Piscataway, NJ: Rutgers University Press.

Rothe, D., and Kauzlarich, D. (2014). *Towards a Victimology of State Crime*. London: Routledge.

Rothe, D., Muzzatti, S., and Mullins, C. W. (2006). Crime on the High Seas: Crimes of Globalization and the Sinking of the Senegalese Ferry Le Joola. *Critical Criminology*, 14(2): 159–180.

Rothe, D. L., and Friedrichs, D. O. (2014). *Crimes of Globalization*. London: Routledge.

Ruggiero, V., and South, N. (2013). Green Criminology and Crimes of the Economy: Theory, Research and Praxis. *Critical Criminology*, 21(3): 359–373.

Stretesky, P., and Lynch, M. (2014). *Exploring Green Criminology: Toward a Green Criminological Revolution*. London: Ashgate.

Sutherland, E. (1939). White Collar Criminality. Presidential address to the American Society of Sociology. *American Sociological Review*, 5: 1–12.

Taylor, A. (2014). *Bhopal: The World's Worst Industrial Disaster, 30 Years Later*. Available at: www.theatlantic.com/photo/2014/12/bhopal-the-worlds-worst-industrial-disaster-30-years-later/100864 (accessed on January 19, 2016).

Thompson, A. (2014). Russian indicted in cyber attack on Erie business. Goerie.com news. Available at: www.goerie.com/article/20140603/NEWS02/306029923/russian-indicted-in-cyber-attack-on-erie-business (accessed on January 19, 2016).

Tifft, L. L., and Sullivan, D. C. (1980). *The Struggle to Be Human: Crime, Criminology and Anarchism*. Sanday, UK: Cienfuegos Press.

Watts, R., Bessant, J., and Hill, R. (2008). *International Criminology: A Critical Introduction*. London: Routledge.

Chapter 2

Media, culture, and crimes of the powerful

Everyday life: how we come to know about crimes of the powerful

> [A] form of communication which has at last attained a unilateral purity, whereby decisions already taken are presented for peaceful admiration. For what is communicated are orders; and with great harmony, those who give them are also those who tell us what they think of them.
>
> (*Comments on the Society of the Spectacle*, Guy Debord, 1988)

We are constantly bombarded with news: 24-hour infotainment. Some of this is relevant to our daily lives, while the majority we ignore as simply background noise. Indeed, news comes in all forms: interpersonal communications, the memos we receive in our mailboxes, the 24-hour television "news" channels (filled more today with opinions and interpretations than news, as Guy Debord's quote illustrates), local news, social media posts, blogs, vlogs, and the daily paper delivered to our doorstep or available at newsstands. One of the many interesting aspects of the news business is the subjects the news media chooses to report on and how they are framed, presented, and inevitably interpreted. It has been argued that this has a subtle effect on our perceptions of the world and the decisions we make (for example, Barak 1994; Hafez 2000; Herman and Chomsky 1988; Mansfield-Richardson 2000).

The agenda-setting hypothesis suggests that if the media chooses to emphasize coverage of an event, issue, or area, then the public will deem it important and will in turn get excited about those events and issues (Mansfield-Richardson 2000). Thus, media plays a role in formulating our perspectives and opinions concerning crimes of the powerful. Additionally, as Debord's opening quote suggests, not only do we see what is selected, but more often than not, the "facts" are burdened by opinions, especially as 24-hour news needs to keep its viewership. For example, "political coverage often focuses on how issues affect politicians or corporate executives rather than those directly affected by the issue. Economics coverage usually looks at how events impact stockholders rather than workers or consumers" (FAIR 2015). See Box 2.1.

It is also believed that news reporting has changed to some degree with the Internet as a major source of news for many. This could translate to mean

---

Box 2.1 Media and opinionated "news"

Between June 5 and 13, 2013, the headlines of *The Guardian* newspaper read, "NSA collecting phone records of millions of Verizon customers daily," "NSA Prism program taps in to user data of Apple, Google and others," "UK gathering secret intelligence via covert NSA operation," "Boundless Informant: the NSA's secret tool to track global surveillance data," "NSA surveillance: anger mounts in Congress at 'spying on Americans.'" In the United States, these stories appeared as front-page headlines and the topic of news panelists' discussions on major networks such as MSNBC and Fox. The framing of these newly realized programs took different shapes, depending on the particular network's corporate master. For instance, while on the (right) hand conservative news groups justified the projects with the unverified and unverifiable assertion that this sort of electronic "Surveillance helped thwart more than 50 terror plots" (Sullivan 2013) on the left, news groups reported, "Progressives' fears stoked in Obama era surveillance" suggesting a degree of disbelief among his liberal supporters that a Democratic president would engage in such sweeping and intrusive tactics.
(From Rothe and Linneman 2015.)

---

that citizens have the *potential* to observe and report more immediately than traditional media outlets do. Yet, even then, we must consider that every day, from newspapers to Internet engines like Yahoo, Bing, or Google, or hundreds of other bloggers, we are shown pre-selected articles of importance and provided with links, reinforcing a new realm of agenda setting. Moreover, we have seen an increasing and alarming set of circumstances when governments and corporations refuse to allow certain newsworthy phenomena to be released to the public, more often than not in the name of national security. For example, *The Times* ran an article titled "The New York Times has come under fire in the past for agreeing to government requests to hold back sensitive stories or information" (Sullivan 2013: 1). Or, consider the case of Sony Pictures in December 2014, which, after being hacked, saw the debut of its film *The Interview* rejected by theaters, and then pulled by Sony. Further, due to the lack of specialization of reporters, when topics of crimes of the powerful are covered, they are often done in a very brief manner and/or without an appreciation of the context and complexities of the case at hand, thus often providing misinformation even propaganda knowingly and unknowingly (see Box 2.2).

As Jewkes (2011) states "despite often being described as a 'window on the world' or a mirror reflecting 'real life', the media might be more accurately thought of as a prism, subtly bending and distorting the view of the world it projects" (Jewkes 2011: 41). If we combine the above with the growing conglomerates or megaplex of media, the control of what we know and how

Box 2.2 Film: *Network* (1976)

Character Howard Beele: Because you people, and sixty-two million other Americans, are listening to me right now. Because less than three percent of you people read books! Because less than fifteen percent of you read newspapers! Because the only truth you know is what you get over this tube. Right now, there is a whole, an entire generation that never knew anything that didn't come out of this tube! This tube is the Gospel, the ultimate revelation. This tube can make or break presidents, popes, prime ministers … This tube is the most awesome God-damned force in the whole godless world, and woe is us if it ever falls into the hands of the wrong people, and that's why woe is us that Edward George Ruddy died. Because this company is now in the hands of CCA – the Communication Corporation of America. There's a new Chairman of the Board, a man called Frank Hackett, sitting in Mr. Ruddy's office on the twentieth floor. And when the twelfth largest company in the world controls the most awesome God-damned propaganda force in the whole godless world, who knows what shit will be peddled for truth on this network? So, you listen to me. Listen to me: Television is not the truth! Television is a God-damned amusement park! Television is a circus, a carnival, a traveling troupe of acrobats, storytellers, dancers, singers, jugglers, side-show freaks, lion tamers, and football players. We're in the boredom-killing business!

Box 2.3 Top 10 media outlets globally

1. Germany's Bertelsmann
2. United States' Gannett Company Inc.
3. United States' CBS Corporation
4. United Kingdom's British Sky Broadcasting Group Plc
5. Liberty Media
6. United States' News Corp (FOX)
7. United States' Viacom
8. United States' Time Warner
9. United States' Walt Disney Company
10. United States' Comcast

we know it, the media's role in shaping our views is far more complex and involves more oversight and control by governments and corporations than at any other time in history. Consider Boxes 2.3 and 2.4, which show the ownership of the major media organizations.

Box 2.4 The megaplex of media: United States' companies

CBS Corporation: CBS and the CW – a joint venture between CBS Corporation and Warner Bros. Entertainment, Showtime Networks, Smithsonian Networks and CBS Sports Network, CBS television stations, CBS Television Studios, CBS Studios International and CBS Television Distribution, CBS Radio, CBS Outdoor, Simon & Schuster, CBS Interactive, CBS Records and 29 television stations and CBS News, CBS Sports, CBS College Sports Network, CBS Television Network.

Comcast: Majority shareholder of NBC Universal from General Electric, the NBC television network, Telemund, USA Network, SyFy, CNBC, MSNBC, Bravo, Oxygen, Chiller, CNBC World, E!, the Golf Channel, Sleuth, mun2, Universal HD, VERSUS, Style, G4, Comcast Sports Net, stakeholders of the Weather Channel, A&E, the History Channel, the Biography Channel, Lifetime, the Crime and Investigation Channel, Pittsburgh Cable News Channel, FEARnet, PBS KIDS Sprout, TV One, MSNBC.com (50 percent), Hulu (32 percent), Fandango.

21st Century Fox (formerly News Corp): *The Wall Street Journal*, the *Daily News, The Times, The Sunday Times, The Sun*, the *New York Post* and *TV Guide*, News Limited (146 newspapers in Australia), Dow Jones, 20th Century Fox, Fox Searchlight Pictures, Blue Sky Studios, FOX Broadcasting Company: FOX Network, FOX News, FOX Business, FOX News Radio Network, FOX News Talk Channel, FX, SPEED; FUEL TV, Fox College Sports, Fox Movie Channel, Dow Jones Local Media, Fox Soccer Channel, Fox Soccer Plus, Fox Pan American Sports, Fox Deportes, Big Ten Network, National Geographic U.S., Nat Geo Adventure, Nat Geo Music, Nat Geo Wild, Fox International Channels: Utilisima, Fox Crime, NEXT, FOX History & Entertainment; the Voyage Channel, STAR World, STAR Movies, NGC Network International, NGC Network Latin America, LAPTV, Movie City, City Mix, City Family, City Stars, City Vibe, the Film Zone, Cinecanal, Elite Sports Limited, BabyTV, STAR India, STAR Taiwan, ESPN STAR Sports, Shine Limited.

Time Warner: Warner Brothers Television, Warner Horizon Television, CW Network (50 percent), TBS, TNT, Cartoon Network, truTV, Turner Classic Movies, Boomerang, CNN, CNN HLN, CNN International, HBO, Cinemax, Space, Infinito, I-Sat, Fashion TV, HTV, Much Music, Pogo, Mondo TV, Tabi, CNN Español, WGN America, CLTV Chicagoland, Tribune Entertainment, Warner Brothers, Warner Brothers Pictures, New Line Cinema, Castle Rock, WB Studio Enterprises, Inc., Telepictures Productions, Inc., Warner Brothers Animation, Inc.,

Warner Home Video, Warner Premiere, Warner Specialty Films, Inc., Warner Brothers International Cinemas, *People*, *Sports Illustrated*, *Time*, *Life*, *InStyle*, *Real Simple*, *Southern Living*, *Entertainment Weekly* and *Fortune*, the *Los Angeles Times*, the *Chicago Tribune*, the *Baltimore Sun* and the *Hartford Courant*.

The Walt Disney Company: ABC television network, cable networks including ESPN, the Disney Channel, SOAPnet, A&E and Lifetime (42 percent), Touchstone, Miramax and Walt Disney Pictures, Pixar Animation Studios; History International (42 percent), ESPN Radio Network; Radio Disney, Marvel Entertainment, ABC Studios, ABC Media Production, Pixar, Walt Disney Pictures, Walt Disney Records, Hollywood Records, Mammoth Records, Buena Vista Records, Lyric Street Records.

(Source: Free Press 2014)

If we consider the portrayal of street crime by the media with the empirical data, we know that viewers are presented with images of the criminal that are not representative of crime perpetrators or victims. We are generally given images of young black males as perpetrators and lower-class or working-class people, in repeated fashion, regardless of the vast numbers of crimes that might occur that same day by white males and the middle to upper classes. Crimes of the powerful are also an area in which media distortion plays a great role (Dowler *et al.* 2006). These crimes and criminals are not as discussed as street crimes and criminals, though they are more prevalent (Tombs and Whyte 2001). For the few cases that make it to the news, we as the audience are given a different perspective, describing the offenders in more positive discourse, painting a picture of a one-time mistake or error in judgment. As a result, "people start to believe the myths and distortions of the mass media and associate certain minorities or individuals with certain crimes" (Han Er 2014: 9). It is not just the coverage of crime or general news that is distorted. Consider also the messages we receive on crimes of the powerful through television, films, movies, and music. The next section provides a discussion of these in relation to the cultural characterization of the crimes/harms of the powerful.

The Hollywoodization of crimes of the powerful

We have all seen Hollywood films depicting the "evil" street criminal and the "good" cops or the glorified yet "bad" organized crime "mobster" that held our attention as the typical story unfolds, leading to the happy and expected outcome of good versus evil. Yet, when it comes to crimes of the most powerful, the depictions in films are quite different, glorifying them or, at best, showing a misguided error of judgment on the part of the powerful superstar.

We call this the "Hollywoodization" of crimes of the powerful; an attempt to socially situate these harms as being less than crimes: good people who made bad judgments, without agency, errors that were made, or where misguided decisions were made, making the costs and harms less than the reality. In some films, legitimizing the criminals as both victim and perpetrator, as holding good intentions overall, make the crimes more acceptable and normalized. After all, "it's no surprise that two of America's favorite things – movies and capitalism – are a match made in heaven" (Brown and Ritz 2012: 1). However, it is not just the US population that is fascinated with Hollywood films or the world of infotainment, it is a global phenomenon for those who can enjoy the luxury.

Film and television Hollywood style

> We have got to realize that we're being conditioned on a mass scale. Start challenging this corporate slave state.
>
> (Alex Jones from the film *Waking Life*, 2001)

Doing a content analysis of Hollywood films over the course of the past decade, the pattern of glorification of and excuses for the powerful and the crimes and harms they commit are present in the majority of cases. The powerful are often depicted in a way that the viewers can identify with and feel bad for, in some cases making them the underdog. For example, in the film *Michael Clayton* (2007), Clayton brings in "fixers" and takes care of a powerful law firm by doing the dirty work needed to accomplish and win their cases. The film's plot is centered on a multi-billion dollar settlement of a class action lawsuit protecting a chemical company; one of the litigators is said to have a nervous breakdown, trying to reveal the harms caused by the chemical company they are representing. Viewers are given glimpses of the personal lives of the main characters, their struggles and challenges, making them "one of us," at times underdogs with pain and sorrow.

Other films depict the powerful as being without agency, merely operating as automatons within the normal system.

Hollywood also depicts the crimes and harms committed by the powerful as necessary, for a greater good. From the film *The Constant Gardener* (2005):

> **Arthur "Ham" Hammond:** So who has got away with murder? Not, of course, the British government. They merely covered up, as one does, the offensive corpses. Though not literally. That was done by person or persons unknown. So who has committed murder? Not, of course, the highly respectable firm of KDH Pharmaceutical, which has enjoyed record profits this quarter, and has now licensed ZimbaMed of Harare, to continue testing Dypraxa in Africa. No, there are no murders in Africa. Only regrettable deaths. And from those deaths we derive the benefits of

Box 2.5 Film: *The Constant Gardener* (2005)

Synopsis: A widower is determined to get to the bottom of a potentially explosive secret involving his wife's murder, big business, and corporate corruption.

Artists: Ralph Fiennes, Rachel Weisz, Hubert Koundé, and Danny Huston.

Protagonist/powerful/criminal: Various.

Depiction of the crimes and harms, and the portrayal of those committing the crimes:

The Constant Gardener is a film that sheds light on the exploitation of a Global South country by British pharmaceutical companies, the British government, and the local government. Draped within a love story between a mild-mannered, passive, and low-ranking diplomat (Justin) and his outspoken activist wife (Tessa), the film implicitly defines the actions of the foreign companies, the local government, and the British government as conspiratorial and corrupt in the pursuit of money and power. Corruption is central to the economic and political structure of this region where responsibility and accountability are not assigned to individuals, but to the structural entities themselves, namely the pharmaceutical companies and the governments. The government official or the pharmaceutical employee, while essentially a representative of a corrupt organization, is portrayed as being corrupt, but not responsible for the corruption: the responsibility for criminal acts or corrupt behavior does not lie with the individuals, but with the institutions. The individuals are without individual agency and simply follow the will of the institution. In this case, the will is to conspire against the African "natives" in the pursuit of power and profit. By eliminating the individual agency of the pharmaceutical and government employees, the conspiracy theory has more support by offering the means by which the complex set of corrupt relationships so heavily ingrained in the region are allowed to continue without any meaningful resistance from the employees themselves or from the exploited victims. The overarching criminal act depicted in the film is perpetrated by the British pharmaceutical companies. In exchange for desperately needed AIDS medication, the pharmaceutical companies give unapproved tuberculosis drugs to unknowing Africans for testing. In the film, this action by the pharmaceutical companies is depicted as abhorrent, and, at the same time, simply part of the normal exercise of economic needs.

civilization, benefits we can afford so easily … because those lives were bought so cheaply.

The film *Edge of Darkness* (2010) is about the death of Detective Craven's daughter that becomes a mini-plot on corporate cover-up (Northmoor), government collusion, and a hired mercenary (hired by a senator) tasked with cleaning up the evidence of their crimes. Emma, the activist daughter that was killed, worked at Northmoor, which was manufacturing illegal nuclear weapons intended to be traced to foreign countries if they were ever used by the government as dirty bombs. The film has the senator and corporation colluding on how to spin the Northmoor "incident" into a positive tale. Here, the victim, Detective Craven, becomes the "criminal" on a killing spree, the mercenary is the good guy, and the corporate CEO and senator are portrayed as good people making bad choices, but doing so for the greater good of national security, and who end up being the victims.

Television rarely has a series or show depicting crimes of the powerful, save for an occasional CEO who commits homicide or some other form of street crime. There is the television series *White Collar*, though the focus is narrow and apolitical, showing instead typical occupational forms of crime such as employee theft, credit card fraud, and embezzlement. The criminals are victimizing the powerful corporations and the government. Viewers are left believing white-collar crimes are financial and committed by middle-class or upper-middle-class people. They do not cover the harms and crimes done by corporations, governments, or international financial institutions. In this way, this particular TV show does more harm than good in terms of education.

On the other hand, *The West Wing* television series' characters make "mistakes," occasionally they are wrong in their judgments or fail to see potential future events, and often appear troubled by their own doubts. In essence, characters are merely individuals making tough choices and mistakes along the way, and never with malice intent. The television show *House of Cards* centers on individual "bad apples" who are ruthless, driven, pragmatic, manipulative, and power hungry. Yet, even these main characters are portrayed as acting in the name of a greater good. One could say viewers are left to wonder if the ruthlessness of the "bad apples," in this case Vice-President Underwood, is really wrong; as such, legitimating as necessary.

The commodification of power or the powerful also permeates popular media through film, television, and video games. From shows like *24* and *Homeland* to films such as *American Sniper*, *Zero Dark 30*, and *United 93*, to video games such as *Battlefield* and *Call of Duty*, these popular depictions of military or covert power amplify the threat of external violence to the state's citizenry and reinforce the message that state violence is a necessary defense, reinforcing nationalism. For example, in the popular show *24*, rogue counter-intelligence agent Jack Bauer frequently engages in the torture of detainees.

More often than not, this leads to the revelation of valuable information that is vital to stopping the threat on our lives and "freedoms." The cultural narrative is overly simple, revolving around a basic morality of good versus evil, with the use of state violence and military power deployed only for "good." In the case of 24, the message to the audience is clear: that torture is not only endorsed by the state, but it is justified when committed against "bad" people. By oversimplifying, the reality of state violence is repackaged and propagated as being a tool effectively and justifiably used against "bad" people, namely those who pose a threat to US citizens and the freedoms that the state represents.

The same argument is more acute with video games whereby ordinary citizens find themselves being able to engage in direct imitations of state violence for the purposes of entertainment. Consumers can deploy military grade weaponry such as drones, missiles, and assault rifles, ride in tanks and military aircraft, deploy aerial and nuclear bombs, as well as engage in drone warfare. Consider that in the video game *Call of Duty Black Ops II*, consumers take the role of a US operative who faces down drones that he or she is unable to defeat due to the pure technological power of the drone weaponry. In order to defeat the enemy drones, the operatives have to deploy their own drone technology because of the power imbalance between soldier and machine. The reality of the power differential between the state and the human soldier is most likely lost on the ordinary consumer of the video game, who, from the safety of his/ her living room, continues to be entertained by the spectacle's violence.

On the media's general depictions of the "crime" and "harm" of the powerful, Michael Levi (2006: 1037) argues that:

> [W]hite-collar crimes are treated by the mass media as extensions of "infotainment." They typically focus on issues like individual and corporate celebrities in trouble; a drugs, gambling or sex craze taking otherwise successful people off the rails; readily visualizable and often quite short fraud events (like credit-card skimming), preferably connected to "organized crime" or "terrorism"; or long-term concealment of fraud that shows up the business and/or regulatory/criminal justice "Establishment" to be incompetent or the offenders to be hypocrites.

Very few crimes of the powerful "constitute 'signal crimes' which evoke and symbolize wider problems in society, for example, whereby seemingly 'low-level' crimes such as graffiti are amplified into indicators of a wider lack of community spirit or social decay" (Levi 2008: 367). When the media does depict crimes of the powerful, they usually focus on individual or corporate defendants that most citizens are aware of. The crimes and harms are generally labeled as misguided acts, wrongdoing, bad choices, errors of judgment, or of being unaware of the circumstances. The crimes are generally minimized and personalized to include the "perpetrator's" victimization as well. Unlike street crime, the "criminals" are interviewed, allowed to give their perspectives and treated with a level of respect. In this sense, there is a demonization of the street criminal from the initial arrest or allegations of committing a crime to the glorification and sensitization of the powerful criminal.

The media also has a tendency to cover some crimes of the powerful, though in a hidden manner. We use several of these examples in later chapters, showing how, if we unpeel the headlines, we often see reporting of crimes and harms of the powerful (see Chapter 7 on "State crime" as an example). Consider the following headline: "US spy agency hacked North Korea before the Sony attack" (Sanchez 2015: 1). The story, while discussing how the US government failed to warn Sony of an approaching hack in North Korea, brings up a larger issue and one that is wholly ignored or presented as legitimate: the US cyberwar on North Korea and the four-year-long practice of hacking into their system. Thus, even media reporting on crimes of the powerful, as we noted previously, is done in a biased manner that does not really challenge the powerful or their actions.

Whistleblowers

In some cases, when we learn of crimes of the powerful, the revelations come from whistleblowers. Consider some of the more well-known cases that resulted in movies depicting them as heroes, such as Erin Brockovich (Pacific Gas and Electric Company of California), Sharon Watkins (Enron), Deep Throat (Watergate), or Daniel Ellsberg, Bob Woodward, and Carl Bernstein (Pentagon Papers). Not all whistleblowers, though, achieve such positive notoriety. One need only recall the names of Bradley (Chelsea) Manning and Edward Snowden to see the other side of whistleblowing, especially for those documenting crimes of states (for example, Marine Corps officer Franz Gayl, who spoke out about lack of protection for United States military personnel against IED attacks in Iraq, and former Lockheed Martin project manager Michael DeKort, who revealed flaws in the United States Coast Guard's Deepwater project). Whistleblowing has exposed ties between government and corporate industries. Consider the Australian case of Guy Pearse, the Greenhouse Mafia and the Australian Industry Greenhouse Network, and the Australian government (see Box 2.6). Yet, the ratio of crimes of the powerful that are exposed to those that remain hidden or never reach the media is bleak at best.

Social media

From Facebook, Twitter, and Instagram to Google+, Flicker, and Reddit, social media outlets have become venues for citizens to post everyday life

Box 2.6 ABC News Australian Broadcasting Station: Lateline interview with Guy Pearse, December 7, 2007

EMMA ALBERICI: Your central thesis is essentially that the Howard Government allows Australia's biggest environmental polluters to write its Cabinet submissions and ministerial briefings. Now that's a serious allegation, is it something you can actually substantiate?

GUY PEARSE: I've got tape recordings of industry lobbyists based here in Canberra saying just that, on half a dozen occasions over more than a decade, they were involved in more than one department writing Cabinet submissions, ministerial briefings and costings on greenhouse policy.

It's worth mentioning that it's not the central argument in the book. That's really one argument. As I've researched the book, I've moved beyond what turns out to be one spoke in the wheel of John Howard's circle of trust on climate change, and what you find when you look around that circle of trust is that he's hearing denial and delay mentalities from all sides.

So either denying the signs or calling on Australia to delay emission cuts at all costs. When you look closely you find the connections all lead back to Australia's worst polluting industries, which are represented here in Canberra by the Australian Industry Greenhouse Network. When you look closely, you find that they represent around 10 per cent of the economy, and about 5 per cent of Australian jobs. They have a vested interest in both denial and delay.

EMMA ALBERICI: And they're the people in your book you refer to as the "Greenhouse Mafia"?

GUY PEARSE: That's correct. I didn't dream that term up, that's their own and when you look closely at all of the different sources that John Howard relies closely on you find that those industries have found a way to get inside those sources, whether it's ABARE, the Government's own economic forecaster, certain sections of CSIRO promoting clean coal and other alternative energy technologies, whether it's economic consultants outside of Government he takes seriously, lobbyists or ministerial colleagues like Andrew Robb, for example, who lobbied for the fossil fuel lobby against Kyoto.

events, including, in some cases, crimes of the powerful. Though, having said this, it should be noted that the use of social media has primarily served as sources of "in-time" crimes of state or social protest movements. Rarely do we see a Facebook or Twitter post that involves information on

Box 2.7 Top 2014 stories in order on Twitter as of December 26, 2014

1. World Cup;
2. Nigeria missing girls: #BringBackOurGirls;
3. Referendum on Scotland's independence: #IndyRef;
4. Hong Kong protests: #occupycentral;
5. Ferguson Mo police shooting: #BlackLivesMatter, combined with New Jersey's shooting: #ICantBreathe and #BlackLivesMatter.

Box 2.8 Top Twitter trends

Table 2.1 Top Twitter trends (past 30 days) as of December 26, 2014

Rank	Trend	Top position	First appeared	Total time in top 10
1	#MTVStars	1	Nov 17, 18:31	8h 5m
2	#icantbreathe	1	Oct 07, 09:58	2h 0m
3	#PeshawarAttack	1	Dec 16, 16:50	1h 35m
4	#RubyPH	1	Dec 04, 09:50	1h 45m
5	#3YearsOf5SOS	1	Dec 02, 14:16	1h 25m
6	#TerriblesMisGanasDe	2	Dec 08, 14:46	1h 35m
7	#sydneysiege	1	Dec 15, 03:00	1h 10m
8	#ÖzgürBasınSusturulamaz	1	Dec 14, 08:05	1h 20m
9	#PeopleWhoMadeMy2014	1	Dec 13, 20:43	1h 20m

Source: Whatthetrend 2015

Box 2.9 Framing

One way to further our understanding of this potential problem is to examine the dynamics and implications of topic "framing," as Lakoff … suggested, helping explain how liberals and conservatives often talk past one another. Thus, if "crime" is too harsh a word for some, what kind of language shifts (e.g., reference to larger justice principles, disproportionate harm, needs, etc.) could be heuristically used to move discourse toward a wider recognition of state violence as criminal? However, if Lakoff's … claim that "if a strongly held frame does not fit the facts, the facts will be ignored and the frame will be kept" is true, then there is little reason to believe that exposure to the facts per se would be all that effective.
(From Kauzlarich 2007: 181.)

corporation or international financial institutions, not to mention the scarcity of organized crime actions or other elite harms and crimes. Of course, viewers can always "like," "repost," or "retweet" news stories that appear on the Web or in print, though these are not the stories that generally make the top 20 Facebook or Twitter stories (see Table 2.1).

As Boxes 2.7 and 2.8 show, there is some interest in and tracking of "live" government crimes, though the priority of tweets surrounds the fascination with celebrity life and input, or votes for "favs" from *The Voice* or *America's Got Talent*. As such, we learn little and share even less from social media sites that uncover or educate on the vast number of crimes of the powerful, and when we do it is generally cases of responses to state crimes such as oppression or crimes of omission.

Additionally, another aspect of "learning" and subsequently posting, tweeting, liking, or sharing stories about crimes of the powerful has to do with individual perceptions of whether or not such acts constitute a crime or harm (see Box 2.9 on "Framing").

Summary

Scholars of crime have often pointed out that news about crime and violence is largely distorted and mostly produced for profit or ratings, not for education. It is naturally understandable, therefore, that people have a poor educational history with crimes of the powerful and that they often do not think of this category of harm when the term crime comes to mind. In addition, with crimes of the powerful, crimes we discuss in this book are often not even labeled as "crimes." Most wars are indeed crimes, and "industrial accidents" are usually not accidents in the sense of there being no fault, but these are not themes that come through most media. Social media allows citizens to connect with one another and an increasing number of independent news sources. Some scholars believe this opens up the conversation and knowledge base that citizens can draw from in understanding social harm and crime. On the other hand, these social media sites, like the film and television industries, are not designed to educate, but to entertain.

Activities and discussion questions

1. How much media do you consume each week and how much of that is about crime or criminal justice? Roughly what percentage of the crime stories are traditional and what percentage could be classified as crimes of the powerful?
2. Search for "state crime" on Twitter and note the content of any search returns. What kinds of news companies, organizations, or groups are tweeting about the topic?

3. Do a quick content analysis of the lead stories on any major newspaper website. How many are devoted to traditional violent crimes versus traditional property crimes and to crimes of the powerful versus crimes of the powerless?

References

ABC News Australian Broadcasting Station (2007). Lateline interview with Guy Pearse and Emma Alberici, December 7. Available at: www.abc.net.au/lateline/business/items/200707/s1977550.htm (accessed on September 11, 2015).

Barak, G. (1994). *Media, Process, and the Social Construction of Crime: Studies in Newsmaking Criminology*. New York: Garland.

Brown, L., and Ritz, T. (2012). 15 Inspirational Quotes from the Greatest Business Movies of All Time. Business Insider, February 4. Available at: www.businessinsider.com/15-inspirational-quotes-from-the-greatest-business-movies-of-all-time-2012-2 (accessed September 11, 2015).

Debord, G. (1988). *Comments on the Society of the Spectacle*. London: Verso.

Dowler, K., Fleming, T., and Muzzatti, S. L. (2006). Constructing Crime: Media, Crime, and Popular Culture. *Canadian Journal of Criminology & Criminal Justice*, 48(6): 837.

FAIR (Fairness and Accuracy in Reporting) (2015). How to Detect Bias in News Media. Available at: http://fair.org/take-action-now/media-activism-kit/how-to-detect-bias-in-news-media/ (accessed on December 11, 2015).

Free Press (2014). Ownership Chart. Available at: www.freepress.net/ownership/chart (accessed on September 11, 2015).

Hafez, Kai (2000). The West and Islam in the Mass Media: Cornerstones for a New International Culture of Communication in the 21st Century. ZEI Discussion Papers: 2000, C 61. Available at: http://aei.pitt.edu/181/ (accessed on December 11, 2015).

Han Er, Hatice (2014). Media Construction of Crime. *Daily Sabah*, September 6. Available at: www.dailysabah.com/opinion/2014/09/06/media-construction-of-crime (accessed on December 11, 2015).

Herman, E., and Chomsky, N. (1988). *Manufacturing Consent: The Political Economy of the Mass Media*. New York: Pantheon.

Jewkes, Y. (2011). *Media and Crime*. New York: Sage.

Kauzlarich, D. (2007). Seeing War as Criminal: Peace Activist Views and Critical Criminology. *Crime, Law and Social Change*, 48: 43–55.

Levi, M. (2006). The Media Construction of Financial White-Collar Crimes. *British Journal of Criminology*, 46(6): 1037–1057.

Levi, M. (2008). White-Collar, Organised and Cyber Crimes in the Media: Some Contrasts and Similarities. *Crime, Law and Social Change*, 49(5): 365–377.

Mansfield-Richardson, V. (2000). *Asian Americans and the Mass Media: A Content Analysis of Twenty United States Newspapers and a Survey of Asian American Journalists*. New York: Garland Publishing, Inc.

Network (1976) [film]. Director Sidney Lume. Writer Paddy Chayefsky. Available at: www.amazon.com/dp/B000I5SY9Q?ref_=imdbref_tt_wbr_aiv&tag=imdbtag_tt_wbr_aiv-20 (accessed on September 11, 2015).

Rothe, D. L., and Linneman, Travis (2015). (Liberal) Democracy Means Surveillance: On Security, Control and the Surveillance Techo-Fetish. In Gregg Barak (ed.), *Routledge International Handbook on the Crimes of the Powerful*, 515–525. New York: Routledge.

Sanchez, R (2015). US Spy Agency Failed to Warn Sony Pictures of North Korea Hacking Plans. *The Telegraph*, January 19. Available at: www.telegraph.co.uk/news/worldnews/asia/northkorea/11355146/US-spy-agency-failed-to-warn-Sony-Pictures-of-North-Korea-hacking-plans.html (accessed on December 11, 2015).

Sullivan, M. (2013). Decision to Publish Against Government Request Was "Not a Particularly Anguished One." *New York Times* blog, September 6. Available at: http://publiceditor.blogs.nytimes.com/2013/09/06/decision-to-publish-against-government-request-was-not-a-particularly-anguished-one/?_r=1 (accessed on December 11, 2015).

The Constant Gardener (2005) [film]. Director Fernando Meirelles. Writers Jeffrey Caine and John le Carré. Available at: www.amazon.com/dp/B0026ISUUQ?ref_=imdbref_tt_wbr_aiv&tag=imdbtag_tt_wbr_aiv-20 (accessed on September 11, 2015).

Tombs, S., and Whyte, D. (2001). Media Reporting of Crime: Defining Corporate Crime out of Existence? *Criminal Justice Matters*, 43: 22–23.

Whatthetrend (2015). Top Twitter Trends. Available at: http://whatthetrend.com/top10 (accessed on September 11, 2015).

Chapter 3

Studying the crimes of the powerful

Researching crimes of the powerful

Science is self-conscious commonsense.

(W. V. Quine 1960)

Within the discipline of criminology, methodological individualism, the systemic character of quantifications–rampant positivism, and belief in the linearity of events combine to create a subjective "acceptable" research approach. As Jock Young (2011: viii) stated, "reality has been lost in a sea of statistical symbols and dubious analysis." This approach is not necessarily the best or most appropriate for researching crimes of the powerful. Of course, this is grounded in our underlying assumption that the phenomena of crimes of the powerful are complex and cannot be reduced to simplistic causal mechanisms; humans are complex beings that cannot be researched in the same manner as a string of DNA or a molecule in the "hard sciences." Tying in with our opening quote, our approach is rather simple and only requires common sense: ask yourself what is your research question and the question always tells you the best method to provide an answer. In the end, what we seek is to understand and analyze the interplay of relationships, factors or variables, and conditions that facilitate crimes of the powerful. In other words, again drawing from Young, do not let "the tools of the trade become magically more important than reality itself" (ibid.: viii).

This is not to say that there are not a variety of ways that criminologists carry out their research. The method and design of a study depends on what the researcher wishes to study, whether theory is to be tested or created, and the previous research on the subject under study. Selecting one method over another can also be based on the time and cost involved, as well as on the researcher's particular skills. The major forms of criminological research include surveys, field research, case studies, comparative and historical approaches, experiments, and content analysis. As we describe below, only a few of these are regularly employed to study elite crime.

The dominant approach to studying crimes of the powerful is grounded in qualitative methods. Qualitative methods are used to interpret observations;

to discover underlying meanings and relationships; to consider the subjective nature of actions, attitudes, beliefs, backgrounds, and social perspectives.
In general, the strengths of qualitative methods include the ability to gain
a more in-depth insight into someone's actions, beliefs, or social reality; to
observe people in their own environments; to observe subjective interpretations often hidden in quantitative measures; to observe body language; and
to obtain unexpected information that may surface within the process of the
method itself. Unlike quantitative research, qualitative research relies on reasons behind various aspects of behavior; it investigates the why and how of
decision-making, as opposed to the what, where, and when of quantitative
research (Frankfort-Nachmias and Nachmias 1996).

Within the parameters of qualitative approaches, the most dominant methodological approach is the case study method. The case study approach can
address processes over time, identify the interplay of meaningful actions and
structural contexts, and interpret the unintended and intended outcomes in
social transformations (Skocpol 1984). In many ways, this approach is no different from what journalists use to uncover complex stories. It is the same
approach a detective uses to try to figure out a homicide. The quintessential
characteristic of case studies is that they strive toward a holistic understanding of systems of action: interrelated acts engaged in by the actors in a specific
social time and space (Feagin *et al.* 1991). A case study method is not a style
of data gathering or an analytical technique; it is a methodological approach
to research. Case studies emphasize detailed contextual analysis of a limited
number of events or conditions and their relationships. This method incor-
porates a systematic gathering of information about specific phenomena to
allow for an effective understanding of how or why the event(s) occurred.
Robert K. Yin (1984: 23) has defined the case study method as an empirical inquiry "that investigates a contemporary phenomenon within its real-life
context; when the boundaries between phenomenon and context are not
clearly evident; and in which multiple sources of evidence are used." The first
statement, we think, highlights the importance of this method for crimes of
the powerful, specifically given that many of the links and relationships are
not clearly evident and researching this subject does require multiple sources
of evidence.

There are different ways to gather and analyze data sources for case studies. To mention a few, there is the use of archival data (historical; see Box 3.1),
primary data (government documents, public records, court records), secondary data (journalistic accounts, scholarly and/or bibliographic texts, media),
interviews, observations, and ethnographic work. The last three form a major
part of qualitative work, but are not easily used for researching crimes of the
powerful. After all, access to boardrooms or high-ranking government offices
for observations is most likely not going to happen. The granting of interviews
by the powerful is also not a likely outcome.

Content analysis is also a viable option for case studies (with a
quantitative—numerical counts—or a qualitative approach). See Box 3.2.

Box 3.1 Historical case study methods

[The] Historical Case Study method is usually regarded as strong in validity though not necessarily reliable. The notion of reliability is at risk due to the inherent danger of subjective and speculative interpretations that cannot be completely controlled for. Archival information contains several innate flaws. Examples of this include missing elements in official documents or missing portions of such documents. For this reason, any research utilizing archival data is subject to receiving or obtaining only partial information. This then limits what can be analyzed. The other side to this limitation is the researcher's decision of what to examine or what information is sought after in archival collections. The process of sedimentation of archived information also limits this study. The sediment in archives is the result of people defining certain materials as "worth keeping" (and excluding other material) in archival situations. This includes primary sedimentation, in which individuals or organizations create, save, collect, or discard material. The deposit of archived information is then reliant on what is "deemed" as relevant information. This puts archival data at risk for incomplete or subjective access. Other limitations include the compartmentalization of social agencies and organizations that contribute to the complex nature of assessing the intent, impact, and social context of the event (pertinent if using the historical case study for more than an individual life account). (From Rothe 2009.)

Box 3.2 Content analysis

Bruce Berg (2007: 3) states that "[q]uality refers to the what, how, when, and where of a thing—its essence and ambience. Qualitative research thus refers to the meanings, concepts, definitions, characteristics, metaphors, symbols, and descriptions of things." This understanding of content analysis is closely aligned with what cultural criminologists call ethnographic content analysis (see Altheide 1987). This extends beyond discourse analysis—or addressing the content as a single entity, allowing the researcher to immerse in the text, identify the relationships, media loops, intended audiences—in essence a part of a larger cultural process.

For example, we can do a content analysis using the count method through LexisNexis or other search engines to see how many times certain terms (truncated) are used in headlines or news stories. Our questions are: does the media report on crimes of the powerful on a regular basis, and, if so, how are they portrayed? For example, we could enter "crimes of the powerful" and see the results, though we would not retrieve many stories; same for "corporate crime." On the other hand, "organized crime" will likely get several hits, as will "environmental crime." If we went no further, we could write up results and say that there was such and such number of stories that appeared and the media neglected to cover the other topics. This would be using the basic form of quantitative descriptive content analysis. Additionally, we could also read the stories and look for descriptive words, themes, and so on, and say we have done a discourse analysis, looking for subtle meaning and hidden innuendos, and then report them as the outcome of media portrayal of crimes of the powerful. However, we would be remiss in our reporting. Weekly, we can scan the media and find stories and coverage of crimes of the powerful, though they are not necessarily easily identified as such. But, with a little digging and a deeper understanding of crimes of the powerful, we can identify the harms and crimes presented. This will be illustrated in several of the chapters in Part II, where headlines appear of major news stories discussing state crimes and crimes of globalization without being framed as crimes of the powerful, though we provide the contextual details of these cases with mini case studies.

Typically, using the case study method involves using different approaches together and collating information from several sources, also called triangulation. With the use of triangulation, researchers can deepen their understanding and obtain a more comprehensive view of the phenomenon under study (Rothbauer 2008). Essentially, this includes combining many pieces of data to obtain (1) a more holistic view of the crimes/harms, (2) some sort of "truth" through confirming and reconfirming information via several sources, and (3) repetition wherein you can feel confident that you have received all the available information.

Reliability, however, has been a debated issue in qualitative research. Very few qualitative projects can be replicated in a controlled manner. Thus, the use of standardized procedures, as are believed to be used in quantitative analysis, to obtain consistent measurement is contradictory to the aim of qualitative research. Instead of seeking consistency in a controlled setting, Richards (2005) suggests qualitative researchers strive for results that the audience can trust, rely on, and have confidence in.

Typically, quantitative approaches concentrate on measuring or counting through collecting and analyzing numerical data and applying statistical tests. The overarching goal is to provide a generalized understanding of patterns, correlations, and causation among variables (Babbie 1998). Quantitative researchers generally assume objectivity. Relying on the accuracy of official data as well as self-reports of surveys, the researcher must interpret the statistics accurately. However, the data, instrument, and analysis are guided by a predisposed notion of findings, thus risking omitting significant variables (issues of spuriousness). While the issue of generalizability is a goal of many quantitative studies, this is not feasible for studying crimes of the powerful: complexities make it difficult to incorporate all the necessary variables, access to an already made data source is nonexistent, and, we suggest, crimes of the powerful do not lend to linear direct causation or correlations; rather they require a method that allows analysis from the micro to the macro and supramacro (international) levels: from agency to organization to structure to political economy and global forces. Braithwaite (1985: 6) notes:

> It may seem odd to argue that quantitative comparisons of offending rates for different companies are the kinds of research least needed when the two most influential studies of white collar crime—those of Sutherland (1983) and Clinard & Yeager (1980)—were precisely of this kind. There are three answers to this. First, the quantification of white collar crimes in both works was important in demonstrating to a disbelieving world that the biggest and best companies are widely involved in criminality; it was not, however, very important for correlational analysis. Second, the major intellectual contributions of both works concerned their syntheses of theory and qualitative data. Third, even if the quantitative aspect of their work did have substantial intellectual as opposed to polemical significance, it is doubtful, given the problems outlined above, that future scholars will be able to advance much upon it.

This is not to say that the positivistic approach has no value or use in studying crimes of the powerful. However, again, coming from our assumption of complexity and the importance of agency to structure and the interplay thereof, we do suggest that quantitative methods alone will not uncover the systematic nature and relationships that perpetuate and facilitate crimes of the powerful. Furthermore, "the quantitative process of data collection, cognitively speaking, must pass through a qualitative process of theoretically guided abstraction, in order to illuminate substantive yet elusive social forces" (Lasslett 2010: 220). In the end, we caution students about being cognizant of a need for a method, rather than using a method for a method's sake. As Ferrell (2009: 1) rightly notes, "Criminology is today crippled by its own methodology, its potential for analysis and critique lost within a welter of survey forms, data sets, and statistical manipulations. Worse, criminology has given itself over to a fetishism of these methodologies."

Toward the death of the positivistic versus qualitative debate

Ferrell's quote directly above suggests that, regardless of the term we use to describe a type of method, in the end these too are socially constructed by disciplines as a means to self-differentiate and create a guise of legitimate, "scientific," and "reputable" findings. If we are to discard these preconceived notions of scientific, non-scientific, academic, or academic politicized rants, we may well find that the value in either approach is only as good as the ability to discern an aspect of social reality as has been constructed.

As students of criminal justice, criminology, socio-legal studies, or law, you will be exposed to the need to remain objective and scientific, and to employ jargon-filled concepts unique to specific methods to help explain phenomena. Depending on the university, specific geographic location, discipline, or professor, the emphasis on one or more of these will vary. However, even quantitative analysis requires some sort of qualitative assessment and interpretation at the onset of data collection or input; many qualitative methods' data can be ascribed numerical values and run through a statistical program as well.

Depending upon the assumptions and beliefs that undergird the researcher, one method may be touted as more "valuable," "objective," or "scientific" without the recognition that each of these concepts is socially constructed. We also emphasize that the idea of objectivity or being objective in your data selection, analysis, and so on is not possible. One is not devoid of worldviews or belief systems. The set of questions we choose to answer are themselves guided by these subjective internal belief systems. In other words, we should recognize that there are always biases in our research and analysis; this does not negate the results. Rather, recognizing them and the underlying assumptions of human nature, and even what we expect to find, allows us to better understand and control the subjective nature of research. In the end, neither qualitative nor quantitative methods hold more value than the other unless the question being asked cannot be answered by the chosen method. In the end, the question that is being asked and the type of answer being sought should be the only determinant of the method.

Having presented in brief some of criminology's own methodological barriers and chains, there are other obstacles that strain research on crimes of the powerful. The following section addresses some of these.

Barriers to researching crimes of the powerful

Beyond the self-imposed divisions within criminological research discussed above, scholarly attention to crimes of the powerful still remains disproportionately weighted in favor of orthodox areas of criminological analysis, namely street crime (Tombs and Whyte 2003), which in part is also due to other more salient obstacles to researching crimes of the powerful, including but not limited to lack of a centralized data source, access to primary data, whether perpetrators or victims, funding for research, institutional support, and, most obvious, due to the ability of the powerful to reframe the events and to their denials, cover-ups, and attempts to legitimate their crimes and harms.

There are institutional barriers including the bureaucratization of research through institutional review boards, pressure to publish in what are subjectively

Box 3.3 Researching crimes of the powerful and neoliberalism

The prospects for researching [crimes of the powerful] have been further diminished in the era of neo-liberalism as a series of changes have swept through universities. In particular, the social credibility of capital, and indeed the importance of the business world as models for and funders of university activity have been augmented. Universities have been subjected to processes of marketization and commodification, with the whip of external funding forcing researchers to turn to external sources of tightly controlled funding. Both within and beyond criminology, these new parameters of academic work have meant that certain types of research and research questions have been increasingly defined as useful, pressing, and legitimate, others as futile, irrelevant, or illegitimate. Within criminology, this trend has perhaps been particularly dramatic given the opening up of a massive pool of funds, funds tied to the Government's narrowing definition of what constitutes crime. Thus questions of corporate or white-collar illegality have clearly slipped further from constructions of acceptable research terrain … Indeed, we may be witnessing a trend akin to that identified in a recent review of state/corporate/university relationships in the United States during the Cold War era: in the short term, power typically selects ideas … while in the long term ideas tend to conform to the realities of power"… [W]ithin criminology and criminal justice research, such processes have particularly helped to construct a terrain of valid, acceptable research for academics, a terrain from which a focus upon corporate and white-collar crimes is more and more likely to be expunged. Certain types of research are therefore further marginalized from academic criminological agendas as academics compete for research grants provided by the state, generating reliance upon direct funding for specific, preordained research projects often with narrowly defined fields of inquiry and outputs. And the increasing penetration of the private sector into state functions creates a further level of obstacles and complexity for the researcher. [Beyond this,] studying relatively powerless groups is much more common than studying elite groups. One reason for this is that, quite simply, "the inner sanctum of the company boardroom and the senior management enclaves within corporate hierarchies still remain a largely closed and secretive world."
(From Tombs and Whyte 2007.)

constructed as top-tier journals for purposes of promotion and tenure that, given the overarching and dominant paradigm of positivism and statistical methods as the legitimate output, also create obstacles for scholars to research crimes of the powerful.

Other barriers include access to primary data: the perpetrators and victims. After all, there is not a data set that tracks and records the instances or reports of crimes of the powerful. This in turn leads us to rely on secondary sources including news reports, and, as we discussed in the previous chapter, this is not without its limitations and drawbacks. Other sources of data that have limitations are formal government documents, though here there are issues with access, redactions, and the over-reliance on national security and classified information to protect states and their vested economic interests, namely the corporations and organizations that are too big to fail.

Summary

There are a variety of methods used by criminologists and social scientists to study crime. Case studies are the most common methods used in the study of crimes of the powerful, but content analysis and historical and comparative research are also employed in some instances. Understanding the causes, correlates, factors, and variables involved in crimes of the powerful is a complex endeavor and no one study—or even a group of studies—has found the "truth" about the phenomena. Instead, care is taken by scholars to understand how events come together on multiple levels of analysis and how parts of a crime or event can be more deeply explained through its constitutive parts, as with puzzle pieces.

Activities and discussion questions

1. Select a classic film on crimes of the powerful, such as *Hotel Rwanda* or *The Killing Fields*, and conduct a content analysis of the themes presented in the film. Look for subtleties as well as direct presentations of the events.
2. How would you develop and design a study of the crimes of the powerful? Would you use more than one method discussed in the chapter? Explain.
3. What would be some ways to get around the barriers to doing research on the powerful?

References

Altheide, D. (1987). Ethnographic Content Analysis. *Qualitative Sociology*, 10: 65–77.
Babbie, E. (1998). *The Practice of Social Research*. Belmont, CA: Wadsworth.
Berg, Bruce (2007). *Qualitative Research Methods for the Social Sciences*. 6th edition. Boston, MA: Pearson Education.
Braithwaite, J. (1985). White Collar Crime. *Annual Review of Sociology*, 11: 1–25.
Feagin, J. R., Orum, A. M., and Sjoberg, G. (1991). *A Case for the Case Study*. Chapel Hill, NC: UNC Press Books.

Ferrell, Jeff (2009). Kill Method: A Provocation. *Journal of Theoretical and Philosophical Criminology*, 1(1): 1–22.

Frankfort-Nachmias, C., and Nachmias, D. (1996). *Research Methods in the Social Sciences*. New York: St. Martin's Press.

Lasslett, K. (2010). Scientific Method and the Crimes of the Powerful. *Critical Criminology*, 18(3): 211–228.

Quine, W. V. (1960). Variables Explained Away. *Proceedings of the American Philosophical Society*, 3: 343.

Richards, L. (2005). *Handling Qualitative Data: A Practical Guide*. Thousand Oaks, CA: SAGE Publications.

Rothbauer, P. (2008). Triangulation. In L. Given (ed.), *The SAGE Encyclopedia of Qualitative Research Methods*, 893–895. Thousand Oaks, CA: SAGE Publications.

Rothe, D. L. (2009). *State Criminality: The Crime of All Crimes*. Lanham, MD: Lexington/Rowman and Littlefield.

Skocpol, T. (1984). *Vision and Method in Historical Sociology*. Cambridge: Cambridge University Press.

Tombs, S., and Whyte, D. (2003). Unmasking the Crimes of the Powerful. *Critical Criminology*, 11(3): 217–236.

Tombs, S., and Whyte, D. (2007). Researching Corporate and White-Collar Crime in an Era of Neo-Liberalism. In Henry N. Pontell and Gilbert Geis (eds.), *International Handbook of White-Collar and Corporate Crime*, 125–144. New York, NY: Springer.

Yin. R. K. (1984). *Case Study Research: Design and Methods*. Beverly Hills, CA: SAGE Publications.

Young, J. (2011). *The Criminological Imagination*. Cambridge: Polity Press.

Chapter 4

Theoretical understandings of crimes of the powerful

The greatest crimes are caused by excess and not by necessity.

(Aristotle, Book II:65)

We should state at the outset that our approach here is not like that of most textbooks on white-collar crime, which introduce you to a host of criminological theories you read small snippets of and attempt to apply (for example, biosocial theories, psychological theories, social control, rational choice, low self-control models, or even social bond models). Although many traditional criminological theories contribute to some understanding of juvenile delinquency, robbery, burglary, and other conventional domestic criminal activities, standing alone or as individual theories, they have serious shortcomings and are able to explain only a small portion of variance (Agnew 2012; Kauzlarich and Barlow 2009). This has resulted in limited understandings and a general over-focus on individuality and subsequent individual "blame." Of course, personality, socialization, and upbringing does matter to a small degree. Further, we have all most likely met the narcissistic, self-aggrandizing, or hedonistic person. Yet, many of the theoretical perspectives noted above tend to result in simplistic interpretations where motivations can be reduced to "greed," "psychopathic traits," or socialization. Additionally, many of these theories need a well-rounded base of personal individual facts, from life background to mental health conditions, that are generally unavailable to researchers and/or omitted from any analysis. Having said this, we return to our opening quote; indeed, crimes of the powerful do not come from having less, rather excess, and, as we highlight later, this is found in the form of power.

We aim to take a much broader approach, given that our underlying assumption is that crimes of the powerful are not parsimonious events, acontextual or ahistorical, but are complex phenomena that must account for a broad array of conditions including individual agency. After all, humans and the human mind are complex. Moreover, individuals do not operate in a vacuum; this is especially the case for the powerful who commit harms/crimes. Their actions, motivations, and responses are situated within a system that fosters and facilitates crimes of the powerful and, as such, should not be ignored or discounted.

We should also note that there remains a divide within criminology of what theory actually is and what it should accomplish (Agnew 2012). As such, let us begin with a brief discussion of theory and its purpose.

Purpose of theory

Theory can be thought of as a set of logically related concepts that can explain a phenomenon. In short, theory aspires to explanation (Barlow and Kauzlarich 2010). An alternative view is that theory is a set of logically related postulates-propositions-hypotheses that can be empirically tested and falsified, and that is capable of being predictive (Lynch *et al.* 2013). The latter is a strict use of the scientific and positivistic interpretation of theory, believing that without the ability to empirically or statistically test or try to falsify, it has no validity or scientific value. Yet, as Bernard (1990: 327) argued, falsification of criminological theories failed insofar as "no theoretical approach to crime has ever been falsified in the history of criminology." Theory that is "testable"—generally understood by orthodox criminologists as quantifiably tested by a sophisticated statistical program—has come to dominate the field and is believed to be "the" proper form, making it falsifiable and parsimonious. However, this assumes a level of simplicity of human nature, a minimalistic means to address the intertwining of a host of factors that explain the phenomenon. After all, humans cannot be understood in terms of natural scientific theories that are used to explain the behavior of an atom or molecule. Parsimonious, simplistic theories and positivist methodologies are unable to capture the complexities of systems and connections between these and the crime they produce, reducing complex human nature to a few measurable variables. A general belief is that theory should explain in a causal fashion and be able to predict. We reject the ideology that a good theory must predict future crime, rather we suggest that attempting to serve as fortune-tellers reduces agency and the recognition of the importance of specific factors combining at specific moments in time. As Karl Popper (1959) argued, though something is not falsifiable—or scientific, as understood by positivistic epistemologies—it does not negate its truth, soundness, or validity.

In light of this, a theoretical model for crimes of the powerful, we argue, should consider the complexities of the system and intertwinement of factors from the structural to the interactional level where agency should not be reduced. Further, focusing more on the explanatory power, rather than the traditions of orthodox criminologists' means of testing and theory falsification, is of more relevance from our perspective. Vaughan (2007: 3) also argues in favor of this approach for theory and theory elaboration: "More specifically, the means to theory elaboration are theoretical tools in general (theory, models, and concepts) rather than a more restricted formal meaning (a set of interrelated propositions that are testable and explain some phenomenon)."

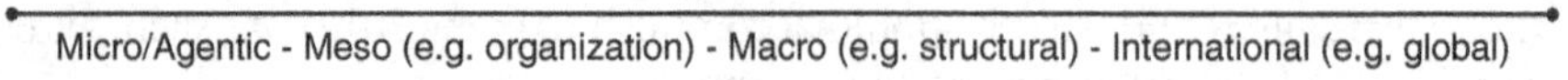

Micro/Agentic - Meso (e.g. organization) - Macro (e.g. structural) - International (e.g. global)

Figure 4.1 Levels of analysis

Figure 4.2 Levels of analysis and relationships

Types of theories

Theories apply to different levels of analysis. Each of these is generally thought of as operating along a continuum from the individual or interactional level of analysis to the macro structural level to the international. The chart in Figure 4.1 may help to contextualize these levels of analysis as they are typically presented.

Here, though, let us be clear that we do not see crimes of the powerful, levels of analysis, or theory as a linear process. We see the interaction of these levels as dialectic, inconsistent, and contingent upon a host factors from the agentic to the international levels. See Figure 4.2.

Utilizing theories that explain only the individual level processes, organizations, structural, or even international are bound to overlook the intricacies and complexities of specific cases of crimes of the powerful. Because of this, we suggest that theory integration is the most viable path forward for understanding crimes of the powerful.

Theory integration can take several forms, it can be specific or general, propositional or conceptual (Liska *et al.* 1989), static or dynamic (Barak 1997). It can combine two or more existing theories, concepts, and/or propositions into one, more comprehensive, model that is closely related, or into what are considered competing theoretical models. There is also side-by-side integration, which involves combining partial theories to explain a phenomenon, or the end-to-end integration that entails shuffling variables from one theory to another, making the dependent variable the independent and vice versa. An up-and-down integration is the development of a "general" theory that includes multiple propositions from specific theories. Integrated macro–micro theories "focus on both the individual and the structure plus on some kind of interaction between the two" (Barak 1997: 198). Integration can combine single level or multilevel analyses as well as intradisciplinary or interdisciplinary critique. Our approach in this chapter is an interdisciplinary multilevel approach. As Jack Douglas (1977: 51) stated, far too often we are guilty of "'simplificationism': the modern scientists' self-imposed professional myopia, the insistence of each specialist on seeing everything as caused by the few particular variables he happens to 'own' professionally." As such, a theoretical framework should recognize the diversity of macro, meso, and micro issues and the totality of the system within which all of these are produced and reproduced. So what would such a theory look like? Which disciplines' theoretical perspectives should be included?

Criminology and beyond

Let us begin by saying that, though we have pointed out the limited utility of criminological theories for explaining crimes of the powerful (as well as street crime), we suggest that in an integrated fashion, some criminological theories aid in our understanding. After all, to ignore extant theory is to be forced to reinvent the wheel. Such a posture is not only myopic in that it ignores decades of established theorizing and theory testing, but it is arrogant in its rejection of what has come before. Over the course of the past few decades, several criminological theories have aided in analyzing various types of crimes of the powerful. These include:

- Anomie
- Strain
- Techniques of neutralization
- Social disorganization
- Learning theories
- Differential association
- Normalization of deviance
- Control/balance
- Rational choice.

However, criminological theories are not sufficient to explain crimes of the powerful if we situate them within the environments where they are produced and reproduced. For that, we must draw from the fields of sociology, history, international relations, and economics to include theories of:

- Power
- Governmentality
- Organizations

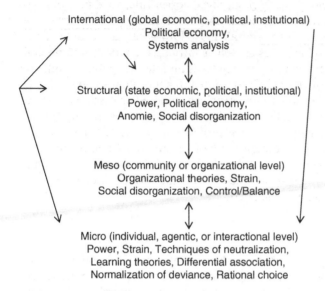

Figure 4.3 Relationships within levels of analysis

- Political economy
- Globalization
- Systems analysis.

Of course, not all of these may be significant factors in their explanatory power for each specific case or instance; however, not including them would be remiss of the broader system and environment. So, how would these theories look in relation to the levels previously discussed and to each other? The chart in Figure 4.3 may help to visualize the relationships and levels of analysis.

Although we present theories at the structural and community/organizational levels, we want to reinforce that these institutions do not act. We may reify them as a person; however, without individuals recognizing the institution and having positions within, they are a shell of a building with or without traces of its previous functions. They have an impact on and help shape the actors within them—their agency then acts—but not as predicated on assumptions of free will or determinism. Additionally, the generic levels of analysis are not always able to be separated or distinct, as noted by the arrows; there is an ongoing dialectic relationship that is specific to time and space. The following provides a brief discussion of most of the theories and concepts noted in the two lists above and their explanatory potential for crimes of the powerful, beginning with the broader structural system within which crimes of the powerful occur.

Systems analysis

The concepts of system criminality and systems analysis can aid our under-standing of crimes of the powerful, as will be discussed more fully in later chapters, and illustrate their symbiotic nature. System criminality has been conceptualized as crimes that are committed by individual actors and organ-izations that constitute a complex whole with varying levels of participa-tion (Nollkaemper and van der Wilt 2009; Rothe and Collins 2011). If we expand and revise the definition of system criminality, the totality of the broader capitalistic system can be included. The meaningfulness of this con-cept is that it provides a tool through which one can analyze the complex web of connections between and amongst various entities and mechanisms of power that are complicit in crimes of the powerful (namely, transnational corporations, international organizations, states, international financial institutions, organized crime syndicates, and other powerful actors). Unlike organizational theories, system criminality is not bound by the confines of a particular organization or its immediate environment. System criminality, as we define it, expands beyond network theories that deal with individual actors, their interactions, and how the structure of ties affects relationships, to the collectivities of a broader system (Freeman 2004, 2006; Moody and White 2003). Recognizing the totality of the globalized system also negates the compartmentalizing of actors, organizations, and policies. After all, if the focus is on atomistic organizations or individuals, we would be limiting our concerns and responses to "small cogs in larger systems" (Nollkaemper and van der Wilt 2009: 2). Additionally, it is within this system that power is exercised, produced, and reproduced to maintain the existing relations of power.

Box 4.1 Small arms trafficking, Charles Taylor and the broader system

While Charles Taylor has been identified as a primary source of the small arms trafficking into Sierra Leone and to the Revolutionary United Front (RUF) of Sierra Leone ... he by no means was able to do this without broad support and actions of other states, corpora-tions, and individuals. Consider that the primary origins of the small arms market are the states that compose the UNSC. Additionally, the global system here is a display of and reification of power, all exercised within the economic, political, and military sphere. To get a sense of the broader system that facilitated the protracted civil war in Sierra Leone through arms support, consider the following list of actors involved. For example, Ibrahim Bah, aka General Ibrahim or Balde, a Senegalese from the southern area of Cassamance was part of the Taylor's trusted inner circle and played a central role as an intermediary in directly set-ting up most of the arms and diamond transactions for Taylor involving Sierra Leone; Daniel Tamba, a Liberian, aka Jungle, actively delivered illicit arms and ammunition to Sierra Leone; Leonid Minin, a Ukrainian arms trafficker, shipped arms from the Ukraine stockpiles to Taylor. Minin was also involved in the diamond and timber trade used as trade for the arms drawn from Ukraine's stockpiles; Foday Sankoh directly purchased small arms for the RUF through Guinea through trading money, coffee, and cocoa; Intermediary arms dealers supplying Liberia arranged arms deals in Kyrgyzstan, Moldova, Serbia, Slovakia, and Ukraine; Sharif al-Masri was contracted to deliver arms from Uganda to Slovakia, in 2000. These arms were rerouted to a company in Guinea, a front company for the Liberian government. The submachine guns were then diverted to Liberia through an elaborate "bait-and-switch" scheme.

The system within which arms trafficking occurred included both direct and indirect involvement of various countries beyond the role as state of origin of sales. In 1997 actors "in the British govern-ment encouraged Sandline International, a private security firm and non-state entity, to supply arms and ammunitions to the loyal forces of the exiled government of President Kabbah." Sandline signed a con-tract with Ahmed Tejan Kabbah, the then exiled President of Sierra Leone to provide a 35-ton arms shipment from Bulgaria. Britain was also at the center of supplying arms to the Air Force Reserve Command (AFRC)/RUF rebels directly by shipping arms to the RUF using two British firms owned and operated by retired British military generals who have strong connections with the [former] British foreign secretary Robin Cook: Sky Air Cargo of London and Occidental Airlines. Other examples include the 200 tons of illegal arms shipped from Belgrade to Monrovia between May and August 2002, with the aid of Mr. Slobodan Tezic, director of the Belgrade based Temex Company.

The United States used Robertsfield Airport in Liberia to supply arms directly to Union for the Total Independence of Angola (UNITA) toward the end of the former President Doe's regime, which were used in the trade of diamonds-for-arms. Likewise, the government of Côte d'Ivoire played a role in the November 2000 diversion of a large ship-ment of ammunition to Liberia, providing the "necessary cover story, documentation, and staging ground for the diversion." Likewise, the president of Burkina Faso, Blaise Compaore, in Abidjan directly facili-tated Liberia's arms-for-diamonds trade, to the benefit of the RUF in Sierra Leone through sales of small arms to Liberia. The Ukraine gov-ernment sold weapons directly to Taylor who then traded the RUF for

diamonds as did Russia. For example, Russian planes directly transported Russian arms on over a dozen occasions directly to Liberia
and at other times employing the use of diversion states including
the Côte d'Ivoire.

To summarize, the illegal trade of arms is a small microcosm
of the relationships that are grounded in the broader capitalistic
system, one which not only fosters economic gain for the few, but
also situates nicely the role of politics and power. (From Rothe and
Collins 2011.)

For a full, in-depth analysis, see Rothe and Collins 2011.

Power

Michel Foucault has been influential in the critical assessment of relations
between power and truth. For Foucault (1977, 1980), power is everywhere,
not solely a coercive force. When analyzing crimes of the powerful, it would
be more than short-sighted to not consider the role power plays in creating the conditions of, supporting, facilitating, and allowing these harms and
crimes to occur. Simply, crimes of the powerful are inherently situated in
and reify existing relations of power. Power is exercised through legitimacy,
relations, resources, and discourse, reaffirming and reproducing itself. These
mechanisms of power—the means through which it is dispersed—produce
"knowledge" that reinforces the exercise of that power. This is done through
several means, including discourse. The idea of discourse (that is, hegemonic
discourse) includes a statement of how a problem is defined, followed by the
rules guiding the ways it is discussed, and how this then frames the authority of "truth" about the subject (Foucault 1980). Truth is a construct of the
political and economic forces that hold the majority of power within and
external to a society. This truth becomes understood as common sense and
accepted as a general way of thinking, reflecting not only what is known but
what should be done. For Foucault (1977: 2), truth is "linked in a circular
relation with systems of power which produce and sustain it, and to effects
of power which it induces and which extend it: a 'regime' of truth." This
regime of truth then aids in the operationalization of authority or truth to
legitimate policy and actions. We suggest that these policies and actions are
to support the existing globalizing political economy that is grounded in a
neoliberal regime of truth.

Political economy

Political economy models are useful to explain the driving forces at the
state and international levels, in terms of motivation. The earliest version

of political economy theory emphasized the relation between the economic system of production and the government and law. This was later revised and expanded to include the international political economy and international relations. The emphasis here, while broadened, remains on the relations between economic systems and politics within and between countries. Specifically, the concern is with the ways political forces shape broader systems through economic interactions and how the economy interacts with these political structures (Oatley 2009). What is ignored by international

---

Box 4.2 International financial institutions (IFIs): power, discourse, truth, and a regime of truth

From a Foucauldian standpoint, IFIs can be said to be a site where capitalistic hegemonic power is exercised. After all, according to Foucault, power extends beyond states' apparatuses, as do politics. This includes soft power wherein political persuasion could be used to advance the "virtues" of neoliberalism. There is, undoubtedly, a genuine belief in the neoliberal strategies that guide the restructuring policies mandated by IFIs. This then becomes the "regime of truth," the authoritative correctness to which discussion occurs and subsequent measures of implementing policy become institutionalized within the organizational culture creating and perpetuating the authority of "a truth." Included within this is the idea of the discourse of "truth," which includes needed statements of, in this case, development, a defining of it, followed by the rules guiding the ways it is discussed, and how this then frames the authority of "truth" about the subject (development) for poverty reduction and economic stability. These are then crystallized by policies such as the structural adjustments that mandate privatization of state-owned entities, removal of tariffs and import protections, reductions in social services, and opening markets to foreign investment, without consideration of the conditions of the extant infrastructure within a given country. This "regime of truth" then serves as the political discourse designed to legitimate the policies of IFIs.

To understand how deeply ingrained this can become, a four-year assessment and report was completed by the World Bank, seven countries, and a multitude of NGOs showing that the Bank's policies and SAP practices had done more harm than good by increasing inequality, unemployment, states' debts, costs of education and healthcare, and environmental degradation. Yet, there were no changes in general policy or procedure, and, more importantly, no change in the underlying belief, the "regime of truth" or subsequent discourse, that such harmful economic policies were sound advice for debtor states. (See Rothe 2010; Rothe and Friedrichs 2014.)

political economy perspectives, however, are the factors that go into political decision-making beyond economic concerns or the impact thereof. This includes ideological and religious interests as well as issues of power, beyond those tied to the economic system, and social/political capital.

Anomie

Emile Durkheim's (1897) classic discussion of anomie argues that it reflects the normlessness associated with rapidly changing societies, wherein traditional norms no longer constrain individuals and new norms are adopted. However, confusion arising out of conflicts between traditional and emerging norms encourages unregulated aspirations and egoism. Again, drawing from Durkheim's work on suicide, the concept of chronic economic anomie with resulting long-term diminution of social regulation is relevant to many crimes of the powerful (see Ross and Rothe 2008). Colvin, Cullen, and Vander Ven (2002) have recognized, however, that over-regulation can also create criminogenic environments. In a Mertonian sense, anomie is the result of a high emphasis on goals with low emphasis placed on institutionalized norms to achieve those goals. The social structure has an inherent contradiction between the expected aspirations (cultural goals) and legitimate means to achieve these culturally emphasized goals. Combining these definitions, anomie can be understood as a condition of the larger environment wherein a great emphasis is placed on goals, but there is a lack of standardized norms that guide the goal achievement (internally and externally): anomic conditions are heightened.

Merton's (1938) classic structure, strain theory, is also of relevance for state actors. According to Merton, strain occurs when attempts to achieve goals and expectations are unattainable due to blocked goals or means. Individuals may respond several ways to this strain: conformity (for example, accepting the organizational/state goals and directed means of achieving them), innovation (for example, accepting the organizational/state goals, but finding different means of achieving them), ritualism (for example, not accepting organizational/state goals, but following the directed means of achieving them), retreatism (for example, not accepting or acting to achieve organizational/state goals), and rebellion (for example, creating an alternative set of goals and means to achieve them). This has been shown to be a factor in many cases of corporate, state-corporate, and state crime (Kauzlarich and Kramer 1998; Michalowski and Kramer 2006).

Social disorganization

Disorganization theories are typically associated with the Chicago school of thought. Here, the shared underlying assumption of individuals is based more on the blank slate perspective or a socially constructed view of human nature. Crime causation is viewed in terms of social causation. For example, the fast-changing occurrences in demographics, agriculture, industrialization, immigration, urbanization, and a newly formed social class all aided the Chicago school's concept that certain effects occur from cultural and societal changes. In other words, the fast-changing cultural and social organization was viewed as related to causes of crime. Rapid changes would damage the existing set of normative controls, leading to the breakdown of consensus, to "dissensus" (Rothe and Mullins 2008). The disorganization that occurs would have two manifestations: (1) long-term, leading to reorganization, and (2) short-term, resulting in deviance. As such, community traits were linked to crime (Shaw and McKay 1942).

Sutherland (1949) took concepts out of the Chicago school of thought and focused on what he called "differential social organization." He paired cultural conflict, occurring due to the social disorganization, with a lack of harmonious social influences, and with the idea that individuals learn patterned criminal behavior. As such, Sutherland contributed to the significance of recognizing the larger social structure while simultaneously introducing individual behavioral catalysts. Bursik and Grasmick (1993) and Sampson and Raudenbush (1999) built on Shaw and McKay's model of social disorganization by introducing the concept of "collective efficacy": a neighborhood is defined in terms of its ability to maintain order amongst the residents. This efficacy can exist only when mutual trust and cohesion of the community are linked to shared intervention of neighborhood social control. Other factors outside of the local residents' control also affect social disorganization and the efficacy of informal control sanctions including the cognitive landscape, socioeconomic status, residential mobility, heterogeneity, and urbanization. In essence, these models view disorganization as a result of structural barriers that affect the development of the formal and informal ties that would promote the ability to solve common problems when communities lack informal mechanisms of social control or exhibit ineffectual levels of collective efficacy; crime rates increase owing to the lack of community self-organization.

Box 4.3 Private military contractors: anomie and social disorganization

Private Military Contractors (PMCs) often operate within a socially disorganized environment. After all, war-torn areas are by definition disorganized. As most PMCs operate in areas of conflict or under tumultuous conditions they are more prone to experiencing the chaos that is a result of the disorganization and indirectly a result of the larger anomic conditions guiding their actions. Their immediate goal accomplishment mechanisms are innately violent and thus prone toward producing additional atrocity when unchecked and constrained. Even corporate social disorganization can undermine or hinder the extant informal social controls within a corporation, thus allowing high rates of criminal activity to occur. This can also occur due to the incongruence associated with intermingling private military with formal military command structures, or the result of a blanket level of disorganization within the corporation or "unit" that is dispatched. For example, circumstances surrounding the deaths of four Blackwater employees in Fallujah (Iraq) speaks of the disorganized environment and corporate structure that led to their "wrongful" deaths. Blackwater intentionally failed to provide the contractors "with the promised levels of protection and information needed, such as armored vehicles, sufficient advance notice of the mission, and sufficient personnel to have a rear-gunner to discourage attacks." They were instead forced to carry out a mission that was disorganized and without the proper support that had been guaranteed in the original contract. Disorganized environments are also created when high rates of turnover are persistent in a corporation. As noted by a Blackwater employee: "Blackwater is like a fucking restaurant. You've got hundreds of people coming through" ... We see a similar pattern of disorganization that surrounded the contractors from CACI and Titan that led to the use of torture in interrogations and security. The command structure at Abu Ghraib, for example, was highly flawed especially given the lack of accountability or knowledge of exactly what the PMCs were doing and their role within the prison walls. There was not only an atmosphere of ambiguity for standards to be used for the PMCs roles, but there was a general level of disorganization at the prison including lack of sufficient personnel, intermixing of roles, the interjection of Central Intelligence Agency (CIA) and other special operating forces.

Additionally, within conflict situations the context is even further disorganized and chaotic, which can create the propensity for individuals to make up their own rules and try to create organization and support, especially given that most PMCs remain isolated and disorganized in the theater of operations. At times, PMCs run vehicles off the road or fire rounds into any car that gets close to their convoy. As noted by one military press officer, the conditions are like "something out of *Mad Max*" [the 1980 Australian movie starring Mel Gibson]. As Robert Fisk wrote: "[t]he power of the mercenaries has been growing ... thugs with guns now push and punch Iraqis who get in their way ... Baghdad is alive with mysterious Westerners draped with hardware, shouting, and abusing Iraqis in the street, drinking heavily in the city's poor hotels."

Not only are conditions of deployment in socially disorganized areas, but PMCs are also finding themselves in environments where they have no social support. As noted by Priest and Flaherty: "Under assault by insurgents and unable to rely on US and coalition troops for intelligence or help under duress, private security firms in Iraq have begun to band together ... with its own rescue teams and pooled, sensitive intelligence." This lack of social support is also evidenced with the case of the contractors with the London-based Hart Group Ltd.: "We were holding out, hoping to get direct military support that never came," said Nick Edmunds, Iraq coordinator for Hart, whose employees were operating in an area under Ukrainian military control.

   Beyond the concept of social disorganization, we believe anomic conditions are core in creating the criminogenic environment from which PMCs operate. Recall that at the forefront of anomie then is the lack of regulation. As Tombs and Whyte state, accountability is stymied through the use of private contractors by absorbing the " 'corporate veil,' 'commercial confidentiality' and the inapplicability of Freedom of Information legislation into their security activities." Conversely, PMCs operate in an ambiguous legal status in theaters of conflict. After all, PMCs and their employees are not subject to the same rules of engagement as the military, if they operate under any rules at all. Further, PMCs can "become very nomadic in order to evade nationally applied legislation which they regard as inappropriate or excessive." As lack of regulation is core to anomic conditions, it seems appropriate to define the problematic nature of controls for PMCs. Beyond traditional corporate activities, it is said that the privatization of the military force makes them "only subject to the laws of the market." Private military forces (PMFs) and private logistical support teams amplify the concept of "loopholes" because they involve minimal oversight, no transparency, and no standing international criminal laws to regulate them. Without some form of control, they are relatively free to behave as they see fit in the socially disorganized environments within which they operate.
   (From Rothe 2006b.)

Organizational theories

Since the 1980s, criminologists have drawn from sociological organizational theories (for example, organizational culture, subunits, role specialization, and task segregation, reward structures, and goal attainment), seeing them as having an important explanatory role for a host of crimes of the powerful (Kauzlarich and Kramer 1998). All organizations and institutions have their own culture. Once an organizational culture exists, it becomes institutional- ized, making it far more difficult to alter short of a major institutional transformation. As organizational theorists point out, organizational cultures and goals remain intact even as employees are replaced. Here, the importance of choice and bounded rationality are widely accepted as parts of organizational analysis.

Broader theories of organizational behavior highlight certain structures that may develop in bureaucratic environments where goal attainment is pushed to an "any means necessary" degree. The very nature of complex organizations provides a host of opportunity-producing elements. Bureaucracies can maintain levels of secrecy with respect to how their resources are utilized; external actors need not know what was done within the organization or by whom. Information may also be hidden from other organizational actors, including those who are actually carrying out elements of criminal activity. Due to internal organizational structures of information control, the ability of external agencies to obtain information on the nature and dynamics of these decision-making events heighten criminal tendencies (Rothe and Mullins 2006). Certain organizations reinforce instrumental rationality within decision-making processes that can enhance the perceived value of criminal behaviors and reduce the perceived harm of the same act. Cultures develop within organizations or subunits that can motivate criminal endeavors (see Sutherland 1949). Situated action—that is, the impact of an environment affects an individual's decision-making and choices—is at the heart of organizational theories. Simply put, a good person can be brought to "evil" action within certain situations and environments. There is the recognition that we all become socialized into the specific organizational contexts in which we find ourselves. As such, it is fitting we now turn to learning theories, techniques of neutralization and normalization of deviance, all of which can take place and be fostered within the organizational structure.

Learning theories

Learning theories share certain assumptions of human nature and their relation to the social environment within which they exist. The suggestion here is that individuals are shaped, and can be reshaped, by specific environments and/or conditions. The process of normal learning generates criminal behavior no different from any other form of knowledge. As such, the key to these theories is the process of learning and the subsequent content of what is learned. Edwin H. Sutherland is the most well-known criminologist associated with learning theories, and is of course the founder of the criminology of white-collar crime. As noted by Sutherland (1949: 300), "Any person can be trained to adopt and follow a pattern of criminal behavior." Through the processes of socialization, individuals learn how to define their environment, favorable or unfavorable attitudes, and specific behaviors.

Sutherland's "Differential Association" theory contains nine postulates that serve as the framework for the process of learning criminal and non-criminal behaviors:

* Criminal behavior is learned.
* It is learned in interaction with others during communication.

- Learning occurs within intimate personal groups.
- The learning includes techniques, motives, drives, attitudes, and rationalization.
- The direction of motives is derived from the definition of law perceived as favorable or unfavorable.
- Delinquency occurs because of excess of favorable definitions over non-favorable.
- Associations vary in time, frequency, priority, intensity, and duration.
- The learning process to criminality is no different from any other learning process.
- Criminal behavior is an expression of general needs and values; it is not explained by those needs and values, as non-criminal behavior is an expression of the same needs and values.

Techniques of neutralization

Sykes and Matza (1957) introduced a model for techniques of neutralization, later expanded on by Matza (1964) when he emphasized that deviant behavior is activated by two impetuses: preparation and desperation, and that the feasibility of deviance involves a moral and technical element. The neutralizing techniques include (1) denial of responsibility, (2) denial of injury, (3) denial of the victim, (4) condemnation of the condemner, and (5) appeal to a higher authority. These techniques can best be understood in terms of the simple process of rationalizing one's own behavior, whether in response to cognitive dissonance, as a precondition to acting, or other factors. Such processes can be prior to an act, aiding a cost–benefit analysis, or post-action to minimize a person's behaviors (Rothe 2009). This model can aid in our understanding of the discourse within the organizational setting, negating the impact of decision-making and subsequent policies as well as the interactional level.

Normalization of deviance

Diane Vaughan (1996) identified what she termed as the "normalization" of deviant practices within the organizational culture. The normalization of deviance occurs when actors define their deviant actions as normal as they conform to the norms and standards of the organization in which they act. "Thus, in some social settings deviance becomes normal and acceptable: it is not a calculated decision where the costs and benefits of doing wrong are weighed because the definitions of what is deviant and what is normative have been redefined within that setting" (Vaughan 2007:11). Organizational deviance is "a routine by-product of the characteristics of the system itself" (Vaughan 1996: 274). Once normalized, a deviant organizational practice becomes a routine activity that is anticipated, expected and used (Vaughan 1996). The

Box 4.4 Abuse, torture and Abu Ghraib: organizational theory, learning theories, and techniques of neutralization

From the onset, the choice of Abu Ghraib for a detention center was troubling. The 280-acre site, with only three towers, was located in civilian neighborhoods where insurgent snipers were easily hidden. This added to the already explosive mixture of emotions that led to the escalation of violence by US troops on civilians at large. Moreover, as the resistance to the US occupation continued to grow, mass roundups were being initiated, detaining thousands of Iraqis. By the Fall of 2003, the numbers of detainees increased and the necessary staff within Abu Ghraib was lacking. Additional organizational factors contributed to an environment where torture and abuses became part of the standard operating procedures in Abu Ghraib. Not only were the MPs' [military police] roles conflicted with multiple tasks such as overseeing prisoners in Iraq, reconstruction efforts, and battle zone security, they were also being "assigned" to tasks of pre-interrogation. In September 2003, Major General Geoffrey Miller, the commander at Guantanamo Bay, was sent to Iraq to assess detention centers and subsequently shared his techniques with interrogators. This included the recommendation that MPs be used to soften up and prepare detainees for MI [military interrogation] interrogators. What did this mean in practice? As one former military intelligence officer, familiar with Miller's directives, put it, "it means treat the detainees like shit until they will sell their mother for a blanket, some food without bugs in it and some sleep." Shortly after his visit, civilian contractors began to show up to aid in the interrogation process. That same month, former Attorney General Sanchez authorized expanded interrogation techniques. These quickly became standard US practice. As these practices became part of the organizational standard operating procedure, a sense of normalization began to occur where it became routine to see naked Iraqi detainees or to hear their screams.

By mid-November the complete takeover of MP supervision by MI had occurred. The chain of command was murky at best. In that environment a growing brutality surfaced as MPs were overwhelmed. This was evidenced by the change in videos MPs and MIs were sending back home to loved ones that were growing more intense, filled with hostilities amongst each other. Moreover, the push for "actionable intelligence" significantly worsened an already hostile environment towards more extreme physical reactions as anger and frustration was growing among US forces. As a constant reminder and motivator, a photocopied letter with Donald Rumsfeld's signature was taped to a column in Abu Ghraib, declaring the "need for actionable intelligence" along with suggested means such as using dogs, and a command to "make sure this happens." Command levels within Abu Ghraib were also aware of daily briefings with the National Security Council for updates on intelligence results: pressuring for intelligence to find out "who the hell is responsible for the insurgency ... who are they." (From Rothe 2006b.)

With any line of command, the need to have success in attaining goals is significant. The notion of necessity was reinforced by the organizational structure of Abu Ghraib. As MPs were put in the position to aid MIs in intelligence gathering, the primary goal was to obtain necessary intelligence to (1) end the insurgency, (2) save their fellow military personnel, and (3) to come closer to a date to return to the States. Soldiers learned that it was acceptable to " 'fuck' (i.e., beat up) and 'smoke' (i.e., bring to collapse through forced physical exertion)" detainees from their initial time of arrival. Consequently, "to a soldier in the field it meant sometimes using ways that were not in accordance with the Geneva Conventions and the law of war" ... This environment had a huge impact on generating the individual motivation to torture. Subsequently, neutralizing one's behavior as "for a greater good or a higher virtue" played a role. This neutralization was reinforced through animalizing the prisoners, Iraqis in general. Detainees were labeled as Gollum, an animalistic character of ignorance and stupidity. Personnel were able to claim a higher good and to neutralize their tactics of torture and abuse through the process of dehumanization.

Ignoring abuse and torture is also an individual response to the processes of socialization within the environment. As Sergeant Davis told CID investigators, "I witnessed prisoners in the MI hold section being made to do things that I would question morally ... but I assumed if they were doing things out of the ordinary or outside the guidelines, someone would have said something." Due to the processes of socialization, studies of torturers have shown that ordinary individuals, regardless of their psychological traits, can be made to torture others by being socialized to atrocity in terms of necessity. Low-ranking personnel witnessed OGA [other government agency] civilian and MI interrogators ignoring the Geneva Conventions and came to believe that anything goes, further reinforcing their socialization into the systematic practice of abuse and torture.

Once the systematic use of abuse and torture was institutionalized within the walls of Abu Ghraib, some individuals then engaged in a competition with each other, which escalated the torture and abuse. For example, in General Fay's Report, one of the cases noted states that "dog handlers were subjecting two adolescents to terror from the dogs for the purposes of playing a game ... dog handlers competed to see who could be the first to get detainees bowel movements and urination to work." At other times, torture occurred in an environment that was filled with frustration, anger, confusion, and most significantly boredom.
(From Rothe 2006a.)

deviance becomes embedded in the organization, culture, and structure where new ideologies are developed to justify the deviance and through socialization it reproduces itself as normal (see, for example, Box 4.5).

Box 4.5 Normalization of deviance and the Deepwater Horizon spill

The explosion of the Deepwater Horizon rig and the blowout of the Macondo well that damaged humans, animals, and ecological systems in the Gulf of Mexico was the end result of policies and actions of three crucial corporations, highlighting the process of normalization of deviance: British Petroleum, Transocean, and Halliburton. Regulation of the offshore industry had deteriorated to little more than a formality. "Created in the era of declining regulation amidst increased privatization, the scandals that plagued the MMS are rooted in the fundamental organizational dynamics of the agency" (Bradshaw 2012:72). Epitomizing the intimate relationship between the Minerals Management Service (MMS) and the offshore oil industry, in 2008 Congressional reports "revealed that up to a third of the MMS department employees involved in the royalties-in-kind (RIK) program had been engaged in serious misconduct over the past several years including rigging oil contracts, taking money as oil consultants and having sexual relationships and using drugs with oil and gas company representatives" (ibid.: 69). The normalization of deviance had infected the organizational culture at the MMS. Without any oversight and regulation, employees of the MMS RIK program and the oil industry had melded to become one. "Far from being perceived as 'deviant' activity, intimate fraternization between MMS and the industry had become the norm, enough to even consider legally codifying the relationship. This normalization of deviance had become so ingrained that employees of the RIK program sought to legalize their intimate relationships with industry that were prohibited by federal law" (ibid.: 70).

Rational choice

Rational choice models are typically associated with the classical school of criminological thought. The underlying assumption of human nature of the classical school, and shared by rational choice theories, is that humans are calculative rational beings with abilities to reason. Individuals make rational choices after a cost–benefit analysis: the doctrine of rationality. This was based on the hedonistic assumptions of human nature wherein individuals are pleasure-seeking animals that need their appetites to be constrained by regulations: perceived pleasure (criminal act) outweighing the pain (punishment). While the classical school viewed humans as free-willed, later developments recognized limitations to this. Alterations to the belief in completely free-willed beings include the concepts of bounded volunteer-ism and/or bounded free will, meaning individuals have free will but that freedom is constrained by their life position and environment.

Cornish and Clarke (1986) developed one version of rational choice the-ory that assumes offenders act after a rational decision-making process that includes (1) the initial choice to become involved, and then (2) the decision of whether to commit a criminal act. The key differentiation here from the classical school of thought is the inclusion of bounded rationality. Simply stated, bounded rationality views the decision-making process as being influ-enced by incomplete or inaccurate information. This is due to social factors and individual estimates of perceived costs and benefits (Rothe 2009). Cohen and Felson (1979) further developed the rational choice theory to include choice constrained by opportunity. The elements of routine activities include a motivated offender (a given), suitable targets (opportunity), and capable guardians (operationality of control). This follows Cornish and Clarke's concept of bounded rationality, but illuminates the situational factors with the aforementioned key postulates of routine activities theory.

While we agree with the generic situational factors, we do not agree that "criminal inclination is a given and ... [we need to] examine the manner in which the spatio-temporal organization of social activities helps trans-late their criminal inclinations into action" (Cohen and Felson 1979: 589). Rather, motivation is an essential variable to be explained. The complex psy-chological, social, and cultural factors (as well as interactions among these factors) that produce motivations are not so easily dismissed. Here we also caution students, as rational choice seems to be a natural "theory" to adopt and claim as present in cases of crimes of the powerful, that it is highly prob-lematic and should never be used as a singular explanation, as this textbook highlights.

Box 4.6 Rational choice limitations: case in point or collective violence

Under the influence of the concept of methodological individualism and rational choice, many within the international criminal law com-munity have come to simplistically regard perpetrators of collective violence as a collection of self-interested actors who act rationally in order to maximize their own self-interests. However, we know that this is not the case: genocide is a collective project! This leads us to the following question: In view of the strong evidence for a negative rela-tionship between group size and collective action, why would tens of thousands of rational, self-interested individuals work together towards a common criminal purpose? In this regard it should be pointed out that the empirical evidence demonstrates that "rational, self-interested individuals will not act to achieve their common or group interests." In contrast to traditional criminological theories, the Micro-Macro-Integrated Theoretical Model recognizes the fact that emotions are essential for flexible and rational decision-making and as a result views emotions as complex, dynamic systems made up of several separate components with different functions: physiological arousal, affect or subjective feelings, cognitive processes and action tendencies. It provides a more nuanced account of agency and responsibility than existing criminological theories—namely rational choice. Furthermore, large scale and complex criminal activities undertaken by a multitude of people will be unsuccessful if they are undertaken without emotions. Further, social identity is the "social glue" that binds participants in collective violence together. The theory views social identity as a function of the emotional significance placed on a particular group membership and emphasizes the critical role played by emotions in this process. In addition, the salience of group membership has a transformative effect on personal self-interests. In other words, it shifts social identity from the self ("my own best interests") to the collective ("our own best interests"), thereby creating a cooperative orientation within the group. From this perspective, it becomes important to recognize that collective violence involves associations between individuals following different pathways and in addition to appreciate the fact that participants in collective violence are motivated by a variety of different incentives (for example positive stimuli such as monetary incentives, opportunities for rape and plunder; or negative stimuli such as group pressures).

(From Olusanya 2014: 5.)

Summary: bringing it all back together

This chapter has attempted to provide you with a basic introduction to an integrated approach for theorizing crimes of the powerful. We have suggested that a specific level of analysis is insufficient. Likewise, one theory is not able to fully explain these types of crimes. As such, we have proposed here that students take into account the dialectic and intertwined relationships that are situated within a broader environment(s) and system(s) in any analysis. This should always include the impact of the broader system, including the global and capitalistic arrangements of today, power, and the conditions that constrain and facilitate actors within specific contexts, groups, organizations, or institutions. The theoretical concepts highlighted here are present in the case studies that you will read in later chapters.

Activities and discussion questions

1. Which of the theories reviewed in this chapter do you find to be the most and least compelling?
2. To what extent do you see the connections between the various theories of crime? Are some more receptive to theoretical integration than others?
3. Some of the theories reviewed in this chapter were originally intended to explain traditional street crime, not crimes of the powerful. Which ones are they and are they strong enough to provide quality explanations of both forms of crime?

References

Agnew, R. (2012). Dire Forecast: A Theoretical Model of the Impact of Climate Change on Crime. *Theoretical Criminology*, 16(1): 21–42.

Barak, G. (1997). *Integrating Criminologies*. Needham Heights, MA: Allyn and Bacon.

Barlow, H., and Kauzlarich, D. (2010). *Explaining Crime: A Primer in Criminological Theory*. New York: Rowman and Littlefield.

Bernard, T. J. (1990). Twenty Years of Testing Theories: What Have We Learned and Why?. *Journal of Research In Crime & Delinquency*, 27(4): 325–347.

Bradshaw, E. (2012). Deepwater, Deep Ties, Deep Trouble: A State-Corporate Environmental Crime Analysis of the 2010 Gulf of Mexico Oil Spill. PhD dissertation, Western Michigan University. Available at: http://scholarworks.wmich.edu/cgi/viewcontent.cgi?article=1078&context=dissertations (accessed on June 6, 2015).

Bursik, R., and Grasmick, H. G. (1993). *Neighborhoods and Crime: The Dimensions of Effective Community Control*. New York: Lexington.

Cohen, L. E., and Felson, M. (1979). Social Change and Crime Rate Trends: A Routine Activity Approach. *American Sociological Review*, 44(4): 588–608.

Colvin, M., Cullen, F. T., and Vander Ven, T. (2002). Coercion, Social Support, and Crime: An Emerging Theoretical Consensus. *Criminology*, 40(1): 19–42.

Cornish, D. B., and Clarke, R. G. (1986). *The Reasoning Criminal: Rational Choice Perspectives on Offending*. New York: Springer-Verlag.

Douglas, J. D. (1977). Shame and Deceit in Creative Deviance. In E. Sagarin (ed.), *Deviance and Social Change*, 59–86. Beverly Hills, CA: SAGE Publications.

Durkheim, É. (1897). *Le Suicide: étude de sociologie*. Paris: Alcan. (Tr. 1951).

Foucault, M. (1980). Truth and Power. In *Power/Knowledge: Selected Interview Writings, 1972–1977*, 109–133. New York: Pantheon Books.

Foucault, Michel. (1977). *Discipline and Punish: The Birth of the Prison*. Translated by Alan Sheridan. New York: Vintage.

Freeman, L. (2004). *The Development of Social Network Analysis: A Study in the Sociology of Science*. Vancouver: Empirical Press.

Freeman, L. (2006). *The Development of Social Network Analysis*. Vancouver: Empirical Press.

Kauzlarich, D., and Barlow, H. (2009). *Introduction to Criminology*. 9th edition. New York: Rowman and Littlefield.

Kauzlarich, D., and Kramer, R. (1998). *Crimes of the American Nuclear State: At Home and Abroad*. Boston, MA: Northeastern University Press.

Liska, A., Krohn, M., and Messner, S. (1989). Strategies and Requisites for Theoretical Integration in the Study of Crime and Deviance. In *Theoretical Integration in the Study of Crime and Delinquency: Problems and Prospects*, 1–20. Albany, NY: State University of New York Press.

Lynch, M. J., Long, M., and Stretesky, P. (2013). Add Parsimony and Stir … Exploring the Explanation of State Crime. *American Journal of Criminal Justice*, 38(1): 99–118.

Matza, David (1964). *Delinquency and Drift*. New York: John Wiley.

Merton, R. K. (1938). Social Structure and Anomie. *American Sociological Review*, 3: 672–682.

Michalowski, R. J., and Kramer, R. (eds.) (2006). *State-Corporate Crime: Wrongdoing at the Intersection of Business and Government*. Piscataway, NJ: Rutgers University Press.

Moody, J., and White, D. (2003). Structural Cohesion and Embeddedness: A Hierarchical Concept of Social Groups. *American Sociological Review*, 68: 103–127.

Nollkaemper, A., and van der Wilt, H. (eds.) (2009). *System Criminality in International Law*. Cambridge: Cambridge University Press.

Oatley, T. (2009). *International Political Economy*. 4th edition. London: Longman.

Olusanya, O. (2014). Understanding Collective Violence: What Are the Advantages of the Macro-Micro Integrated Theoretical Model Over the Rational Choice Model?. *Newsletter Criminology and International Crimes*, 9(1): 5–6.

Popper, K. R. (1959). *The Logic of Scientific Discovery*. London: Hutchinson.

Ross, J., and Rothe, D. (2008). The Ironies of Controlling State Crime. *International Journal of Law, Crime, and Justice*, 36(3): 196–210.

Rothe, D., and Mullins, C. (2006). International Community: Legitimizing a Moral Collective Consciousness. *Humanity and Society*, 30(3): 254–276.

Rothe, D. L. (2006a). The Masquerade of Abu Ghraib: State Crime, Torture, and International Law. PhD dissertation, Western Michigan University.

Rothe, D. L. (2006b). War Profiteering and the Pernicious Beltway Bandits: Halliburton and the War on Terror. In R. Michalowski and R. Kramer (eds.), *State-Corporate Crime: Wrongdoing at the Intersection of Business and Government*, 215–238. Piscataway, NJ: Rutgers University Press.

Rothe, D. L. (2009). *State Criminality: The Crime of All Crimes*. Lanham, MD: Lexington/Rowman and Littlefield.

Rothe, D. L. (2010). Facilitating Corruption and Human Rights Violations: The Role of International Financial Institutions. *Crime, Law and Social Change*, 53(5): 457–476.

Rothe, D. L., and Collins, V. (2011). An Exploration of System Criminality and Arms Trafficking. *International Criminal Justice Review*, 21(1): 22–38.

Rothe, D. L., and Friedrichs, D. O. (2014). *Crimes of Globalization*. London: Routledge.

Rothe, D. L., and Mullins, C. (2008). Genocide, War Crimes and Crimes Against Humanity in Central Africa: A Criminological Exploration. In Alette Smeulers and Roelof Haveman (eds.), *Supranational Criminology: Towards a Criminology of International Crimes*, 135–158. Antwerp: Intersentia.

Sampson, R. J., and Raudenbush, S. W. (1999). Systematic Social Observation of Public Spaces: A New Look at Disorder in Urban Neighborhoods. *American Journal of Sociology*, 105(3): 603–651.

Shaw, C. R., and McKay, H. D. (1942). *Juvenile Delinquency and Urban Areas*. Chicago, IL: University of Chicago Press.

Sutherland, E. (1949). *White Collar Crime*. New York: Holt, Rinehart, and Winston.

Sykes, G., and Matza, D. (1957). Techniques of Neutralization: A Theory of Delinquency. *American Sociological Review*, 22: 664–670.

Vaughan, D. (2007). Beyond Macro- and Micro-Levels of Analysis, Organizations, and the Cultural Fix. In Henry N. Pontell and Gilbert Geis (eds.), *International Handbook of White-Collar and Corporate Crime*, 3–24. New York: Springer.

Vaughan, D. (1996). *The Challenger Launch Decision: Risky Technology, Culture and Deviance at NASA*. Chicago, IL: University of Chicago Press.

Chapter 5

The symbiotic nature of crimes of the powerful

The problem with typologies and separating crimes of the powerful

The introductory chapter presented several typologies of crimes of the powerful with the caveat that separating the various divisions—white-collar crime, corporate crime, state-corporate crime, state crime, crimes of globalization, organized crime, and even environmental crime—or looking at them as *divisions within divisions* misses the broader symbiotic nature and relationships they have with each other, at times making it nearly impossible to claim one form or another. Put simply, it is difficult to see how corporate crimes are not related to the state, and in many cases to international financial institutions. Likewise, environmental crimes are generally committed by states, corporations, international financial institutions, and organized crime groups. State crime can rarely be separated from the complicit roles of corporations, and in some cases international financial institutions or organized crime groups. Organized crime groups, too, have some sort of implicit or complicit relationship with states and, in many cases, corporations and international financial institutions as well. As such, typologies that separate out these crimes may be convenient to highlight a primary role of one organization, but, in the end, this abstract and artificial division within divisions blinds the broader problem: the current power and economic structures and their reproduction.

Moreover, students of crimes of the powerful would be amiss in assuming these harms occur within a vacuum devoid of the broader social, political, and economic, and power structures. Likewise, any assumptions that these crimes are the result of individuals devoid of context, assuming pure agency, should be disabused. On the other hand, to assume it is all about capitalism, the political economy, or neoliberalism misses the historical legacy and pattern of crimes of the powerful pre-capitalism and in former non-capitalistic systems. Rather, there is symbiosis between the various types of harms/crimes, the perpetrators, and the structures/systems, where one perpetuates the other in a cyclical fashion. The driving forces behind crimes of the powerful are reproduced and reinforced by the powerful, thus, reproducing the

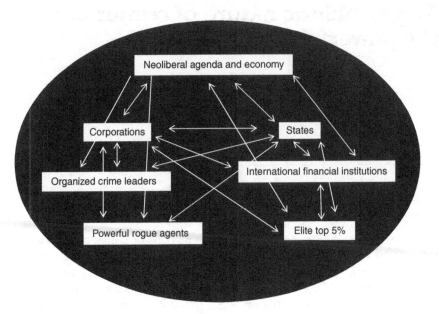

Figure 5.1 Fundamental social and political relationships

conditions that facilitate and legitimate these behaviors, which wax and wane throughout time.

Figure 5.1 may appear complicated and hard to follow given all the arrows that highlight relationships, though we contend this mirrors the reality of the symbiosis between all of the institutions and elite actors that produce and reproduce the structure that currently resides within the neoliberal agenda and that facilitates the harms and crimes of the powerful.

Students are most likely asking what drives these behaviors if we cannot blame it on individual choice, capitalism, politics, political economy, culture, or power. The "reality" is that it is all of the factors that we presented in Chapter 4. We emphasize the role of power as it is primary to the reproduction of relationships (social capital), harms of the powerful, and capital accumulation in a broad sense (prestige, knowledge, money, political will, the ability to create and spread hegemonic discourse and propaganda, the ability to pursue or maintain economic or military might, organizational legitimacy, etc.).

In the end, it is the relationship between them all that combines with specific intersections of time and opportunity, drawing from and reproducing relationships, power, and capital accumulation. As such, having these typologies and divisions of "type" for the crimes or harms of the powerful is problematic and retracts from the system component that is present. Likewise, we caution students to critically access various resources that suggest there are a host of other "types" of crimes of the powerful (for example, financial crime, political crime, crimes of empire, transnational crime), making the divisions within divisions more pronounced rather than the nuances of artificial typologies. Here again, we can be accused of reproducing some of these same problems with our separation of "types," though we reiterate that these are artificial and used for convenience to present to you as the reader, rather than a recognition of their uniqueness or atomistic nature.

Driving forces behind crimes of the powerful

Neoliberal agenda and globalization

The current state of crimes of the powerful is immersed within the trajectory of neoliberal economic policies and globalization, the combination of which provides a host of opportunities for the accumulation of capital and power. Whether we focus on transnational corporations, international financial institutions, states, organized crime syndicates, or the powerful that hold positions in multiple institutions and situations, their decision-making, policies, and actions all fall within the parameters set by the broader structure. This structure currently emphasizes privatization, open markets, deregulation of corporations, and transfusion of economic policies and culture from the Global North to the Global South.

> Within the discourse of neoliberalism, democracy becomes synonymous with free markets, while issues of equality, racial justice, and freedom are stripped of any substantive meaning and used to disparage those who suffer systemic deprivation and chronic punishment ... As Fredric Jameson has argued in *The Seeds of Time*, it has now become easier to imagine the end of the world than the end of capitalism.
>
> (Giroux 2005: 9)

Consider that a state's vested interest is in the growth of the economy, which is needed for it to maintain its legitimacy and political and military power. As such, corporations, their growth and profits, are a primary concern. Additionally, states both impact and are impacted by the international financial institutions in their ongoing push for global open markets and privatization. These financial institutions also play a primary role in facilitating corporate growth, expansion, and profit maintenance, generally at the expense of the non-powerful. Corporations need the state for charters, but more importantly to ensure an ongoing healthy market for them to exist without the over-regulation that would stymie their "successes," namely, profit. Having said this, we do note that corporations do not oppose all regulations, only those that could potentially hinder their goals, and indeed favor those that ensure protection, from legal rights to financial security, in cases of economic meltdowns like the one we have witnessed in the past few years, which saw mega government bailouts of the banking sector. As noted by Fasenfest (2010: 630–631), perversely, the cause for the current crisis is presented as the solution, and the major culprits have been put in charge of the recovery.

Within each of these sectors, there is an ongoing revolving door of relationships and power:

> Globalization can be seen as a mirror that reflects the status quo in terms of power relations in the global economy. Individual corporations that are most often hosted in the North, or the developed countries, are gigantic monolithic structures that have colossal amounts of power and resources to make changes and decisions to their favor. The support and backing of their mother countries which themselves are some of the most powerful in the world make this integrated world economy one that is controlled by the reins of a few is a view that is held by some.
>
> (Fernando 2007: 11)

The current geopolitical and economic sphere conveniently reproduces these symbiotic relationships between states, corporations, and international financial institutions. This theme will continuously reappear in the chapters devoted to various types of crimes of the powerful. Here again, we note that it is this interdependent relationship that makes the divisions between the types of crime (corporate, state, state-corporate, etc.) artificial and at times misleading, assuming a more monolithic form of criminality. Capital should not be misunderstood, however, as an economic term. Rather, capital can be understood as a site of gaining or maintaining power: social, political, cultural (including knowledge and language), and economic.

Capital accumulation: from social to political to economic gain

Capital accumulation is a central theme that runs through each of the crimes discussed here: capital accumulation or capital maintenance. As Bourdieu (1986) suggests, it is impossible to account for the structures and functions of the "objective" and "subjective" social worlds without reconsidering capital beyond an economic understanding. Social, economic, and political capital are resources in the larger social struggles that are carried out in different social/political arenas and can be used to produce or reproduce inequality. Capital types, such as economic, social, cultural, and political, interact with each other and can be exchanged for one another, increasing power in circumstances. Whether it is a head of state, leading political players within a regime or region, militia, or paramilitary, an organized crime syndicate, or a rogue criminal, the interest or desire to attain and utilize some form of capital is omnipresent. Consider the following quote by former President George W. Bush:

> You asked, do I feel free. Let me put it to you this way: I earned capital in the campaign, political capital, and now I intend to spend it. It is my style. That's what happened in the—after the 2000 election, I earned some capital. I've earned capital in this election—and I'm going to spend it for what I told the people I'd spend it on, which is—you've heard the agenda: Social Security and tax reform, moving this economy forward, education, fighting and winning the war on terror.
>
> (PBS 2004)

Likewise, former Prime Minister of Australia Paul Keating states, "I always believed in burning up the government's political capital, not being Mr Safe Guy, you know?," in an effort to pass market reforms (The Conversation 2013).

Social capital can be understood as the culmination of and expansion of networks that serve to provide greater cultural, economic, and political capital (see the resource section at the end of this chapter for additional information here on the revolving door between economic and political capital). Consider the case of Goldman Sachs in Box 5.1, where the revolving door relationships have recently been highlighted in the news. Additionally, beginning in 2012, Jin-Yong Cai serves as the current World Bank Group Executive Vice-President and CEO of the International Finance Corporation, after he had served as Participating Managing Director in Goldman Sachs Group and Chief Executive of Goldman Sachs with extensive involvement in Goldman's management globally through his membership on the Investment Banking Operations Committee, the Asia Executive Committee, the Growth Markets Committee, and the Partnership Committee, to name a few (World Bank 2012).

Likewise, the revolving door between the corporate sector and the state includes the "military industrial complex." In 2008, the Government Accountability Office found that 52 of the biggest defense contractors employed 2,435 former generals, senior executives, and acquisition officers. Of those, 422 were in a position to work on defense contracts directly related to their former agencies and at least nine may have been working on the same contracts they previously oversaw (Davenport 2014).

The networks and social capital extend beyond state borders or the corporate world. Consider this example from October 2014:

> India's government on Thursday appointed the Washington-based development economist Arvind Subramanian as its chief economic adviser ... [he has also been a] senior fellow at the Peterson Institute for International Economics in Washington ... [and] held positions at the International Monetary Fund ... [and] at the World Bank and the World Trade Organization.
>
> (Bagri 2014: 1)

Box 5.1 Revolving door: government, corporate, and back

Joshua Bolten

Government: President George W. Bush's Chief of Staff from 2006–2009; Director of Office of Management and Budget from 2003–2006; White House Deputy Chief of Staff from January 20, 2001–June 2003.
Goldman: Executive Director of Legal Affairs for Goldman based in London aka the bank's chief lobbyist to the EU from 1994–1999.

Kenneth D. Brody

Government: President and Chairman of the Export-Import Bank of the United States (1993–1996).
Goldman: Former general partner and member of the Management Committee at Goldman Sachs where he worked from 1971–1991.

Kathleen Brown

Government: Former California State Treasurer.
Goldman: Senior Advisor responsible for Public Finance, Western Region.

Mark Carney

Government: Governor of the Bank of Canada since 2008.
Goldman: Mr. Carney had a thirteen-year career with Goldman Sachs in its London, Tokyo, New York, and Toronto offices. His progressively senior positions included Co-Head of Sovereign Risk; Executive Director, Emerging Debt Capital Markets; and Managing Director, Investment Banking. He stated at Goldman in 1995.

Robert Cogorno

Government: Former Gephardt aide and one-time floor director for Steny Hoyer (D-MD.), the No. 2 House Democrat.
Goldman: Works for [Steve] Elmendorf Strategies, which lobbies for Goldman.

Kenneth Connolly

Government: Staff Director of the Senate Environment & Public Works Committee 2001–2006.
Goldman: Vice President at Goldman from June 2008–present.

E. Gerald Corrigan

Government: President of the New York Fed from 1985 to 1993.
Goldman: Joined Goldman Sachs in 1994 and currently is a partner and managing director; he was also appointed chairman of GS Bank USA, the firm's holding company, in September 2008.

Jon Corzine

Government: Governor of New Jersey from 2006–2010; U.S. Senator from 2001–2006 where he served on the Banking and Budget Committees.
Goldman: Former Goldman CEO. Worked at Goldman from 1975–1998.

Gavyn Davies

Government: Former chairman of the BBC from 2001–2004.
Goldman: Chief Economist at Goldman where he worked from 1986–2001.

Paul Dighton

Government: Chief executive of the London Operating Committee of the Olympic Games (LOCOG).
Goldman: Former COO of Goldman where he worked for 22 years beginning in 1983.

Mario Draghi

Government: Head [Governor] of the Bank of Italy since January 2006.
Goldman: Vice Chairman and Managing Director of Goldman Sachs International and a member of the firm-wide management committee from 2002–2005.

William Dudley

Government: President Federal Reserve Bank of New York City (2009–present).
Goldman: Partner and Managing Director. Worked at Goldman from 1986–2007.
(From CBS News 2010; see for a more detailed list.)

Economic capital is a constant source of power for states, corporations, and the elite. The extremely wealthy have an abundance of social and political capital due to the ability to use their economic capital to influence policies and politics. Consider the $100 billionaires Charles and David Koch, who own Koch Industries and actively fund pro-business, conservative political candidates. Sheldon Adelson, a billionaire casino tycoon, the chairman and CEO of the Las Vegas Sands Corporation and owner of the Israeli daily newspaper *Israel Hayom*, spent nearly $100 million in an effort to defeat President Barack Obama in 2012 and another $100 million to influence the 2014 Senate elections in the United States.

As the above examples highlight, it is not possession of one form of capital, but the accumulation and ability to "exert" and trade capital that facilitates the incestuous relationships that support and reify the existing structure. We do caution students, however; when discussing the role of neoliberalism, it should be clear that this is an ideology that guides economic policy. Likewise, the economy is not an objective entity—it is not an entity at all—only a system that is continuously socially constructed and played out using socially constructed objects as value (that is, tender or silver).

Finally, Charles Wright Mills (1959) pointed out a very long time ago that the sociological imagination—the ability to see the differences and connections between the personal and social—is a critical tool in understanding our world and ourselves. This is especially true in thinking about the crimes of the powerful. As offenders or victims, resisters or regulators, or witnesses to any of these, we are all tied together while also experiencing reality in unique ways. That crimes of the powerful are so consequential and profound, such as in the case of state and corporate complicity in global warming, makes this common experience all the more urgent to resist.

Summary

While the classification and typologizing of crime can be intellectually useful, the gravest harms are all wrapped up in larger systems of economics, politics, and social order, so they can all be understood as interdependent and multi-directional. This means that the organizing themes of political economy in the modern world are based on activities like the constant drive for profit, the buying off and corruption of political systems, and the disproportionately powerful driving most aspects of law, justice, and social policy. To understand crimes of the powerful, then, means to understand them as being epiphenomenal or as outcomes of broader economic and political relationships, both domestically and internationally.

Activities and discussion questions

1.   Develop a list of crimes and discuss the extent to which they are connected to political and economic structures in society.

2. Do you see law and social and criminal justice policy as issues best thought of as the outcome of democratic processes or capitalist influence on political systems?
3. Provide some examples of organizations that can commit crime with differing levels of social, cultural, and economic capital.

References

Bagri, N. (2014). India Picks Top Economic Aide, Formerly of I.M.F. *New York Times*, October 17. Available at: www.nytimes.com/2014/10/17/business/international/india-picks-top-economic-aide-formerly-of-imf.html?_r=0 (accessed on April 10, 2015).

Bourdieu, P. (1986). The Forms of Capital. In J. Richardson (ed.), *Handbook of Theory and Research for the Sociology of Education*, 241–258. New York: Greenwood.

CBS News (2010). Goldman Sachs' Revolving Door. April 8. Available at: www.cbsnews.com/news/goldman-sachs-revolving-door/ (accessed on September 11, 2015).

The Conversation (2013). Keating, Reform and the Difficult Notion of "Political Capital." December 15. Available at: http://theconversation.com/keating-reform-and-the-difficult-notion-of-political-capital-21315 (accessed on December 11, 2015).

Davenport, C. (2014). Pentagon Not Properly Tracking "Revolving Door" Data, Report Says. *Washington Post*, July 4. Available at: www.washingtonpost.com/business/economy/pentagon-not-properly-maintaining-revolving-door-data-report-says/2014/04/07/c65f27bc-be7f-11e3-b195-dd0c1174052c_story.html (accessed on February 17, 2015).

Fasenfest, D. (2010). Neoliberalism, Globalization and the Capitalist World Order. *Critical Sociology*, 36(5): 627–631.

Fernando, A. (2007). Globalization and the Neo-liberal Agenda: The Role of Corporations, International Financial Institutions and the WTO in Shaping the Processes. Position Paper 2, IGD Project, SPARC, Faculty of Arts, University of Colombo.

Giroux, H. A. (2005). The Terror of Neoliberalism: Rethinking the Significance of Cultural Politics. *College Literature*, 32(1): 1–19.

Jameson, F. (1994). *The Seeds of Time*. New York: Columbia University Press.

Mills, C. W. (1959). *The Power Elite*. New York: Oxford University Press.

PBS (2004). President Bush Announces Agenda for Second Term. November 4. Available at: www.pbs.org/newshour/bb/white_house-july-dec04-second_11-04/ (accessed on December 11, 2015).

World Bank (2012). World Bank Group Announces Jin-Yong Cai as New Executive Vice President and CEO of the International Finance Corporation. October 8. Available at: www.worldbank.org/en/news/press-release/2012/08/10/world-bank-announces-jin-yong-cai-new-executive-vice-president-and-ceo-the-international-finance-corporation (accessed on December 11, 2015).

Part II

Types of crimes of the powerful

Chapter 6

Corporate crime

Corporate crime is not new, nor is it a commonly taught area within criminology or criminal justice. Rather, the focus of the majority of textbooks, television shows, systems of social control, even the federal white-collar consortium, remains on what we define as occupational crimes—those committed by individuals during the course of employment for their own self-gain: the forgers, embezzlers, tax evaders, and fraudsters. Generally speaking, these are not what we would consider to be the "powerful." Additionally, corporate crimes are far more costly financially, physically, and mentally than those occupational crimes considered a priority by social control systems. We follow the Sutherland tradition and define corporate crimes as those crimes and harms committed in the name of or on behalf of the organization and major stakeholders for the gain of the organization, with the recognition of self-gain as a component though not a necessity. Additionally, we do not believe or suggest that all corporations are "bad" or "evil," rather they exist and operate within a system that facilitates criminogenic behavior as we discussed in the previous chapter. Before we begin discussing cases of corporate crime, let us first turn to a brief discussion on the personhood or legal standing and rights of corporations, as we suggest that it is the changes in legal standing and rights that have fueled corporate criminality and harms.

The corporation, personhood, rights, and legal power

In the United States, corporations began as a service to the community and were given charters, calling them into existence by states, and these charters could be revoked at any time if the corporation was found not to be a service or no longer needed. It was not until 1886 when corporations were first granted any of the rights that are typically thought of for persons. In the 1886 Supreme Court ruling in *Santa Clara County* v. *Southern Pacific Railroad Company*, Chief Justice Morrison Waite announced: "The court does not wish to hear argument on the question whether the provision in the 14th Amendment ... applies to these corporations. We are all of the opinion that it does" (Oyez Project n. d.). This was the beginning of a controversy and the onset of corporate personhood. It has been argued that the ruling and quote noted above was actually an error that the court stenographer made, and that the judge did not in fact make this ruling. Nonetheless, the transcript decision stood as legal precedent. In 1919, in the case of *Dodge* v. *Ford Motor Company*, the Michigan Supreme Court stated that "A business corporation is organized and carried on primarily for the profit of the stockholders. The powers of the directors are to be employed for that end." This decision in essence supported the notion of stockholder primacy. In 1922, the Supreme Court decided the Pennsylvania Coal Company enjoyed the Fifth Amendment rights and in 1967, the Fourth Amendment rights were extended to corporations. In 1970, in the case of *Ross* v. *Bernhard*, corporations were granted rights under the Seventh Amendment: the right to a jury trial. In 1978, in the case of *First National Bank of Boston* v. *Bellotti*, the First Amendment right of free speech was granted to corporations, allowing, for the first time, a legal standing for corporations to use their wealth and profits, without limitations, to influence politics (Yeoman 2006). This was reinforced in 2010 with the case of *Citizens United* v. *Federal Elections Commission* removing any doubt that Congress did not have the right or authority to regulate federal elections. Further, this case provided the most explicit justification of corporate personhood.

Box 6.1 Analogy: robots and corporations

The robots take over ... People create what looks to be a nifty machine, a robot, called the corporation. Over time the robots get together and overpower the people. They redesign themselves and reconstruct law and culture so that people don't remember they created the robots in the first place, that the robots are machines, are not alive. For a century the robots propagandise and indoctrinate each generation so it grows up believing that robots are people too, gifts from God and Mother Nature; that they are inevitable, and the source of all that is good. How gullible we've been.
(From Grossman 2001.)

In the United Kingdom, a similar situation exists where corporations are viewed as "persons." In 1600, the East India Company was the first chartered corporation, even though this was considered unlawful and, until 1825, corporations were primarily chartered by parliament for specific projects. In 1844, the Joint Stock Companies Act created the contemporary form of corporation and in 1855 they were granted limited liability, meaning shareholders were not responsible for any corporate debts and could not be assumed or forced to lose any financial costs other than the shares they owned, and this also protected them from any civil or criminal offenses committed by the corporation, save if the stakeholders could be shown to be personally involved in the criminality.

Originally, the courts controlled corporations in that, if they acted outside of their mandate or objectives, it could be challenged and declared void. While cases had previously watered this control down, it was the Companies Act 1989 that made the "objects" clause a statement or philosophy with no legal force or standing and the court or vested parties could no longer restrict the company's activities (Spenser 2004). Under the 1998 Human Rights Act, corporations were given the right to a fair trial, privacy, freedom of expression, and property.

Given the global and multinational character of corporations that are considered "powerful" in the sense that we are using it, these characteristics, rights, and personhoods have expanded and are the case in almost all regions. These legal rights, afforded as personhood and the conglomeration of ownership, have provided an environment that, when undergirded by neoliberalism, results in the many growing cases of corporate harms and crimes where, more often than not, profit is above humanity.

Corporate wealth and conglomerate ownership

Global inequality most students are aware of, yet many do not realize that the majority of products and services are owned by just a few corporations. A report by Vitali, Glattfelder, and Battiston (2011) analyzed all 43,060 transnational corporations and share ownerships and found that 147 of them own interlocking stakes of one and another, controlling 40 percent of the wealth (see Table 6.1). A total of 737 control 80 percent of the value of all transnational corporations.

Most of the corporations listed in Table 6.1 are investment firms. When it comes to products and services beyond investments and banks, of the top 100 companies, the US corporations dominate with 47 companies listed (see the list in Box 6.2). Breaking them down by type, we see the following: financial institutions have 21 in the top 100; technology has 13; consumer goods has 16; oil and gas has 14; health care has 12; consumer services has 7; industrials have 7; telecommunications has 5; and basic materials has 5. So who are some of these?

• Technology:

Apple Inc.; Google Inc.; Microsoft Corp.; IBM Corp.; Oracle Corp.; Facebook Inc.; Tencent Holdings Ltd.; Qualcomm Inc.; Intel Corp.; Cisco Systems Inc.

Table 6.1 The top 50 of the 147 corporations

1. Barclays plc	26. Lloyds TSB Group plc
2. Capital Group Companies Inc.	27. Invesco plc
3. FMR Corporation	28. Allianz SE
4. AXA	29. TIAA
5. State Street Corporation	30. Old Mutual Public Limited Company
6. JP Morgan Chase & Co.	31. Aviva plc
7. Legal & General Group plc	32. Schroders plc
8. Vanguard Group Inc.	33. Dodge & Cox
9. UBS AG	34. Lehman Brothers Holdings Inc.
10. Merrill Lynch & Co. Inc.	35. Sun Life Financial Inc.
11. Wellington Management Co. LLP	36. Standard Life plc
12. Deutsche Bank AG	37. CNCE
13. Franklin Resources Inc.	38. Nomura Holdings Inc.
14. Credit Suisse Group	39. The Depository Trust Company
15. Walton Enterprises LLC	40. Massachusetts Mutual Life Insurance
16. Bank of New York Mellon Corp.	41. ING Groep NV
17. Natixis	42. Brandes Investment Partners LP
18. Goldman Sachs Group Inc.	43. Unicredito Italiano SPA
19. T Rowe Price Group Inc.	44. Deposit Insurance Corporation of Japan
20. Legg Mason Inc.	45. Vereniging Aegon
21. Morgan Stanley	46. BNP Paribas
22. Mitsubishi UFJ Financial Group Inc.	47. Affiliated Managers Group Inc.
23. Northern Trust Corporation	48. Resona Holdings Inc.
24. Société Générale	49. Capital Group International Inc.
25. Bank of America Corporation	50. China Petrochemical Group Company

Source: Vitali, Glattfelder and Battison (2011)

• Consumer goods:

Nestle; Procter & Gamble Co.; Samsung Electronics Co. Ltd.; Toyota Motor Corp.; Anheuser-Busch InBev; The Coca-Cola Co.; Philip Morris International; PepsiCo Inc.; Unilever; Volkswagen AG; L'Oréal SA.

• Consumer services:

Wal-Mart Stores Inc.; Amazon.com Inc.; Walt Disney Co.; Comcast Corp.; Home Depot Inc.; McDonald's Corp.; CVS Caremark Corp.

• Industrials:

General Electric Co.; Siemens AG; Boeing Co. United States.
Globally, of the 100 companies with the most foreign assets, meaning those operating beyond their base country, 17 have over 90 percent of their assets abroad including Nestlé, Anheuser-Busch InBev, and Vodafone (*The Economist* 2012).

Box 6.2 Top 20 US corporations out of Top Global 100

- Apple Inc. (technology)
- Exxon Mobil Corp. (oil and gas)
- Google Inc. (technology)
- Microsoft Corp. (technology)
- Berkshire Hathaway Inc. (financials)
- Roche Holding AG (health care)
- Johnson & Johnson (health care)
- General Electric Co. (industrials)
- Wells Fargo & Co. (financials)
- Nestlé SA (consumer goods)
- Wal-Mart Stores Inc. (consumer services)
- Royal Dutch Shell plc (oil and gas)
- PetroChina Co. Ltd. (oil and gas)
- Novartis AG (health care)
- Chevron Corp. (oil and gas)
- JPMorgan Chase & Co. (financials)
- Procter & Gamble Co. (consumer goods)
- Samsung Electronics Co. Ltd. (consumer goods)
- Pfizer Inc. (health care)
- Ford Motor Company (motor vehicles)

Source: Vitali, Glattfelder and Battison (2011)

If we combine all the information from above, what we see is a few major multinational or transnational corporations controlling much of the global market from financials to services and products. We may feel we have many choices and products available for consumption and use today; yet, when we delineate these major corporations, we find out the products and services may be vast, but the ownership is very limited. Having looked at the broader environment of legal standing and regulation, conglomeration of ownership and wealth, let us also consider the power of these corporations in terms of lobbying, especially in the case of the United States, though this is not unique and happens in various fashions across the globe including bribery, as we will discuss later.

Lobbying power

Lobbying power is about more than direct campaign contributions to politicians; it also includes lobbying Congress and federal agencies. Each year, billions of dollars are spent on US lobbying to impact the special interests and privilege of corporate vested interests. Some corporations retain their own lobbying firms and others have lobbyists who work in-house or in the government (see Table 6.2 as an example).

Table 6.2 Monsanto's federal lobbying expenditures, 2008–2013

Year	Q1	Q2	Q3	Q4	Total
2008	$1,280,000	$1,980,000	$3,380,000	$2,188,120	$8,831,120
2009	$2,094,000	$2,080,000	$1,990,000	$2,530,000	$8,694,000
2010	$2,460,000	$2,180,000	$1,920,000	$1,470,000	$8,030,000
2011	$1,440,000	$1,710,000	$2,010,000	$1,210,000	$6,370,000
2012	$1,410,000	$1,520,000	$1,800,000	$1,240,000	$5,970,000
2013	$1,590,000	$1,400,000	$2,440,000	$1,510,000	$6,940,000

Source: Union of Concerned Scientists 2015

Box 6.3 Top pharmaceutical spenders for lobbying

Five pharmaceutical companies have reported million-dollar increases in their spending on lobbying the United States federal government during the first quarter of 2014. The top pharmaceutical spenders in the first quarter of 2014:

Pharmaceutical Research & Manufacturers (PhRMA) $4,680,000—up from $4,050,000 in 2013 Q4.

Pfizer Inc. $3,190,000—up from $2,090,000.
Novartis $2,580,000—up from $920,000.
Amgen USA Inc. $2,560,000—up from $2,330,000.
Eli Lilly & Co. $2,086,000—down from $2,430,000.
Johnson & Johnson Services $2,110,000—up from $860,000.
Bayer $2,040,000—up from $1,000,000.
Merck & Co. $2,000,000—up from $820,000
Glaxosmithkline $1,630,000—up from **$421,000. (Corrected)**
Sanofi US Services Inc. $1,570,000—up from $790,000.
AbbVie $1,450,000—up from $600,000.
Genentech Inc. $1,152,000—down from $1,220,700.
Teva Pharmaceuticals USA Inc. $1,160,000—up from $800,000.
AstraZeneca $1,030,000—up from $560,000.
Novo Nordisk Inc. $710,000—down from 820,000.
Bristol-Myers Squibb Co. $520,000—down from 740,000.
Abbott Laboratories $410,000—down from $700,000.
(From Cooper 2014: 1.)

The Center for Responsive Politics gathered data from the United States Senate Office of Public Records and reported that the known total amount of spending on recorded lobbying efforts by corporations between 2012 and 2014 looked like this:

Table 6.3 Overall top spenders for lobbying in 2014

Lobbying client	Total
US Chamber of Commerce	$91,935,000
National Association of Realtors	$41,624,253
Blue Cross/Blue Shield	$15,651,221
American Medical Association	$15,070,000
American Hospital Association	$14,652,342
National Association of Broadcasters	$13,910,000
Google Inc.	$13,680,000
Pharmaceutical Research and Manufacturers of America	$12,650,000
Dow Chemical	$12,520,000
General Electric	$12,480,000
Boeing Co.	$12,440,000
National Cable and Telecommunications Association	$11,960,000
Comcast Corp.	$11,940,000
United Technologies	$11,438,000
CVS Health	$10,977,640
AT&T	$10,960,000
Lockheed Martin	$10,688,325
Business Roundtable	$10,540,000
Verizon Communications	$10,220,000

Source: Open Secrets 2014

2012: $3.31 billion; 2013: $3.24 billion; 2014: $2.41 billion.
Moreover, the overall number of known lobbyists is astounding:
2012: 12,437; 2013: 12,359; 2014: 11,509.

The top spenders for lobbying in 2014 are provided in Table 6.3:
Given this, the intersections between business and government are more than blurred; rather, it is a cooperative system where vested interests vie for priority, ensuring corporate interests are heard and addressed and impacting decisions from regulations to monopolies and beyond. This is not unique to the United States. The United Kingdom has a similar situation where "Lobbyists are paid to influence government decisions. So, whether it's the private healthcare lobby pushing for the current NHS reforms; or banks lobbying against reform of the financial system; or the construction industry wanting to get their hands on greenbelt land," lobbyists affect politics, and eventually us and our daily lives (Alliance for Lobbying Transparency 2015). As Steve Tombs (2012: 170) notes, states and corporations are increasingly in a symbiotic relationship leading to the systematic, routine production of crime and harm. In many circumstances, disentangling "state interests" from "corporate interests" is highly problematic owing to the intersecting

agendas of those at the top of both the state and the corporate hierarchies, and the multiple "interlocks" reflected in movements in and out of high-level state and corporate positions (Friedrichs and Rothe 2014; Michalowski and Kramer 2006).

Criminology and corporate crime

From a criminological sense, concern over corporate crimes has been a long and highly marginalized road. The term "white-collar crime" was coined in 1939 by Edwin H. Sutherland. He defined it as crimes committed by people of respectability and high social status in the course of their occupations. Sutherland also observed that criminologists had virtually ignored the illegal activities of those in business, politics, and the professions, concentrating instead on the world of lower-class criminality emphasized in crime statistics and in the criminal justice system. Lawbreaking, he argued, goes on in all social strata. Restraint of trade, misrepresentation in advertising, violations of labor laws, violations of copyright and patent laws, and financial manipulations were a part of what Sutherland called "whitecollar crime."

Over the years since Sutherland's groundbreaking work, other criminologists have refined the definition of white-collar crime. As touched upon in Chapter 1, one of the earliest of these was Clinard and Quinney's (1973) effort to define white-collar crime in more operational terms. They split the concept of white-collar crime into corporate crime—crimes organizationally based and directed toward reaching *corporate* goals—and occupational crime—acts committed by individuals in the course of their occupations for their own *personal* gain. Today, the study of corporate crime is firmly entrenched into the field of criminology, although most criminologists still prefer to study forms of traditional street crime.

Examples of corporate crime

> I live in the Managerial Age, in a world of "Admin." The greatest evil is not now done in those sordid "dens of crime" that Dickens loved to paint. It is not even done in concentration camps and labour camps. In those we see its final result. But it is conceived and ordered (moved, seconded, carried and minuted) in clean, carpeted, warmed and well-lighted offices, by quiet men with white collars and cut fingernails and smooth-shaven cheeks who do not need to raise their voices.
>
> (C. S. Lewis 1941)

As the above quote suggests, crimes of the powerful are often borne out in boardrooms, executive offices, parliaments, congress, and state rooms. The following sections provide some examples of common corporate crimes.

Restraint of trade

The first relevant federal statute relating to trade was the Sherman Antitrust Act of 1890. Designed to curb the threat to a competitive free-enterprise economy posed by the nineteenth-century spread of trusts and monopolies, this act made it a criminal misdemeanor for individuals or organizations to engage in restraint of trade by combining or forming monopolies to that end. In 1974, Congress made restraint of trade a felony, thus making it possible for convicted offenders to receive prison terms of a year or more. Antitrust violations contribute to the persistence of a "closed enterprise system," the very antithesis of what American business is supposed to be.

There are three principal methods of restraint of trade: (1) consolidation so as to obtain a monopoly position; (2) price fixing to achieve price uniformity; (3) price discrimination, in which higher prices are charged to some customers and lower ones to others. From the standpoint of those engaging in these practices, they make sense: the lower the competition and the greater the control over prices, the larger the profits. But, small and independent businesses will lose business, and the public at large will face higher prices and lose its discretionary buying power.

The most common violations of restraint of trade laws are price fixing and price discrimination. Price fixing is an example of "horizontal" restraint of trade because it involves people or organizations at the same level in the chain of distribution (manufacturing, wholesaling, or retailing). Examples of price fixing include any agreement or understanding among competitors to raise, lower, or stabilize prices. Price discrimination represents "vertical" restraint in that it involves conspiracies across different levels, for example, between manufacturers and retailers. Sutherland (1949) describes a case involving Sears, Roebuck, and Goodyear Tire Company: Goodyear charged Sears a lower price than its own independent Goodyear dealers for identical tires, allowing Sears to charge a lower retail price to the disadvantage of the Goodyear independents.

In his investigation of 70 of the largest US corporations over a 50-year period, Sutherland found that many of the suits charging restraint of trade through price fixing or price discrimination were brought by private interests rather than by the Federal Trade Commission or the Department of Justice, the two agencies given primary responsibility for enforcing restraint of trade provisions. When corporate officers break the law on behalf of their organizations, criminal justice officials do not seem particularly aggressive in ferreting out violations and bringing charges. But this should hardly come as a surprise, given the close relationship between business and politics. Indeed, in Europe and the Far East, governments have historically encouraged cartels, whose price-fixing activities are legendary.

Price-fixing conspiracies

In 1961, 21 corporations and 45 high-ranking executives in the heavy electrical equipment industry were successfully prosecuted for criminal violations of the Sherman Antitrust Act. They had been involved in a price-fixing and bid-rigging scheme that, over nearly a decade, had bilked local, state, and federal governments (and taxpayers) out of millions of dollars on purchases averaging nearly $2 billion a year.

In carrying out their scheme, called by trial judge J. Cullen Ganey (1961) "the most serious violations of the antitrust laws since the time of their passage at the turn of the century," executives of the conspiring companies would meet secretly under fictitious names in hotel rooms around the country. Referring to those in attendance as "the Christmas card list" and to the meetings as "choir practice," the conspirators arranged prices for equipment, allocated markets and territories, and agreed on which companies would supply the low bids on pending government contracts. The participants covered their tracks well and were discovered only because officials of the Tennessee Valley Authority had received identical sealed bids on highly technical equipment. The companies involved in the conspiracy ranged from such giants in the electrical equipment business as General Electric, Westinghouse, and Allis Chalmers, to such smaller firms as the Carrier Corporation, the I.T.E. Circuit Breaker Company, and Federal Pacific.

This price-fixing conspiracy illustrates extensive collusion among corporations which have found a way to prosper without having to compete. Needless to say, cooperation is preferred when the benefits outweigh the risks of competition. Equally important, the cooperators usually gain over those who refuse to, or simply cannot, participate in the collusion. This advantage is precisely what restraint of trade laws are designed to curb, for its consequence is obvious: fewer firms stay in business, and the prices of goods and services rise when the survivors exercise their monopoly on power, keeping new competitors away and setting artificially high prices and, in effect, stealing from their customers. The cost of those higher prices can be staggering. In the heavy electrical equipment conspiracy, the cost approached $3 billion, "more money than was stolen in all the country's robberies, burglaries, and larcenies during the years in which the price fixing occurred" (Geis 1978: 281). There are countless illustrations of price fixing, although rarely will those accused of it admit the practice. Cullen, Maakestad, and Cavender (1987: 60) have argued that "conspiracy to set prices has become a way of life in some industries."

The savings and loan failures

When savings and loan (S&L) companies began to fail around the country in the late 1980s, alarm bells sounded in homes and businesses everywhere and in Washington, DC. Long thought to be among America's most stable and trustworthy institutions, the local S&L suddenly looked weak and vulnerable. Since the government insures savings up to $100,000 in individual accounts, small investors were not hurt; however, the private aggregate cost to taxpayers has been estimated at over $500 billion. Mismanagement and mistakes in operating a business are not necessarily indications of criminal activity. Many believe that the S&L collapse was a product of systemic changes resulting from the deregulatory frenzy of the Reagan years and the rise of the junk bond market. Deregulators took the position that "the free enterprise system works best if left alone" (Calavita and Pontell 1990: 312). The opportunities and incentives for S&Ls to embark on risky ventures were simply too compelling given the freeing of controls and the prospects of huge short-run profits. A sort of "casino" economy emerged where speculation and deregulation created expanded opportunities for fraud and embezzlement (Calavita and Pontell 1991). "Participants in this epidemic of fraud included both those who deliberately entered the thrift industry in order to loot it and legitimate thrift operators who found themselves on the 'slippery slope' of insolvency, unlawful risk taking, and cover-up" (Pontell and Calavita 1993: 240).

As details surrounding the collapse of Lincoln Savings and Loan, the largest thrift failure in US history, emerged it became clear that deceit, conspiracy, political corruption, and all manner of financial irregularities were involved. A sort of "collective embezzlement" occurred, in which S&L executives siphoned off funds for personal gain at the expense of the institution, "but with implicit or explicit sanction of its management" (Calavita and Pontell 1990: 321). On December 4, 1991, a Los Angeles jury convicted S&L owner Charles H. Keating, Jr., on 17 counts of securities fraud. On April 10, 1992, he was sentenced to ten years in prison and fined $250,000. How does one measure this punishment against the estimated $2.6 billion that the collapse of Lincoln is estimated to have cost American taxpayers?

Frauds in advertising, sales, and repairs

Consumers become the victims of fraud in many different ways, including misrepresentation in advertising and sales. Misrepresentation in advertising means that what prospective buyers are told about a product is untrue, deceptive, or misleading. Sometimes the misrepresentation concerns the quality of a product or the actual contents of a package or container; sometimes it concerns the effectiveness of a product; and sometimes it involves lack of or insufficient information about a product or service such that buyers are misled. An illustrative case involved Chrysler Corporation. In 1987, the company admitted selling as "new" cars that had in fact been previously driven by executives. Another example is an advertising campaign by Ralston Purina, the makers of Puppy Chow, in which the company seemed to be claiming that its product cured cancer.

The fact that a fine line divides fraudulent from legitimate sales promotion becomes evident as one considers a problem faced by nearly all businesses: creating a need for their products and services. Many of the things considered necessities today—canned foods, refrigerators, automobiles, insurance policies—either did not exist several decades ago or were thought of as luxuries, certainly not necessities. They have come to be thought of as necessities largely because the companies selling them have convinced the public that they are. When things are necessities, people "need" to purchase them.

In their efforts to convince people of a need for goods and services, businesses use a variety of different ploys. A fraudulent ploy is to make false claims as to the effectiveness of a product in doing what it is supposed to do. Those who believe the claims will see a need for the product. An example is the advertising plan followed some time ago by the makers of Listerine. In their campaign, the makers sought to create a need for Listerine as a mouthwash, a fairly new idea at the time; to establish that need, they presented fake claims about the mixture's germ-killing powers.

It is only a short step from these strategies to those that the common swindler uses. Consider the activities of the Holland Furnace Company. This company was in the business of selling home-heating furnaces. With some 500 offices and a sales force in the thousands, the company put its resources to work on a fraudulent sales promotion involving misrepresentation, destruction of property, and, in some cases, what amounted to extortion. Salesmen, misrepresenting themselves as "furnace engineers" and "safety inspectors," gained entry into their victims' homes, dismantled their furnaces, and condemned them as hazardous. They then refused to reassemble them, on the grounds that they did not want to be "accessories to murder." Using scare tactics, claiming that the furnaces they "inspected" were emitting carbon monoxide and other dangerous gases, they created, in the homeowners' minds, a need for a new furnace and proceeded to sell their own product at a handsome profit. They were so ruthless that they sold one elderly woman nine new furnaces in six years for a total of $18,000. The Federal Trade Commission finally forced the company to close in 1965, but, in the meantime, it had done some $30 million worth of business per year for many years (Leiser 1973: 270).

In another example of corporate theft and fraud, a lawsuit costing $238 million accused State Farm Insurance of several fraudulent practices involving the sale of whole life and universal life policies from January 1982 to December 1997. This lawsuit, which State Farm settled without admitting wrongdoing, claimed that policyholders were told to switch policies so they could receive greater benefits. In reality, these greater benefits were for the company, not the customer. Customers were also intentionally deceived about the rate of return on their policies and were given unreasonable predictions about the possible dividend. At about the same time, State Farm was found guilty of fraud in the use of generic replacement parts in auto body repairs.

Auto body shops generally need the permission of insurance companies when installing replacement parts. State Farm mostly approved the use of generic replacements parts, not the more reliable original equipment parts from car manufacturers. While State Farm acknowledges that it did recommend and approve the use of aftermarket parts rather than the "true" replacements, it claimed the practice was not illegal. The judge did not agree and slapped a $1.2 billion fine on the insurance company. This is believed to be the largest cash settlement against an insurance company.

The BCCI case

The Bank of Credit and Commerce International (BCCI) was established in 1972 by Pakistani financier Agha Hassan Abedi. BCCI became the first multinational bank originating out of the Global South. At that time headquartered in London, regulated (in a very loose way) by Luxembourg, and backed by Middle East oil revenues, BCCI had by 1990 over $20 billion in assets in 75 countries with more than 400 branches and subsidiaries (Potts *et al.* 1992). It gained a reputation for offering first-rate service to its large depositors, and for asking no questions. BCCI also knew exactly where to go in the political hierarchy of Western nations to get counsel and representation for its expansion, for example to Clark Clifford, who was a very powerful actor in multiple state and financial contexts. Clifford, a man of formerly unquestioned respectability and integrity, became chairman of First American Bankshares following its purchase by Saudi investors in 1981 with money loaned by BCCI. The investors eventually defaulted and BCCI (secretly, according to Clifford in Congressional testimony) became the owner of First American.

In 16 years of expansion, BCCI was not the legitimate banking operation it appeared to be and there is evidence that officials in many countries, including the United States, England, Peru, and Argentina, knew it. They knew that BCCI was heavily involved in shady activities, but, far from doing anything about it, found their own illegal uses for the bank.

Drug trafficking was arguably BCCI's downfall. Indicted by a federal grand jury in 1988 for laundering millions of dollars in drug money, BCCI eventually pleaded guilty and was fined $14 billion in 1990 (Potts *et al.* 1992). Subsequent investigations produced an incredible array of charges: gunrunning, bribery and corruption, smuggling, terrorism, securities theft, property theft of all sorts, influence peddling, insurance fraud, covert operations for the CIA, bank fraud, espionage, extortion, kidnapping, and the violation of other domestic and international laws. The bank was closed down in July, 1991, its assets frozen. In January, 1992, BCCI pleaded guilty to racketeering; Clifford was indicted seven months later, along with his law partner, and many more indictments and convictions will surely follow.

The Enron case

Perhaps the most infamous case of corporate fraud in US history took place in the late 1990s to 2001 when it was revealed that the energy giant Enron had seriously misrepresented its financial status for several years. At its core, the Enron case involved the company's fraudulent financial reports (concealment of debt and inflation of profits) and premeditated actions to cover up the company's declining value and forthcoming bankruptcy. It is also widely known that Enron company executives consistently provided messages to its employees and stockholders that the company was "doing great" and specifically encouraged others to buy more stock and invest more money into their pension plans because of the company's record "successes." Further, Enron executives Kenneth Lay and Jeffrey Skilling often took exorbitant bonuses and loans out for themselves through the company and its subsidiaries (some of which were shell companies), thereby diminishing the company's profitability and obligations to its line employees and stockholders (Friedrichs 2009). All told, it is estimated that the crimes of the Enron Corporation cost $2 billion in pension plans and $60 billion in lost markets shares/values (McLean and Elkind 2004).

In 2006, both Lay and Skilling were convicted of multiple charges of securities and wire fraud, with Skilling receiving a prison sentence of 24 years. Lay died shortly after the guilty verdicts. Over a dozen other Enron executives have also been convicted or pleaded guilty to corporate fraud charges, such as investor relations manager Paula Rieker, who in September of 2006 received two years' probation in exchange for her cooperation with authorities in other related cases. Another corporate giant, Arthur Anderson Accounting, was implicated in the Enron affair as well. Convicted on charges of obstruction of justice as a result of the shredding of Enron's financial documents, Arthur Anderson is now almost as defunct an organization as Enron.

Corporate violence

While many corporate crimes result in economic harms, a sizable amount of corporate crimes are violent. This violence includes corporations' involvement, from environmental harms to direct violence, such as hiring mercenaries to "protect" their interests, from mines to electric projects to dam building, that has resulted in immense harms, violence, forced displacement, and deaths across the Global South. Additional forms of corporate violence include the role of corporations in human trafficking, as Box 6.4 highlights.

Global profits from forced labor exploitation are estimated at $51.2 billion in general, with a significant amount that directly and indirectly involve corporations, where these types of violent crimes are hidden in plain sight and occur across the United States and the globe. It is clearly a myth that white-collar crimes can be correctly called "economic crimes." Here, we

---

Box 6.4 Corporations and human trafficking

A trial involving one of the biggest human trafficking cases in the United States began in a New Orleans Federal Court (January 2015), where it was alleged that Signal International, a US Gulf Coast ship-building company, had recruited individuals from India under false premises, then forcing them to live in "fenced-in labor camps and work for little to no pay" (Mississippi Press 2015: 1). Specifically, hundreds of welders and pipefitters were recruited to repair oil rigs damaged by Hurricane Katrina, paying up to $25,000 for the chance to come to the United States and work. They were promised full employment, green cards, and employee housing. However, their reality become one where they were forced to live in crowded shipping containers with up to 24 individuals in one unit, they were not fed, forced to work around the clock, and charged over a $1,000 for rent to live in the shipping containers along with other fees directly taken from their checks, leaving them with near zero balances. The premises were isolated compounds surrounded by barbed wire and armed guards, ensuring no one left the grounds. Furthermore, if they left the grounds, their H2B visas would be retracted; having not been given the proper green card or other work visa, they remain trapped, giving their forced labor.
(From Urban Institute 2015.)

---

review several instances of violent corporate crimes committed as part of a company's pursuit of profit, a major cause of most forms of corporate crime.

Violence against consumers

Most of us rely on corporations to provide us with the commodities we use in our daily lives. We assume these products will not expose us to unreasonable threats to our life and safety. Unfortunately, this assumption can be a serious error, as we shall see in the following examples.

Ford Motor Company's Pinto was designed in the late 1960s to compete in the "small car for a small price market," which at the time was controlled by Volkswagen. Ford president Lee Iacocca and other executives directed the Pinto to be produced quickly, weigh under 2,000 pounds, and cost less than $2,000. While the Pinto was being tested prior to its release into the marketplace, a major problem in the fuel system was discovered. When rear-ended, the Pinto's gas tank often ruptured. The problem could be fixed by placing a rubber bladder or flak within and/or around the tank or by locating the tank in a safer area. Ford executives rejected these avenues because the assembly line was already tooled for production and it would have cost the company several millions of dollars to redesign and produce a safer car. As a direct result of the deadly design of the Pinto, dozens of drivers and passengers of the vehicle were killed or seriously burned in rear-end collisions over the next several years (Cullen *et al.* 1987).

In the course of several successful civil suits against Ford and one unsuccessful criminal prosecution, it came to light that the company had made a conscious decision to risk the lives of consumers in order to make a profit. Ford calculated that a burn death would result in an average $200,000 loss and any injury less than death would cost them $67,000. Ford officials also calculated that the cost of fixing the problem with the Pinto's fuel tank placement would be a paltry $11 per vehicle. But, with 11 million cars to fix, paying the estimated $49.5 million it would cost in lawsuits for deaths and injuries would be a better business deal for the corporation. Ford was eventually forced to recall the Pinto after several successful product liability lawsuits (Mokhiber 1988). No one was ever sentenced to prison for the deaths.

Two widely publicized cases of corporate violence against consumers are also crimes against women and children (Fox and Szockyj 1996; Rynbrandt and Kramer 1995). First, the Dalkon Shield, an intrauterine birth control device, was marketed and sold by the A. H. Robins Company in the 1960s. The device was popular in part because it supposedly did not have negative side effects like the pill. It was also marketed as an extremely effective way of blocking pregnancy (Mokhiber 1988). But, because the Shield was poorly designed (and poorly tested), it often caused severe pelvic infections, sterility, poor pregnancy protection, and the spontaneous abortions of fetuses. Twelve women also died from using this device. The A. H. Robins Company, which knew of many of the problems with the Shield but did nothing to protect consumers, has escaped criminal charges but has paid nearly $1 billion in lawsuits (Mokhiber 1988).

Another corporate crime against women and children involved the sale and distribution of the drug thalidomide. Many women were given prescriptions for thalidomide as a tranquilizer and to combat morning sickness while pregnant. The producer of the drug, the German company Chemie Grünenthal, had information that the drug could cause major health problems, including severe disturbances to the nervous system. This information was ignored and downplayed by Grünenthal for years, but the company was finally forced to come clean after overwhelming evidence of the drug's horrible side effects on fetuses. At least 8,000 children, the "thalidomide babies," were born with deformed genitals, eyes, and ears, brain damage, and shortened limbs. While Grünenthal escaped criminal fines, Distillers Ltd., a company later distributing thalidomide under the name of Distaval in Britain, was forced to pay millions of dollars to British and German victims of this drug (Mokhiber 1988).

A more recent case involving widespread consumer violence includes the Blue Bell Creameries company, a US regional ice cream chain that recalled all of its products in April 2015 due to listeria. While that may seem to be the appropriate and corporately responsible thing to do, it should be noted that the company knew for over two years (since 2013) that they had a serious problem with listeria in their Oklahoma plant. Still, Blue Bell failed to improve its cleaning and manufacturing practices. Food and Drug Administration (FDA) inspectors also "found water condensation inside the Oklahoma plant dripped into frozen sherbet containers during production ... Blue Bell's own testing in 2014 found coliform bacteria levels in finished products higher than what the state of Oklahoma allows" (Collette 2015: 2). Even with the previous knowledge and citations from the FDA, Blue Bell failed to change its inadequate sanitation policies. This resulted in several deaths and sickness across several states. This is not unique to the United States. Consider that in the past year (2014–2015), Sainsbury's, a popular UK supermarket, had several recalls for tainted food products. Sainsbury's was forced to recall their own-brand watercress (with E. coli O157) that resulted in nearly two dozen people falling seriously ill; they also had issues with Salmonella and recalled their fruit and nut mix along with their lemon thyme herb. The Germany-based company, Milchwerke Mittelelbe GmbH, under the label of Mars, was forced to recall their chocolate drinks after it was found that they contained elevated levels of Bacillus bacteria.

Violence against workers

According to the Occupational Safety and Health Administration (OSHA 2015), there were 3 million work-related injuries and illnesses in 2013. OSHA also estimates that just under 5,000 workers died on the job that year. However, these statistics are conservative estimates of the risks involved in work. There is strong evidence to show that up to 100,000 workers in the United States lose their lives each year in the context of work (Reiman and Leighton 2016). Many illnesses and injuries are simply not reported to the authorities, whether that authority is the company, OSHA, or the US Department of Labor. Some workers also know that whistleblowing to agencies like OSHA could cost them their jobs.

A study of mining disasters in five countries concluded that most of them were related to violations of workplace safety laws (Braithwaite 1985). Some of the violations were a cause of the disasters and others made the disasters worse than they should have been. Workers are not the only ones at risk in the mining industry. In 1972 in Buffalo Creek, West Virginia, an entire community was virtually destroyed from a dam break.

During the twentieth century, at least 100,000 US miners were killed and 1.5 million injured (Mokhiber 1988). Black lung disease is still a major problem today. It is now called "coal worker's pneumoconiosis," and usually results from inhalation and exposure to assorted coal dusts and silica. There is no doubt that many coal companies knew of the dangers of black lung but did nothing to prevent worker exposure to dangerous coal dust (Mokhiber

1988). Even today, a few companies do not adequately protect their workers from contracting the disease (OSHA 2015).

Even if we use the conservative OSHA statistics, we get some sense of how routine violations of worker safety laws actually are in the United States. Federal and state OSHA agencies conducted 100,000 inspections in 2006, resulting in the uncovering of over 200,000 violations of worker safety laws (OSHA 2015). Here are two examples of these violations:

1. Cintas Corporation was fined $2.78 million for 42 willful violations of equipment safety regulations which contributed to the death of an employee in 2007. The employee fell into an industrial dryer as he tried to clear washed laundry from a conveyor belt (OSHA 2015).
2. Two Milwaukee companies were fined over $50,000 for failing to ensure proper safety measures and inspections pertaining to underground propane gas connections. Three employees of the companies lost their lives in an explosion and fire resulting from underground gas leaks (OSHA 2015).

Corporate violence to the natural environment

The natural environment can also be a victim of corporate violence. Like most corporate crimes, corporate degradation of the natural and physical environment is largely an outcome of the pursuit of profit. The costs of compliance with federal and state regulations are often greater than the costs of paying fines.

A most devious environmental crime in US history involves the actions of the Hooker Chemical Corporation, who in the 1940s bought the Love Canal near Niagara Falls and filled it with dangerous toxic chemicals. The Canal was eventually turned into a neighborhood playground and recreational area for nearby residents. Hooker had sold the land for $1 to the local school board and did not notify the board or the community of the hazardous material buried there (two hundred or so dangerous chemicals were dumped there over several years). As time passed, residents complained of terrible odors emanating from the area, and high rates of emotional problems, miscarriages, and other illnesses were documented. It was also claimed that several died as a result of exposure to the chemicals (Mokhiber 1988). For years Hooker claimed it was not responsible for the problems, but eventually it was forced to pay millions of dollars to victims as well as to the federal government for the clean-up of the area (Mokhiber 1988).

In another case, when the Exxon Valdez ran aground in 1989, about 12 million gallons of oil fouled the ocean near Prince William Sound, Alaska. Roughly 1,300 miles of beach were affected by the spill. At least 250,000 seabirds, 2,800 sea otters, 300 harbor seals, 250 bald eagles, and 22 killer whales were killed. Billions of salmon and herring eggs were eliminated as well (Cruciotti and Matthews 2006). Thousands of people have been directly affected by the spill. Millions of dollars have been lost in tourism income and several commercial fishing enterprises have folded.

Hearings eventually determined that Exxon was responsible for the disaster: the company had allowed an incompetent crew to run the ship under a captain known to have a drinking problem. It had also made cuts to necessary staffing. Exxon entered into a criminal plea agreement in the US District Court which allowed them to pay only $25 million of a $150 million criminal fine. The company also has paid $100 million in restitution and $900 million toward the clean-up (Cruciotti and Matthews 2006).

More recently, 210 million gallons of oil was released into the Gulf of Mexico by the energy company BP resulting in untold damage to wildlife, tourism income, and fishing and other seafood industries. The company was fined at least $12 billion and pleaded guilty to 11 manslaughter charges, one felony count of obstruction of Congress, and two environmental misdemeanors. The technical cause of the event was the use of inferior cement in the well and malfunctioning valves. BP, as most corporations do, put profits before safety and this was a direct cause of the deaths and injuries.

Summary

Corporate crimes are tied to the pursuit of profit and whether they emerge as fraud, theft, or violence, their consequences are almost always profound. In virtually any industry there are examples of corporate crime, from oil drilling, insurance sales, food industry, to retail and manufacturing, and, like traditional street crimes, the fundamental causes are deeply entrenched in social and political phenomena. As corporations control so much wealth and so many political activities and actors, their crimes might be said to be the most pressing across the world.

Activities and discussion questions

1. Why do you think crimes by corporations get so little attention compared with traditional street crimes?
2. Research the Exxon Valdez and BP Deepwater Horizon oil crimes and note the similarities and differences between the cases.
3. Do you think the rise in technology has increased or decreased a corporation's ability to commit financial crimes?

External links and additional resources

Center for Corporate Policy: www.corporatepolicy.org/topics/walmart.htm.
Corporate Watch: www.corporatewatch.org/company-profiles/corporate-crimes-0.
Global Exchange: Most Wanted Corporate Criminals: www.globalexchange.org/ corporateHRviolators.

Box 6.5 Films

The top 50 corporate crime movies are:

(* indicates documentary)

American Dream (1991) (Workers vs. Hormel)*
An Injury to One (2002) (Butte, Montana vs. Anaconda Mining)*
Barbarians At the Gate (1993) (Corporate greed, '80s style)
Blue Vinyl (2002) (Toxic PVC)*
Bulworth (1998) (Beatty vs. corporate corruption)
The China Syndrome (1979) (Nuclear near meltdown)
A Civil Action (1989) (Leukemia in Woburn)
Class Action (1991) (Unsafe automobiles)
The Constant Gardener (2005) (Big pharma)
Coma (1978) (Hospital nightmare)
The Corporation (2004) (The big picture)*
The Distinguished Gentleman (1992) (Eddie Murphy, power lines and
    cancer clusters)
The Dogs of War (1981) (Corporate mercenaries overthrow dictator)
Enron: The Smartest Guys in the Room (2005) (Fraud)*
Erin Brockovich (2000) (Water pollution and illness)
The Formula (1980) (Oil company snuffs out people in the know)
Fun with Dick & Jane (2005) (Jim Carrey meets Enron)
Harlan County USA (1976) (Mining industry vs. workers)
The Insider (1999) (Tobacco whistleblower)
Libby, Montana (2004) (W. R. Grace contaminates a community)*
Living With the Spill (1991) (Exxon Valdez)*
Lord of War (2005) (Arms industry)
McLibel (2005) (Up against McDonald"s)*
Manchurian Candidate (2004) (Corporate puppet in the White House?)
Matewan (1987) (Coal industry)
Other People's Money (1991) (Corporate raider vs. family business)
The Parallax View (1974) (Corporate assassinations)
Poletown Lives! (1980) (GM tears down a neighborhood)*
Pootie Tang (2001) (A CEO who wants kids to smoke, drink and eat
    fast food)
Power Trip (2004) (An American power company in Tblisi – not pretty)*
Quiz Show (1994) (Prime time fraud)
The Rainmaker (1997) (Law firm vs. insurance company)
Robocop (1987) (Robo takes on Detroit Inc.)
Roger & Me (1989) (Michael takes on Detroit Inc.)*
Rollerball (1975) (Globocorps divert the masses)
Salt of the Earth (1953) (NM mineworkers stick it to the man)

Silkwood (1983) (Nuclear whistleblower)
Super Size Me (2004) (Fast food nation)*
Syriana (2005) (Oil companies dominate)
Taken for a Ride (1996) (Auto, oil company campaign to destroy mass transit)*
Thank You for Smoking (2006) (Big tobacco gets kids to smoke)
Tucker (1988) (Trying to build a different car)
Vietnam: The Secret Agent (1983) (Agent Orange disaster)*
Wal-Mart: The High Cost of Low Price (2005) (Retail Giant Dominates)*
Wall Street (1987) (Greed is good)
Walker (1987) (Corporate interests take over Nicaragua)
Who Framed Roger Rabbit? (1988) (Auto, oil companies rip up the tracks)
Who Killed the Electric Car? (2005) (Auto companies)*
Why We Fight (2005) (It's a cash proposition)*
Wild Palms (1993) (Corporate takeover through virtual reality)

(From *Corporate Crime Reporter* 2006.)

Third World Traveler: Corporate Crimes: www.thirdworldtraveler.com/Corporate_Crimes/Corporate_Crimes.html
Third World Traveler: International Corporate Crime Watch: www.thirdworldtraveler.com/Transnational_corps/IntlCorpCrime_CorpWatch.html
White-Collar Crime Watch: www.whitecollarcrimewatch.com/

References

Alliance for Lobbying Transparency (2015). Available at: www.lobbyingtransparency.org/ (accessed on December 20, 2015).

Braithwaite, J. (1985). *To Punish or Persuade: Enforcement of Coal Mine Safety*. Albany, NY: SUNY Press.

Calavita, K., and Pontell, H. (1990). Heads I Win, Tails You Lose: Deregulation, Crime, and Crisis in the Savings and Loan Industry. *Crime and Delinquency*, 36: 309–341.

Calavita, K., and Pontell, H. (1991). Other People's Money Revisited: Collective Embezzlement in the Savings and Loan and Insurance Industries. *Social Problems*, 38: 94–112.

Citizens United v. *Federal Election Commission*. (2010). United States Supreme Court No. 08-205, 558 U.S. 310.

Clinard, M. B., and Quinney, R. (1973). *Criminal Behavior Systems: A Typology*. New York: Holt, Rinehart & Winston.

Collette, M. (2015). Blue Bell Knew About Listeria Contamination, Feds Say. Chron.com, May 7. Available at: www.chron.com/business/article/Blue-Bell-knew-about-listeria-contamination-feds-6249023.php (accessed on December 11, 2015).

Cooper, K. (2014). Drug Companies Give Million-Dollar Boost to Lobbying. Roll Call, April 22. Available at: http://blogs.rollcall.com/moneyline/drug-companies-give-million-dollar-boost-to-lobbying/ (accessed on September 11, 2015).

Corporate Crime Reporter (2006). List of Top 50 Corporate Crimes Movies Released. January 26. Available at: www.corporatecrimereporter.com/topmovies012606.htm (accessed on December 20, 2015).

Cruciotti, Tricia, and Matthews, Rick (2006). The Exxon Valdez Oil Spill. In R. Michalowski and R. Kramer (eds.), State-Corporate Crime: Wrongdoing at the Intersection of Business and Government, 149–171. Piscataway, NJ: Rutgers University Press.

Cullen, Francis T., Maakestad, William J., and Cavender, Gary (1987). Corporate Crime Under Attack: The Ford Pinto Case. Cincinnati, OH: Anderson.

Cullen Ganey, Judge J. (1961). In Application of the State of California. Federal Supplement, 195 (Eastern District, PA): 39.

Dodge v. Ford Motor Company (1919). Michigan Supreme Court 170 N.W. 668.

The Economist (2012). Biggest Transnational Companies. July 10. Available at: www.economist.com/blogs/graphicdetail/2012/07/focus-1 (accessed on January 10, 2014).

First National Bank of Boston v. Bellotti (1978). United States Supreme Court 435 U.S. 765.

Fox, James G., and Szockyj, Elizabeth (1996). Corporate Victimization of Women. Boston, MA: Northeastern University Press.

Friedrichs, D. (2009). Trusted Criminals: White Collar Crime in Contemporary Society. Belmont, CA: Wadsworth.

Friedrichs, D., and Rothe, Dawn L. (2014). State-Corporate Crime and Major Financial Institutions: Interrogating an Absence. State Crime, 3(2): 146–162.

Geis, Gilbert (1978). Deterring Corporate Crime. In M. David Ermann and Richard J. Lundman (eds.), Corporate and Governmental Deviance, 278–296. New York: Oxford University Press.

Grossman, R. (2001). Corporations, Accountability and Responsibility. In D. Ritz (ed.), Defying Corporations, Defining Democracy, 300–303. New York: Apex Press.

Leiser, B. (1973). Liberty, Justice and Morals. New York: Macmillan.

Lewis, C. S. (1944). The Screwtape Letters, by C. S. Lewis. New York: The Macmillan Company. [c. 1943].

McLean, B., and Elkind, P. (2004). The Smartest Guys in the Room: The Amazing Rise and Scandalous Fall of Enron. New York: Penguin.

Michalowski, R.J., and Kramer, R. (eds.) (2006). State-Corporate Crime: Wrongdoing at the Intersection of Business and Government. Piscataway, NJ: Rutgers University Press.

Mississippi Press (2015). Testimony Begins in Signal International Labor Trafficking Trial in New Orleans Federal Court. January 10. Available at: http://blog.gulflive.com/mississippi-press news/2015/01/testimony_begins_in_signal_int.html (accessed on September 11, 2015).

Mokhiber, Russell (1988). Corporate Crime and Corporate Violence. San Francisco, CA: Sierra Club.

Open Secrets (2014). Top Spenders. Available at: www.opensecrets.org/lobby/top.php?indexType=s&showYear=2014 (accessed on December 20, 2015).

OSHA (United States Department of Labor) (2015). OSHA Data and Statistics. Available at: www.osha.gov/oshstats/commonstats.html (accessed on December 11, 2015).

Oyez Project (n. d.). Santa Clara County v. Southern Pacific Railroad Company. The Oyez Project at IIT Chicago, Kent College of Law. Available at: https://supreme. justia.com/cases/federal/us/118/394/ (accessed January 25, 2016).

Pontell, H., and Calavita, K. (1993). The Savings and Loan Industry. In Michael Tonry and Albert J. Reiss, Jr. (eds.), *Beyond the Law: Crime in Complex Organizations*, 203–246. Chicago: University of Chicago Press.

Potts, M., Kochan, N., and Whittington, R. (1992). *Dirty Money: BCCI – The Inside Story of the World"s Sleaziest Bank*. Washington, DC: National Press Books.

Reiman, J., and Leighton, P. (2016). *The Rich Get Richer and the Poor Get Prison*. 10th edition. New York: Routledge.

Ross v. *Bernhard* (1970). United States Supreme Court 396 U.S. 531.

Rothe, D. L., and Friedrichs, D. O. (2014). *Crimes of Globalization*. London: Routledge.

Rynbrandt, Linda J., and Kramer, Ronald C. (1995). Hybrid Nonwomen and Corporate Violence: The Silicone Breast Implant Case. *Violence Against Women*, 1(3): 206–227.

Sutherland, E. (1949). *White Collar Crime*. New York: Holt, Rinehart & Winston.

Spenser, R. (2004). Corporate Law and Structures: Exposing the Roots of the Problem [resource document]. Corporate Watch. Available at: www.corporatewatch.org.uk/ sites/default/files/corporate_structures.pdf (accessed on April 1, 2015).

Tombs, S. (2012). State-Corporate Symbiosis in the Production of Crime and Harm. *State Crime*, 1(2): 170–195.

Union of Concerned Scientists (2015). Monsanto Outspends All Other Agribusinesses on Efforts to Persuade Congress and the Public to Maintain the Industrial Agriculture Status Quo. Available at: www.ucsusa.org/food_and_agriculture/our-failing-food-system/genetic-engineering/lobbying-and-advertising.html (accessed on September 11, 2015).

Urban Institute (2015). Why the Human Trafficking Case Against Signal International Matters. January 16. Available at: www.urban.org/urban-wire/why-human-trafficking-case-against-signal-international-matters (accessed on September 11, 2015).

Vitali, S., Glattfelder, J. B., and Battiston, S. (2011). The Network of Global Corporate Control. *PloS one*, 6(10).

Yeoman, B. (2006). When Is a Corporation Like a Freed Slave? *Mother Jones*, November/December. Available at: www.motherjones.com/politics/2006/10/when-corporation-freed-slave (accessed on December 11, 2015).

Chapter 7

State crime

Genocide, human rights violations, war crimes, illegal wars, and crimes against humanity are all actions that fall under the category of state crime and that most people recognize and accept as such. However, there are others that we consider to be state crimes such as general oppression, overt and covert surveillance, denial of due process, perpetuation of classism, racism, sexism, the lack of care for the homeless, the use of drones and targeted assassinations, the treatments and policies for the mentally ill and illegal immigrants, and a host of other serious harms. State crimes are historically and currently ubiquitous and result in more injury and death than traditional street crimes such as robbery, theft, and assault. Consider that genocide during the twentieth century in Germany, Rwanda, Darfur, Albania, Turkey, Ukraine, Cambodia, Bosnia-Herzegovina, and other regions claimed the lives of tens of millions and rendered many more homeless, imprisoned, and psychologically and physically damaged (Rothe and Kauzlarich 2010). Unlike political white-collar crime in which offenders benefit personally from an act or omission, state crime is organizational in nature, wherein motivation is tacitly or explicitly related to larger structural or cultural goals and objectives of government or its agencies (Faust and Kauzlarich 2008).

Crimes and harms perpetrated by states, directly and indirectly, had been occurring long before the modern state, whether under the rule of a church, monarchy (kings and queens), lords, or chiefdoms. Crimes of omission and commission, committed by what is often referred to as the modern state, remain a common occurrence. Yet, most people do not see the socially harmful and illegal actions of state officials to be a problem, let alone a crime. Despite the brutal and murderous impact of state crimes around the world, few government officials, and fewer still average citizens, think much about these offenses. Recent news headlines highlight the common occurrence of state criminality: "Palestinian President: Closing Jerusalem holy site 'a declaration of war'" (Yan 2014); "Iran foils attempt to sabotage nuclear heavy-water tanks" (*The Jerusalem Post* 2014); "UK government can be sued over rendition claims, judges rule" (BBC News 2014a); "Suspected US drone strike kills 2 militants in northwest Pakistan" (Fox News 2014); "UN

Rebukes Israel Over Jerusalem Settlements" (BBC News 2014b). These are but a few that made it to the running headline news in the early part of the day. Furthermore, it is not what the headlines state that lets us know that state crime is occurring, it is in the story and events prompting the news coverage. Consider this headline that met with little response or outrage: "Pentagon unilaterally grants itself authority over 'civil disturbances'" (Morey 2013). This report notes that "By making a few subtle changes to a regulation in the U.S. Code titled 'Defense Support of Civilian Law Enforcement Agencies' the military has quietly granted itself the ability to police the streets without obtaining prior local or state consent, upending a precedent that has been in place for more than two centuries." According to Federal Register No. 2013–07802, "Federal military commanders have the authority, in extraordinary emergency circumstances where prior authorization by the President is impossible and duly constituted local authorities are unable to control the situation, to engage temporarily in activities that are necessary to quell large-scale, unexpected civil disturbances" (Federal Register 2013). Within weeks, the following headline made its way into the media: "Pentagon bracing for public dissent over climate and energy shocks," but what is more disturbing is the final paragraph, well backed up by original data:

> The Pentagon knows that environmental, economic and other crises could provoke widespread public anger toward government and corporations in coming years. The revelations on the NSA's global surveillance programmes are just the latest indication that as business as usual creates instability at home and abroad, and as disillusionment with the status quo escalates, Western publics are being increasingly viewed as potential enemies that must be policed by the state.
>
> (Ahmed 2013)

Before going further with examples and discussions of state crime, we will address two possible questions students may have: what is a state and what is state crime?

What is a state?

While research on crimes of the state can be criticized for not clearly defining what a state is, to us this critique should be situated within a historical context with the understanding that, since the rise of the modern state, theorists have put forth many different versions of what a state actually is, many of which compete with each other or offer partial answers. Philosophers such as Aristotle, Hobbes, Locke, and Rousseau all attempted to explore the political components of society and civil governance. Classical theorists, such as Marx (1906), Weber (1947), and Durkheim (1933), also developed theories of the state and its function. By the mid-twentieth century, contemporary theorists continued to explore theories of states. These works come from several scholars including Miliband (1970), Poulantzas (1969, 1976), Habermas (1975), O'Conner (1973), and Gramsci (1971). The modernity and dependency schools also explored state theory in terms of globalization (see Santos 1971; Smelser 1964; So 1990; and Wallerstein 1974). During the 1980s, state theory waned considerably, so much so that the last decade was "notable for the impoverishment of state theory" (Barrow 2005: 1). There were negligible theoretical advances and many radical scholars, including critical criminologists, drifted away from state models. This was in part due to the complexities of the topic itself and a stalemate between "proponents of various theories."

In addition, there was a broad abandonment of grand theory and grand-scale meta-narratives. The move from a neo-Marxist model to post-structuralist and post-modern theory shifted analysis from the macro to the micro forms of power and to "technologies of power" (Foucault 1972; Henri-Levi 1977; Mitchell 1991). The recognition that a meta-theory of the state was unrealistic resulted in a shift in focus of the state in general to the capitalistic state in particular. "What is perfectly legitimate is a theory of a capitalist state ... made possible by the separation of the space of the state and that of the economy" (Poulantzas 1980: 20). Moreover, the concept of one grand economy, the global economy, took center stage and was reified where a capitalistic world economy was seen as "self-perpetuating."

At the same time, recognition of the state as a more complex political apparatus surfaced where the state was recognized as a peculiar political entity composed of an assemblage of impersonal and anonymous functions distinct from economic power (Poulantzas 1978: 54). The state "is a specific and highly complex phenomenon, and it can by no means be reduced to, or treated as a simple variant of, the capitalist state" (ibid.: 24). This included recognition of the relative separation of the political from the economic. Nonetheless, the political, as conceived, still failed to take into account agency or the forces of individuals' ideological, religious, and moral interests framed as state interests. As Seabrooke (2002) noted, the state was effectively a faceless rational actor. The notion of sovereignty erosion was becoming popular leading to a further decline in state theories that focus more broadly on state functions domestically and internationally (Krasner 1995).

As such, we agree with Faulks (2000: 20) when he notes, "defining the state is a notoriously difficult task." Given this, we accept a more common-sense understanding of the state: the institution (and all-encompassing agencies and actors within them) that has the legitimacy to hold political power to govern or rule the population as defined and recognized within a specific geographical territory. We suggest state crime can be defined *as an act or omission of an action by actors within the state that results in violations of domestic and international law, human rights, or systematic or institutionalized harm of its or another state's population, done in the name of the state regardless of whether there is or is not self-motivation or interests at play.*

This recognizes agency, the organizational context, lack of action as well as direct and indirect perpetration, encompasses harms not officially "criminalized," and provides some limitations by recognizing the systematic or institutionalized component. Having provided the above discussion of what a state is, the long historical debates and definitions, we do point out that, as with the others, this discussion and our own lay definition play into the legitimation, reification, or reproduction of the discourse of "states," as if they are a normal or expected entity, as the only game in town.

Criminology and state crime

While criminology has been around for over six decades, it has only been over the course of the past two and a half decades that criminologists have studied state crime. Yet, state crime has been approached in a number of ways by a number of disciplines (criminology, history, political science, and sociology). For example, at the end of the nineteenth century, a French judge, Louis Proall (1898), in his book *Political Crime* focused on the crimes of statesmen and politicians. Becker and Murray (1971) analyzed how state governments break the law, as did Lieberman in 1972. Sociologists, such as Giddens (1987) and Tilly (1985), explored the use of organized violence by states. Keelman and Hamilton (1989) analyzed crimes committed by individuals acting in obedience to government authorities.

The intellectual history behind white-collar crime can be traced back to Edwin Sutherland (1939), who called attention to a then-neglected form of crime, namely the crimes of respectable people in the context of a legitimate occupation, and of corporations. Although the significance of such crime—white-collar crime—was conceded by some criminologists in response to Sutherland, only a few began to focus on white-collar crime until several decades after his 1939 speech and the publication of his landmark book, *White Collar Crime* (1949).

Since the 1970s, however, a fairly rich literature and substantial interest in white-collar crime developed within criminology (for example, Friedrichs 2004). Yet, Sutherland himself was not at all interested in crimes of states. For him, "war crime" referred to the black market activity of businessmen, and he disregarded the massive crimes of the Nazis that were taking place during the time that he was working on *White Collar Crime* (Rothe and Friedrichs 2006). But his extension of the concept of crime beyond its conventional parameters did provide an important foundation.

Generally, scholars of state crime recognize that it was not really until William Chambliss gave his 1989 American Society of Criminology presidential address (Chambliss 1990) that more direct and immediate inspiration for attention to crimes of the state began. Since that time, there has emerged a growing and strong body of literature examining crimes of the state. There are now two state crime research centers, one in the United Kingdom and one in the

United States, that focus on current events, scholarship, and state crime. There are sole-authored and edited books examining state crime and victims of state crime, and hundreds of articles ranging in topic from state responses to natural disasters, immigration policies, mass incarceration, the use of drones, illegal wars, torture, and illegal detention to the abuse of whistleblowers and systems of control. The following section provides many examples of state crime including mini case studies that students may find beneficial to their own research interests.

Media headlines and the man behind the curtain

We started this chapter with headlines related to crimes of the state and now focus our attention to more details of some of those cases to show how, with a little understanding of state crime and the framing of these acts by the media, the headlines highlight significant and long-standing forms of state criminality. For example, the headline read, "Iran foils attempt to sabotage nuclear heavy-water tanks" (*The Jerusalem Post* 2014). This is a microcosm of state-sponsored cybercrime that is becoming the new warfare frontier.

Cybercrime

Cybercrime, cyber security, and political hacktivism are issues that are now at the forefront of media, political agendas, academic subdisciplines, and the corporate sector. Consider the words of President Obama in 2012, stating that the "cyber threat to our nation is one of the most serious economic and national security challenges we face" (Protalinski 2012). Likewise, the UK Prime Minister and the UK Home Affairs Select Committee state that the threat of cybercrime is of greater concern than nuclear war (Bell 2013) and that it, alongside terrorism, is the key danger to UK security. These types of cybercrime include the general hackers and organized crime syndicates that pose threats in their attempts to gain secretive information, credit cards, infiltrate businesses and economic structures, as well as a host of other cybercrimes that are conducted by individual and organized criminal networks, most often portrayed as Chinese or Russian groups. Likewise, media reports abound on the criminal nature of cybercrime with cases of arrests and thwarted plots by governments around the world. Scholars are also joining the call to fight cybercrime through research centers, and consultation with various think tanks and governments dedicated to the issue.

While we are not suggesting that the forms of cybercrime that typically garner attention do not merit focus, we suggest that the explicit focus by governments, media, and academics on non-state actors as "the cybercriminal" and "threat" to nations' national security supports both the legitimation of funneling vast funds to fight cybercrime and the claims that these *are* the most significant threats. Meanwhile, this masks the larger, more ominous, forms of state cyber criminality, or what some have called "World War C" or "cyberwarfare": state-sponsored cyberwarfare (government warfare using internet technologies) and the militarization of cyberspace to achieve specific military, economic, political advantages as well as a means of counterinsurgency. After all, states across the globe have been investing, and continue to invest, vast resources in developing and implementing cyberwarfare weaponry to target an adversary's critical infrastructure system, prevent nuclear uranium enrichment, alter their view of the battlefield, delegitimize regimes or political parties, and to spread propaganda: a form of cyberterrorism aimed at generating fear or instilling a populace movement to overthrow a regime.

Box 7.1 Botnets

The use of botnets in cybercrime is where a large amount of information is sent to targeted websites simultaneously, causing them to freeze in what is called "distributed denial-of-service disruptions" (Geers *et al.* 2013). While most of these are carried out by states directly or indirectly through the renting or funding of individuals to carry out their agendas, they are done in such a manner as to allow plausible deniability to regimes. Consider the case of Estonia when, in April and May 2007, an extensive denial-of-service attack brought one of the most wired countries in the world to a standstill. Banks, news websites, utility networks, including those of the Prime Minister's Office, ceased to function. The botnet attack began within hours of the relocation of a Soviet-era war memorial out of the center of Tallinn. In conjunction with the initiation of the internet attacks,

> [E]thnic Russians in Estonia staged violent street protests against the removal of the statue—during which 1,300 people were arrested, 100 people were injured, and one person was killed. On the same day in Moscow, a Kremlin-run youth movement attacked and sealed off Estonia's embassy. The occurrence of these three events almost simultaneously suggests that these were not a haphazardly-planned series of protests, but a deliberate and concerted effort to pressure the Estonian government.
>
> (Applegate 2009)

The attacks peaked on May 9—Victory Day in Russia—with the last wave on May 18. In September 2007, the website of the Ukrainian Party of Regions, platforming for former Ukrainian Prime Minister Viktor Yanukovych, was the target of a denial-of-service attack during his re-election campaign. Botnets also attacked the website of the anti-establishment Russian politician Gary Kasparov. These botnets are able to take down candidate sites, send free advertising or free smear campaigns, and potentially have an impact on who becomes a presidential running mate. In October 2007, a Ukrainian-sponsored botnet carried out a large spam campaign in support of then US presidential candidate Ron Paul. This botnet artificially inflated Paul's online support by spamming online poll results and message boards with votes and comments in his favor. His seemingly massive internet support translated into widespread mainstream media coverage. While having a limited scope, this was the first botnet that explicitly attempted to influence a US presidential election (Senor 2008).

Invasive and threatening forms of cybercrime against states range from temporary suspensions to the destruction of major infrastructures. The United States has conducted the most significant, damaging, and highly engineered cyberattacks to date, including Stuxnet, 74 Duqu, Flame, and Gauss. However, they are not alone in the technophelia mania that continues to redefine the face of warfare. In 2007, Israel used a tactic of cyberwarfare when it disrupted Syrian air defense networks to enable the Israeli Air Force's destruction of Dayr az-Zawr, a Syrian nuclear facility (Geers *et al.* 2013). Israel used a combination of electronic attacks coupled with precision bombing by engaging a Syrian radar site at Tall-Abuad to enter Syrian airspace undetected as the entire Syrian radar system was shut down.

Perhaps one of the more invasive and destructive forms of state cybercriminality that caused major infrastructure destruction was the case of the United States and the use of the Stuxnet worm in 2010—operation code name "Olympic Games"—to sabotage and dismantle Iran's nuclear power plants by destroying approximately 1,000 of the 5,000 Iranian centrifuges. Originally put in place by former President George W. Bush's administration, the final phases of the operation were conducted by the Obama administration. To expand a little on this case, in 2006, when Iran resumed uranium enrichment at Natanz, the US military and intelligence officials proposed a cyberwar program (Sanger 2012). The following year, a virtual replica of the Natanz plant was built for testing the worm. The original worm, while having crashed some of the centrifuges in 2008, was not perceived to be effective enough. The following year, Obama agreed to carry out the cyberwarfare plan against Iran, focusing on enhancing capabilities by targeting a critical array of centrifuges composed of nearly 1,000 machines. Even with the discovery of the worm when it was accidently plugged into the Internet, Obama continued the program successfully, taking out nearly a fifth of the operating centrifuges.

A similar virus, found to be from the Stuxnet originators, is Duqu, the purpose of which is to gather information related to control systems and trade relationships between particular organizations in Iran. While "Stuxnet and Duqu belonged to a single chain of attacks, which raised cyberwar-related concerns worldwide," said Eugene Kaspersky, CEO and co-founder of

Kaspersky Lab., "the Flame malware looks to be another phase in this war, and it's important to understand that such cyber weapons can easily be used against any country" (Zetter 2012). As with the other two viruses, the Flame was used to steal and delete information from computers belonging to the Iranian Oil Ministry and the Iranian National Oil Company in the ongoing cyberwar that the United States has declared against Iran. In a similar vein, there is the Gauss Trojan, which is the first known cyberespionage campaign with a banking Trojan component that is either monitoring finance/funding sources for specific targets or transferring funds for targets deemed to merit having their assets frozen, using the same path as the Flame and Stuxnet, through a USB port. Targeted banking institutions are primarily located in Iran, Saudi Arabia, Sudan, and Syria, followed by Egypt, Iraq, and Turkey. Some of the banking institutions include several Lebanese banks: Bank of Beirut, EBLF, BlomBank, ByblosBank, FransaBank, and Credit Libanais. In addition, it targets users of Citibank and PayPal.

On a more simplistic level, cyberwarfare can include the complete shut-down of the Internet to enforce a point of power or for revenge. Consider the recent case of the hack against the film industry's Sony in late 2014, where the United States government declared, rightly or wrongly, that North Korea was responsible for the hack in retaliation for the upcoming release of the film, *The Interview*. In response, President Obama warned that the United States would launch a "proportional response" to North Korea's hack against Sony (Fisher 2014). For several days, beginning December 24, 2014, the Internet was effectively shut down in the whole of North Korea.

The above cases are but a few examples of state-sponsored cyberwarfare. Given the facts of the US activities in Iran, the abovementioned headline noting Iran's accusations holds much more plausibility. Given the difficul-ties of tracking, tracing, or removing the veil of state secrecy, deception, and plausible deniability—common characteristics of state covert warfare—other cases are bound to occur or be occurring at this time (as we know the United States was considering engagement in cyberwarfare against Libya and Syria a couple of years ago to institute regime change, and in this past year an eighteen-page presidential memo from Obama reveals that he has ordered intelligence officials to draw up a list of potential overseas targets for US cyberattacks), making this form of cybercrime a common tactic of states' exercising of power.

Dronefare and the exercise of power

The headline "Suspected US drone strike kills 2 militants in northwest Pakistan" (Fox News 2014) may, at first glimpse, appear to be nothing more than the killing of some "enemy" in the "war on terror." However, when we dig a little deeper into what is actually occurring, a different picture emerges; one where states, most notably the United States, are using drones in a broad

---

Box 7.2 Cyber as the fifth domain

The United States has officially declared "Cyber" as the 5th domain, after land, sea, air, and space. One can see the incorporation of this new realm into the militarization of state violence, the exercise of geo-political interests and power—cyberpower. In October 2013, President Obama institutionalized an 18-page Presidential Policy Directive 20 for Offensive Cyber Effects Operations (OCEO) that "can offer unique and unconventional capabilities to advance US national objectives around the world with little or no warning to the adversary or target and with potential effects ranging from subtle to severely damaging." It says the government will "identify potential targets of national importance where OCEO can offer a favorable balance of effectiveness and risk as compared with other instruments of national power." As Dr. Lani Kass asserts: "Cyber is a war-fighting domain. The electromagnetic spectrum is the maneuver space. Cyber is the United States' Center of Gravity—the hub of all power and movement, upon which everything else depends. It is the Nation's neural network" [Kass cited in Burghardt 2013: 3]. Kass continues with "cyber superiority is the prerequisite to effective operations across all strategic and operational domains—securing freedom from attack and freedom to attack" ... This is further reflected in the US' investment and support for offensive cyber technologies to be included into the defense infrastructure as the Pentagon requested $4.7 billion for cyberspace operations in their 2014 budget, $1 billion more than the 2013 allocation.
(From Rothe and Collins 2014.)

---

theater that is harmful, damaging, and a perfunctory mechanism of recruitment for those we "fight" against.

Drones are only another example of the state using violence to achieve and maintain global domination, power, and the suppression of those deemed unworthy. The United States' use of drones and targeted assassinations has significantly increased over the course of the past decade, especially so under the Obama Administration. As noted by Miller (2012: 2), "over the past few years, the Obama administration has institutionalized the use of armed drones and developed a counterterrorism infrastructure capable of sustaining a seemingly permanent war." Despite a lack of official statistics, data collected by independent sources, based on a variety of methods, indicate that the United States currently has 60 military and CIA bases across the globe directly connected to the drone program, with 375 armed drones operating in the Middle East (for example, in Afghanistan, Iraq, Iran, Pakistan, and Yemen) and Africa (for example, in Ethiopia, Mali, Nigeria, the Seychelles, and Somalia) (Cole 2013). Table 7.1 shows the numbers of known drone attacks and casualties by country.

Table 7.1 Known US drone strikes between 2002 and August 2014

Country	Total drone strikes	Total reported killed	Civilians	Children	Total reported injured
Pakistan 2004–2014	390	2,347–3,796	416–957	168–202	1,099–1,660
Yemen 2002–2014	65–77	339–494	64–83	7	78–196
Additional unverified	97–116	324–515	24–48	6–9	87–120
US covert	14–79	150–386	60–89	25–27	22–115
Somalia 2007–2014	5–8	10–24	0–15	0	2–24
Covert	8–11	40–141	7–47	0–2	11–21
Syria Sep–Nov 2014	9–14	6	50–54	5–9	27

Source: Cole (2013)

The accuracy rate for hitting the intended target is approximately 1.5–2 percent. The Bureau of Investigative Journalism has estimated that 98 percent of the victims of drone strikes are "collateral damage," or, in more human terms, civilians, children, or suspected militants, who were either minor, low-level affiliates or whose involvement with militants has never been proven.

The precision of these attacks, not to mention the alleged targets, has been in question since the first use of drones over a decade ago, though this is rarely acknowledged by the US government. Rather, the political statements tend to ignore and downplay any civilian deaths with statements such as "there have been 'no' or 'single digit' civilian casualties." However, as Box 7.3 illustrates, that was not, nor is, the case.

Box 7.3 Drone strike cases

On the morning of March 17, 2011, more than three dozen village elders and local government leaders gathered in an open-air bus depot in the town of Datta Khel, in North Waziristan, Pakistan. Under discussion: how to avoid being drawn into the insurgency raging there and across the border in Afghanistan. At about 10:45 a.m., a drone hovering overhead fired a supersonic missile into the gathering. One man remembers hearing a slight hissing noise before the blast threw him, unconscious, several yards away. An immediate second strike killed many of the wounded (Wood 2013: 2).

On 7 January, 2013, eight people "were killed in similar attacks in the village of Haiderkhel in the Miranshah district of North Waziristan. Sixteen people had been also killed in a drone strike on South Waziristan a day before" (Press TV 2013).

Box 7.4 Targeted assassinations: Terror Tuesday

The use of these drones for targeted assassinations has reached the level where the Obama administration holds what have been deemed "Terror Tuesday sessions," where kill lists are given to President Obama for approval and for overseeing the Predator drones (Scahill 2013). A disposition matrix is used, which is a system to codify and streamline the killings that are carried out by drones (Miller 2012). It was developed by a group of military and intelligence officers and is now overseen by the Director of the CIA, John Brennan. In 2012, President Obama granted a CIA request to launch drone attacks even if the identities of those who are to be killed are unknown. They refer to this as a "signature" strike policy (Democracy Now! 2012). The "targets" have expanded from the initial "al-Qaeda terrorist" to "terrorist" to "terrorist-like group" to "associated with a terrorist or terrorist-like group," including US civilians. Terrorists and those associated with them, or perceived to be, fall under the scope of national security risk management (Rothe and Ross 2014). As noted in the United States Department of Justice White Papers (2011: 2), while "we recognize that there is no private interest more weighty than a person's interest in his life that interest must be balanced against the United States' interest in forestalling the threat of violence and death." The White Papers continue: "The threat posed by al-Qaeda and its associated forces demands a broader concept of imminence in judging when a person continually planning terror attacks presents an imminent threat."

In many cases, drones hover twenty-four hours a day over communities, particularly in northwest Pakistan. "Those living under drones have to face the constant worry that a deadly strike may be fired at any moment, and the knowledge that they are powerless to protect themselves. These fears have affected behavior" (Global Research News 2013). See Box 7.4.

Drones "are woven up in myths of technological superiority, objectivity, and control that help support their adoption" (Wall and Monahan 2011: 250). This "truth" of efficiency, conciseness, and the savior of "our boys'" lives obfuscates the underlying exercise of state violence. As noted by Cole (2013: 1), "as this technology proliferates, as it is sure to do, the prospect of many different countries around the globe remotely controlling armed drones to carry out lethal attacks is nothing short of terrifying." As stated by Wall and Monahan (2011: 247), "knowing when to say 'when' is not a 'decision' that is made in a vacuum but is rather a sovereign act shaped by social and political norms, which are encoded in both the institutional practices and technological systems of drones."

Here again we note that these forms of state crime require the support of corporations as well as other countries. For example, the corporations making the most profit from this dronefare include Boeing, General Atomics, Lockheed Martin, Northrop Grumman, AeroVironment, Prox Dynamics AS, Denel Dynamics, SAIC, Israeli Aerospace Industries, Textron, General Dynamics, and DJI. As these companies vie for technological superiority and government contracts, they are supporting and participating in the exercise of state violence.

As the above two cases have highlighted, often a quick glimpse at news headlines does not serve the population well for knowing there is a darker history associated with these stories of state crime. The following section provides mini case studies of other forms of state criminality.

Cases of state criminality

When we think of state crime, more often than not the more horrific images of war, genocide, and torture, to name a few, come to mind. While these are more visible and easy to identify as state crimes, there are more subtle forms that impact our lives as citizens across the globe, as we noted in the introduction to this chapter. These can be thought of as part of a continuum from the extreme subtle to the obvious and public. Consider state crimes from harming the environment through policies such as failure to address global warming, to nuclear weapon waste, to the environmental impact of war, to environmental harms that result from ignoring major infrastructural defaults and deterioration.

Box 7.5 War on Iraq/Afghanistan: the environmental costs

The war on Iraq and Afghanistan by the United States and its allies has rightly been considered a state crime. What is less thought of are the secondary forms of state crime as a result of the initial criminality of the illegal war and occupation. There are significant environmental harms that should be considered as a continuation of the primary crimes committed by the United States and its allies in their war. There has been a significant amount of damaged forests, wetlands, and marshlands, of forest-cover destruction and high levels of carbon emissions due to the massive numbers of military machinery, from the ground to the sky. "Military vehicles used in both Iraq and Afghanistan produced many hundreds of thousands of tons of carbon monoxide, oxides of nitrogen, hydrocarbons, and sulfur dioxide in addition to CO_2" (Eisenhower Study Group 2011: 11). Chemical residue of weapons and other military operations, including bombing, soils the earth leaving depleted uranium, trichloroethylene, benzene, and perchlorate which have impacted the water supply in both countries (ibid.: 10). Wildlife populations from animals to birds have also been adversely impacted. The initial bombing campaign released toxins, as did the intentional setting of fire to oil fields as a form of warfare during the initial invasion in 2003. All of this has not only harmed the environment but further victimized innocent civilians and low-ranking military personnel and insurgency groups through exposure to these chemicals, leading to a host of medical conditions. Additionally, hundreds of service personnel including foreign soldiers, private contractors, and Iraqi troops and civilians were exposed to chemical weapons when old stored caches were discovered and interrupted, releasing chemicals such as sarin or a sulfur mustard agent.

Along the same continum, we can consider crimes that are the result of government policy. For example, as *The Guardian* reported on October 9, 2014:

> The Mediterranean has become Europe's sea of death. More than 3,000 refugees and migrants have already been killed this year trying to escape war and poverty in Africa and the Middle East and break into the continental fortress to the north ... this is the direct result of a system that favours the free movement of cheap European labour over providing refuge for victims of conflagration and destitution on our periphery ... But it's not so different on the US–Mexican border or in sea-lanes between Indonesia and Australia ... In the past 15 years, at least 6,000 migrants have died trying to cross into the US, and 1,500 have perished on their journey to Australia. The Australian government boasts that it has cut the death toll by interning or dumping migrants on impoverished states and turning back boats by force. That is the grim face of 21st-century global privilege up against the consequences of its actions in the rest of the world.
>
> (Milne 2014: 1)

Likewise, when Australia does not "discard" the immigrants, they utilize Christmas Island, where it is well documented that basic care is not available, particularly for specific populations such as children and pregnant women.

It is not only "illegal" migrants or asylum seekers who are the victims of state crime owing to government policy, it also includes citizens who are denied the basic right to have their families with them. Consider the United Kingdom's immigration law of 2012, which states:

> Nobody earning less than £18,600 per year can bring their partner into the UK and the amount increases with children and does not alter for different costs of living, pay, or any other conditions in different regions. "The income is for the British partner ONLY, so if for example, the overseas

Box 7.6 The highway of death

Since the early 1990s, hundreds of unauthorized border crossers have died every year in the deserts north of the US–Mexico border in their attempt to reach safe havens somewhere in the Southwest. Many more suffer illness and injury as a result of their efforts to reach the United States via ever more hazardous border crossings.

There have always been some migrant deaths during unauthorized crossings into the United States. They were, however, relatively few until 1994 when Operation Gatekeeper established a new border enforcement strategy. The logic of Gatekeeper, in contrast, was based on deterring would-be migrants from trying to cross the border by flooding popular crossing areas around San Diego with Border Patrol agents, erecting fences and other barriers, and engaging in active "internal enforcement," that is, detecting, detaining and deporting undocumented immigrants in cities, towns and other places well away from the immediate border.

Prompted by the politics of a growing anti-immigration movement, the US government embarked upon the Sisyphusian task of making the entire US–Mexico border impermeable to unauthorized border crossers. As a result, by 2005, with border militarization now extending from San Diego to El Paso, the death toll reached 500 ... With the onset of the Great Recession and the corresponding shrinking of the US labor market, border deaths dropped slightly to 375 in 2011, but surged back to 476 in 2012, even as the number of people attempting to cross dropped ... As grim as they are, these figures underestimate the actual number of migrant deaths. According to the GAO (2006), the Border Patrol's Tucson Sector undercounted migrant deaths by 32% in 2002, 43% in 2003, and 35% in 2004. This undercounting is a consequence of Border Patrol practices that record deaths as "migration related" only if they occur in counties adjacent to the US–Mexico border and a Border Patrol agent either found or was led to a corpse or remains *in situ*. As part of this protocol, the Border Patrol also excludes skeletal remains from unknown years, or bodies determined to be those of human smugglers.

Migrant deaths are the visible tip of an iceberg of human suffering. In addition to the risk of dying in the desert, undocumented immigrants crossing the borderlands are injured as pedestrians while attempting to cross roads or highways in border regions and as passengers in vehicles operated by human smugglers.

Days spent afoot in the borderlands of California, Arizona and Texas can result in other physical trauma, including broken bones, cuts, bruises, blisters, and snake, scorpion, or centipede bites, as well as exposure to both killing heat in the deserts and dangerously cold temperatures in the mountains. Although some of these physical problems are annoyances, others can be lethal. Volunteers from migrant aid groups working in Arizona, such as the Samaritans and No More Deaths, report encountering border crossers suffering from medical problems such as cerebral stroke, heart attacks, insulin shock, dysentery from drinking contaminated water, and heat stroke.

It Doesn't Happen by Accident

The death, injury, and illness suffered by irregular migrants crossing the Southwestern borderlands are not the unintended collateral damage of otherwise benign immigration policies. They are the known and predictable results of border militarization strategies designed to force migrants toward dangerous crossings. US policy planners made the deadly consequences of border militarization part of their overall plan to gain "control" of the US–Mexico border. In 1994, the US Border Patrol acknowledged that Operation Gatekeeper would force migrants to take routes that placed them in "mortal danger" due to "extremes of heat and colds." Forcing desperate migrants to make hazardous journeys was seen as an important "deterrent" rather than a violation of human rights and thus, a state crime.

US border militarization policies are also responsible for the emergence of a new breed of organized crime along the US–Mexico border—human smuggling syndicates. These new organized crime cartels offer point-to-point services that, for a substantial fee, will transport migrants from Mexican border towns such as Agua Prieta and Altar to their desired destination somewhere in the United States. This system has transformed unauthorized migrants from human beings into commodities. Groups of migrants are now a valuable load, *un cargo*, to smugglers. All of the practices connected with transporting and protecting shipments of illegal drugs now apply to human cargos of migrants: loading as much "product" into transport vehicles as possible, jettisoning anything that might increase risk of capture (i.e., migrants unable to keep up the pace of marching across the desert), and in some cases, raiding rival syndicates to steal their loads.

The application of military technology and tactics, and increased deployment of heavily armed agents to control the US–Mexico boundary, promotes a conceptual shift in the popular understanding of irregular migrants. In popular consciousness, armies exist to fight enemies. Consequently, the deployment of military personnel, machinery, and tactics throughout the US–Mexico borderlands reframes immigration control as war-fighting, and unauthorized immigrants as enemies.

The United States and several of its individual member states can and should be held accountable for the victimization of undocumented immigrants rooted in border militarization and the pursuit of attrition through enforcement, which is attempting to drive undocumented immigrants out of the country by depriving them of the basic requirements for human lives.

(From Michalowski and Harding 2014.)

partner is the main earner, it makes it almost impossible for expatriate Brits to return to the UK. An example may be a British woman in Japan who is a housewife, with a middle-class husband. That family would now face exile under the new rules."

(Outer Nationalist 2012: 1)

More identifiable forms of state crime include, for example, acts of torture and renditions that occurred during the US war on Iraq and the subsequent "war on terror"; forced displacement and disappearances that were commonplace in Columbia, Chile, and other countries involved in civil war; assassinations including those being carried out by the United States and the United Kingdom in the name of "fighting terrorism"; genocide as we saw in Darfur, Rwanda, and the former Yugoslavia; forced sterilization that occurred in China (and less formally in India today), or through prison experiments and as a mean to rehabilitate sex offenders in the United States; systematic rape as a tool of warfare, as is and has been a common tactic of war; corruption, which is a common occurrence, especially so through the funding by many international financial institutions of various projects or the expansion of private oil ventures in war-torn countries; and the violent oppression of populations, including of dissent.

One need only recall the vast number of cases since 2011 of militarized government responses to demonstrations and protests across the globe from Egypt to Sudan to North Korea and to the United States during Occupy Wall Street. In Venezuela, at "the one-year anniversary of the death of strongman Hugo Chavez, his successor Nicolás Maduro continued his crackdown against protestors demanding an end to corruption, rampant crime, and economic mismanagement. Since nationwide demonstrations began a month ago, clashes between Venezuelan security forces and protestors have resulted so far in at least 18 deaths and over 250 injuries" (Christy 2014: 1). In October of 2014 in Turkey, the Euro-Mediterranean Human Rights Network (EMHRN

2014: 1) condemned "the excessive use of violence, including firing of tear gas, water cannon and live ammunitions by police forces to disperse pro-Kurdish demonstrators, leading to the tragic death of over 30 civilians, the injury of hundreds and the mass arrest of more than a thousand civilians." The types of state crime are vast in number and, unfortunately, cannot all be covered here; however, we do provide a list of potential resouces that you may find helpful at the end of this chapter.

Summary

This chapter has provided a brief introduction to the crimes of governments and has summarized several illustrations of cases, highlighting those less often thought of as a "crime" or even a "harm" in an effort to have students critically think through state actions that, on the surface, may seem "logical," "acceptable" or "necessary." After all, as we have previously discussed, when it comes to crimes of the powerful, there is a strong hegemonic discourse that dominates the way these acts are framed and discussed which is a general dissentive for alternative discourse. As such, we think it is critical to examine not only the political rhetoric, but the state acts, policies, and their outcomes that, more often than not, can and should be defined as state crimes.

Activities and discussion questions

1. Go to the United Nations website and examine international laws dealing with human rights violations. Which laws seem to be the most significant in terms of controlling crimes of the powerful?
2. Research the use of technologies by the US government to gather intelligence on citizens. Do you think these violate constitutional rights?
3. What is your view on the US use of drones?

Films to watch

Congo: White King, Red Rubber, Black Death (2003)
Death in Gaza (2004)
The Devil Came on Horseback (2007)
Ghost Writer (2010)
No Fire Zone: The Killing Fields of Sri Lanka (2013)
Sometimes in April (2015)

Resource links

http://statecrime.org/
http://statecrimecenter.com/

References

Ahmed, N. (2013). Pentagon Bracing for Public Dissent Over Climate and Energy Shocks. *The Guardian*, June 14. Available at: www.theguardian.com/environment/ earth-insight/2013/jun/14/climate-change-energy-shocks-nsa-prism (accessed on September 3, 2015).

Applegate, S. (2009). Cyber Warfare: Addressing New Threats in the Information Age. Available at: www.academia.edu/1098261/Cyber_Warfare_-_Addressing_ New_Threats_in_the_Information_Age (accessed on September 10, 2015).

Barrow, C. (2005). The Return of the State: Globalization, State Theory and the New Imperialism. *New Political Science*. Available at: www.umassd.edu/cfpa/docs/ annrpt05.pdf (accessed on March 3, 2009).

BBC News (2014a). UK Government Can Be Sued Over Rendition Claims, Judges Rule. October 30. Available at: www.bbc.com/news/uk-29831112 (accessed on September 3, 2015).

BBC News (2014b). UN Rebukes Israel Over Jerusalem Settlements. October 30. Available at: www.bbc.com/news/world-middle-east-29801841?utm_source= Sailthru&utm_medium=email&utm_term=%2AMorning%20Brief&utm_cam-paign=2014_MorningBrief-%20RD%20PROMO (accessed on December 11, 2015).

Becker, T., and Murray, V. (1971). *Government Lawlessness in America*. New York: Oxford University Press.

Bell, L. (2013). Cyber Crime is a Bigger Threat than Nuclear War, UK Government Warns. *The Inquirer*, July 13. Available at: www.theinquirer.net/inquirer/news/ 2285740/cyber-crime-is-a-bigger-threat-than-nuclear-war-uk-government-warns (September 3, 2015).

Burghardt, T. (2013). Cyber Command Prepares for High-Tech War Crimes: "Computer Network Attacks to Protect U.S. Interests." Global Research, November 14. Available at: www.globalresearch.ca/cyber-command-prepares-for-high-tech-war-crimes-computer-network-attacks-to-protect-u-s-interests/21919 (accessed on September 10, 2015).

Chambliss, W. (1990). State Organized Crime. *Criminology*, 27(2): 183–208.

Christy, P. (2014). A Growing Crisis in Post-Chavez Venezuela. RealClearWorld, March 6. Available at: www.realclearworld.com/articles/2014/03/06/a_growing_ crisis_in_post-chavez_venezuela_110347.html (accessed on September 3, 2015).

Cole, C. (2013). First British Drone Strike Carried Out From UK RAF Waddington [resource document]. January 5. Available at: http://dronewars.net/2013/05/01/first-british-drone-strike-carried-out-from-uk-raf-waddington/ (accessed on August 20, 2013).

Democracy Now! (2012). As Obama Expands Drone War, Activists and Victims' Advocates Join D.C. Summit on Growing Civilian Toll. April 27. Available at: www.democracynow.org/2012/4/27/as_obama_expands_drone_war_Activists (accessed on September 10, 2015).

Durkheim, E. (1933). *The Division of Labor in Society*. Translated by G. Simpson. New York: Free Press.

Eisenhower Study Group (2011). The Costs of War Since 2001: Iraq, Afghanistan, and Pakistan. Executive Summary. Eisenhower Research Project, July. Available at: http://www.whale.to/c/costs-of-war-2001-2011.pdf (accessed on December 11, 2015).

EMHRN (The Euro-Mediterranean Human Rights Network) (2014). Turkey's Violent Denial of the Right to Peaceful Protest Turns Tragic Again. October 15. Available at: www.euromedrights.org/eng/2014/10/15/turkeys-violent-denial-of-the-right-to-peaceful-protest-turns-tragic-again/ (accessed on January 10, 2015).

Faulks, K. (2000). *Political Sociology: A Critical Introduction*. New York: New York University Press.

Faust, K., and Kauzlarich, D. (2008). Hurricane Katrina Victimization as a State Crime of Omission. *Critical Criminology*, 16(2): 85–103.

Federal Register (2013). Federal Register Volume 78, Number 71 (Friday, April 12, 2013) Rules and Regulations: Pages 21826–21839. Federal Register Online via the Government Printing Office, FR Doc. No. 2013–07802. Available at: www.gpo.gov/fdsys/pkg/FR-2013-04-12/html/2013–07802.htm (accessed on September 3, 2015).

Fisher, M. (2014). North Korea's Internet Appears to be Under Mass Cyber Attack. VOX World News, December 22. Available at: www.vox.com/2014/12/22/7433873/north-korea-internet-down (accessed on September 3, 2015).

Foucault, M. (1972). *The Archaeology of Knowledge and The Discourse on Language*. New York: Harper and Row.

Fox News (2014). Suspected US Drone Strike Kills 2 Militants in Northwest Pakistan. Fox News Asia, October 30. Available at: www.foxnews.com/world/2014/10/30/suspected-us-drone-strike-kills-2-militants-in-northwest-pakistan/ (accessed on September 3, 2015).

Friedrichs, D. (2004). White-Collar Crime in a Globalized World. Paper given at Western Michigan University.

Geers, K., Kindlund, D., Moran, N., and Rachwald, R. (2013). *World War C: Understanding Nation-State Motives Behind Today's Advanced Cyber Attacks*. Milpitas, CA: FireEye Inc.

Giddens, A. (1987). *The Nation State and Violence*. Berkeley, CA: University of California Press.

Global Research News (2013). Living Under Drones. September 26. Available at: www.globalresearch.ca/living-under-drones/5306110 (accessed on September 3, 2015).

Gramsci, A. (1971). *Selections from the Prison Notebooks*. New York: International Publishers.

Habermas, J. (1975). *Legitimation Crisis*. Translated by Thomas McCarthy. Boston, MA: Beacon Press.

Henri-Levi, B. (1977). *Barbarism With a Human Face*. New York: Harper and Row.

The Jerusalem Post (2014). Iran foils attempt to sabotage nuclear heavy-water tanks. October 30. Available at: www.jpost.com/International/Iran-says-foils-bid-to-sabotage-nuclear-heavy-water-tanks-380292 (accessed on September 3, 2015).

Keelman, H. C., and Hamilton, V. (1989). *Crimes of Obedience*. New Haven, CT: Yale University Press.

Krasner, S. (1995). Compromising Westphalia. *International Security*, 20(3): 115–151.

Marx, K. (1906). *Capital, Vol. I: The Process of Capitalist Production*. Translated from 3rd German edition by Samuel Moore and Edward Aveling. Edited by Frederick Engels. Chicago, IL: Charles H. Kerr.

Michalowski, R., and Harding, L. (2014). The Highway of Death. In D. L. Rothe and David Kauzlarich (eds)., *Towards a Victimology of State Crime*, 87–109. New York: Routledge.

Miliband, R. (1970). The Capitalist State: Reply to Nicos Poulantzas. *New Left Review*, 59: 53–60.

Miller, G. (2012). Plan for Hunting Terrorists Signals U.S. Intends to Keep Adding Names to Kill Lists. *The Washington Post*, October 23. Available at: www.washingtonpost.com/world/national-security/plan-for-hunting-terrorists-signals-us-intends-to-keep-adding-names-to-kill-lists/2012/10/23/4789b2ae-18b3-11e2-a55c-39408fbe6a4b_story.html (accessed on September 3, 2015).

Milne, S. (2014). Europe's Sea of Death for Migrants is a Result of War and Escalating Inequality. *The Guardian*, October 9. Available at: www.theguardian.com/commentisfree/2014/oct/09/europe-sea-death-migrants-war-inequality (accessed on September 3, 2015).

Mitchell, T. (1991). The Limits of the State: Beyond Statist Approaches and Their Critics. *American Political Science Review*, 85(1): 77–96.

Morey, J. (2013). U.S. Military "Power Grab" Goes Into Effect: Pentagon Unilaterally Grants Itself Authority Over "Civil Disturbances." Long Island Press, May 14. Available at: www.longislandpress.com/2013/05/14/u-s-military-power-grab-goes-into-effect/ (accessed on September 3, 2015).

O'Conner, J. (1973). *The Fiscal Crisis of the State*. New York: St. Martins Press.

Outer Nationalist (2012). UK Government's Tightening of Immigration Laws Clear Violation of Basic Human Rights. December 11. Available at: http://outernationalist.net/?p=3042 (accessed on September 3, 2015).

Poulantzas, N. (1969). The Problem of the Capitalist State. *New Left Review*, 58: 67.

Poulantzas, N. (1976). The Capitalist State: A Reply to Miliband and Laclau. *New Left Review*, 95: 63–83.

Poulantzas, N. (1978). *Classes in Contemporary Capitalism*. London: Verso.

Poulantzas, N. (1980). *State Power and Socialism*. New York: Verso.

Press TV (2013). US Assassination Drone Attack Kills 4 in NW Pakistan. April 14. Available at: www.presstv.com/detail/2013/04/14/298274/us-drone-strike-kills-4-in-pakistan/ (accessed on December 11, 2015).

Proall, L. (1898). *Political Crime*. New York: D. Appleton.

Protalinski, E. (2012). Obama: Cyber Attack Serious Threat to Economy, National Security. ZDNet, July 21. Available at: www.zdnet.com/article/obama-cyber-attack-serious-threat-to-economy-national-security/ (accessed on September 3, 2015).

Rothe, D. L., and Collins, V. E. (2014). Beyond Conventional Cyber Crime Concerns: "Beacons" to Botnets to Centrifuge Virus-"Olympic Games" to "Titan Rain" and More. Paper presented at Oxford Cyber Harassment Research Symposium, University of Oxford, UK, March 25–28.

Rothe, D. L., and Friedrichs, D. (2006). The State of the Criminology of State Crime. *Social Justice*, 33(1): 147–161.

Rothe, D. L., and Kauzlarich , D. (2010). State-Level Crime: Theory and Policy. In Hugh D. Barlow and Scott Decker (eds.), *Crime and Public Policy: Putting Theory to Work*, 166–187. 2nd edition. Philadelphia, PA: Temple University Press.

Rothe, D. L., and Ross, Jeffrey Ian (2014). Dronefare: The Normality of Governance and State Crime. In William J. Chambliss and Christopher J. Moloney (eds.), *State Crime*, Vol. II, 93–105. London: Routledge.

Sanger, D. E. (2012). *Confront and Conceal: Obama's Secret Wars and Surprising Use of American Power*. New York: Broadway Paperbacks.

Santos, D. T. (1971). *The Structure of Dependence*. Boston, MA: Extending Horizons.

Scahill, I. (2013). *Dirty Wars: The World Is a Battlefield*. Philadelphia, PA: Nation Books.

Seabrooke, L. (2002). Bringing Legitimacy Back in to Neo-Weberian State Theory and International Relations. Department of International Relations, Research School of Pacific and Asian Studies, Australian National University, Working Paper 2002/6.

Senor, T. (2008). Intel Brief: Cybercrime Gets Political. June 19. Available at: www.isn.ethz.ch/Communities-and-Partners/Partner Network/Detail/?ord655=grp1&lng=en&id=88484 (accessed on September 10, 2015).

Smelser, N. (1964). Towards a Theory of Modernization. In A. Etzioni and E. Etzioni (eds.), *Social Change: Sources, Patterns, and Consequences*, 258–274. New York: Basic Books.

So, A. (1990). *Social Change and Development: Modernization, Dependency, and World System Theory*. Newbury Park, CA: SAGE Publications.

Sutherland, E. (1939). White Collar Criminality. Presidential Address to the American Society of Sociology. Reprinted 1940. *American Sociological Review*, 5: 1–12.

Tilly, C. (1985). War Making and State Making as Organized Crime. In P. Evans, D. Rueschemeyer, and T. Skocpol (eds.), *Bringing the State Back In*, 169–191. Cambridge: Cambridge University Press.

United States Department of Justice (2011). Lawfulness of a Lethal Operation Directed Against a U.S. Citizen Who is a Senior Organizational Leader of Al-Qa'ida or an Associated Force. Department of Justice White Paper. Available at: http://msnbcmedia.msn.com/i/msnbc/sections/news/020413_DOJ_White_Paper.pdf (accessed on September 10, 2015).

Wall, T., and Monahan, T. (2011). Surveillance and Violence From Afar: The Politics of Drones and Liminal Security Scapes. *Theoretical Criminology*, 15(3): 239–254.

Wallerstein, I. (1974). *The Modern World – System I: Capitalist Agriculture and the Origins of the European World-Economy in the Sixteenth Century*. New York: Academic Press.

Weber, M. (1947). *The Theory of Social and Economic Organization*. Edited by T. Parsons. New York: Oxford University Press.

Wood, D. (2013). Drone War Expansion Sparks Questions About Effectiveness, Oversight In Obama's Second Term. *The Huffington Post*, January 16. Available at: www.huffingtonpost.com/2013/01/16/drone-war-obama_n_2454901.html (accessed on September 10, 2015).

Yan, H. (2014). Palestinian President: Closing Jerusalem Holy Site a Declaration of War. CNN World News, October 30. Available at: www.cnn.com/2014/10/30/world/meast/temple-mount/ (accessed on September 3, 2015).

Zetter, K. (2012). Meet "Flame," the Massive Spy Malware Infiltrating Iranian Computers. WIRED, May 28. Available at: www.wired.com/threatlevel/2012/05/flame/ (accessed on December 20, 2015).

Chapter 8

State-corporate crime

The two previous chapters introduced you to corporate crime (Chapter 6) and state crime (Chapter 7). Likewise, Chapter 5 discussed the symbiotic nature of all forms of crimes of the powerful. So why a chapter called "state-corporate crime"? What if the harms and crimes of corporations and states are the result of more than the symbiotic nature? As C. Wright Mills (1956) stated, a "circulation of elites" occurs between major economic and political decision-makers and they are typically from the same pool of the powerful, pursuing a shared vision. What if crimes of the powerful are the results of direct collusion? These were the questions that provided the foundation for a separate typology of corporate and state crime in the early 1990s: state-corporate crime.

Criminological origins

The concept of state-corporate crime first appeared in a series of papers that were presented in 1990 (Kramer 1990; Kramer and Michalowski 1990). Yet, its origins and evolution has a longer history spanning more than eight decades of collaborative efforts to understand crimes of the powerful, from Sutherland and white-collar crime to political and organizational crime. However, Kramer and Michalowski (1990: 4) provided the most widely cited definition of state-corporate crime: "State-corporate crimes are illegal or socially injurious actions that occur when *one* or more institutions or political governance pursue a goal in direct cooperation with one or more institutions of economic production and distribution." State-corporate crime increasingly came to be seen as taking two forms, although these types often interacted with each other. Accordingly, a distinction emerged between state-facilitated and state-initiated crimes (Kramer 1992; Kauzlarich and Kramer 1993). These earlier works proposed and explored a "framework for examining how corporations and governments intersect to produce social harm" (Kramer *et al.* 2000: 263). See Box 8.1.

It should be noted that crimes carried out either by the state or by corporations involved some level of implicit or explicit cooperation between states

Box 8.1 Original onset of framework for state-corporate crime

Ron [Kramer] began a project focused on unraveling the organizational origins of the Space Shuttle Challenger explosion. As he examined the relevant documents, he became increasingly sensitized to how the controversial Challenger launch decision involved interactions between a political organization, The National Aeronautics and Space Administration (NASA), and Morton Thiokol, Inc., a private business corporation. Acting in concert, these two organizations produced a technological failure of far-reaching consequence ... This clearly suggested a need for criminology to develop clearer conceptualizations of deviant inter-organizational relationships between business and government. In 1989, over dinner at the Society for the Study of Social Problems (SSSP) meeting in Berkeley, we [Kramer and Michalowski] discussed the issue, and Ray [Michalowski] suggested labeling harms resulting from these interactions "state-corporate crime." Ron thought the term fit the problem, and began incorporating it into his work on the Challenger ... including "State-Corporate Crime: A Case Study of the Space Shuttle Challenger Explosion," which he presented at the Edwin Sutherland Conference on White Collar Crime: 50 years of Research and Beyond ... We [Kramer and Michalowski] continued working together to refine the concept of state-corporate crime, and to develop a more elaborated theoretical framework for it. We presented our first efforts at the American Society of Criminology meeting in November of 1990 in a paper titled "Toward an Integrated Theory of State-Corporate Crime." We used the term state-corporate crime to denote these types of crimes and offered the following definition, "State-corporate crimes are illegal or socially injurious actions that occur when one or more institutions of political governance pursue a goal in direct cooperation with one or more institutions of economic production and distribution" (Kramer and Michalowski 1990). In the years following our initial inquiry into state-corporate crime, other scholars began adapting the concept and its associated theoretical model to a number of other social harms. Thus, within a capitalist economy, state-corporate crimes are the harmful consequences of deviant inter-organizational relationships between businesses and governments. This definition can be applied to illegal or socially injurious actions in societies organized around private-production systems and to those based on centrally planned economies. The deviant inter-organizational relationships that serve as the basis for state-corporate crime can take two forms. One is state-initiated corporate crime, and the other is state-facilitated corporate crime. State-initiated corporate crime occurs when corporations employed by a government engage in organizational deviance at the direction of, or with the tacit approval of, that government. State-facilitated corporate crime occurs when government institutions of social control are guilty of clear ... failure to create regulatory institutions capable of restraining deviant business activities, either because of direct collusion between business and government, or because they adhere to shared goals whose attainment would be hampered by aggressive regulation.

(Reprinted with permission of Rutgers University Press.)

(From Kramer and Micalowski 2006.)

and corporations (Friedrichs and Rothe 2014). More recently, Steve Tombs (2012) has advanced the claim that states and corporations are increasingly in a symbiotic relationship, leading to the systematic, routine production of crime and harm. In many circumstances, disentangling "state interests" from "corporate interests" is highly problematic due to the intersecting agendas of those at the top of both the state and the corporate hierarchies and the multiple "interlocks" reflected in movements in and out of high-level state and corporate positions.

Such intersections can work in a myriad of fashions, as noted in Box 8.1. States can create laws that facilitate corporate wrongdoing and crimes (for example, the infamous savings and loan debacle within the United States), and regulatory and advisement agencies can simply fail to do their appointed tasks (for example, OSHA's failure to provide remedy to safety violations at an Imperial Chicken plant in Hamlet, North Carolina [Aulette and Michalowski 1993], and the FAA's failures to ground ValuJet [Matthews and Kauzlarich 2000]).

Since these early works, the concept of state-corporate crime has taken off with research on fraud in the Dutch construction industry and collusion as a concept between corruption and state-corporate crime (van den Heuvel 2005); state-corporate crime and the Paducah gaseous diffusion plant (Bruce and Becker 2007); the Democratic Republic of Congo and gold and diamond industries (Mullins and Rothe 2008); state-corporate crime symbiosis and the transnational security industry (O'Reilly 2010); Blackwater in Iraq (Welch 2010); global warming and state-corporate crime (Kramer and Michalowski 2012; Lynch *et al.* 2010); the Canadian-Alberta tar sands: a case study of state-corporate environmental crime (Smandych and Kueneman 2010); OxyContin and a regulation deficiency of the pharmaceutical industry (Griffin and Miller 2011); Steve Tombs' (2012) research on the financial bailouts, suggesting that the bailouts can also be understood in terms of a symbiotic state-corporate crime relationship. Lines of demarcation between state and corporate entities, and between the public and the private realms, are blurred and opaque. This is by no means an exhaustive list, but does provide students with an array of topics where the state-corporate crime concept has been utilized. Additionally, there is a book edited by Michalowski and Kramer in 2006, *State-Corporate Crime: Wrongdoing at the Intersection of Business and Government*, that brings together the classic works as well as several new chapters (these are discussed more fully in the following section). This was the first anthology specifically dedicated to state-corporate crime and includes a series of articles documenting the daunting costs of state-corporate crime in a wide range of settings and contexts. More recently, in 2014, a special issue in the journal *State Crime* was dedicated to the concept of state-corporate crime, covering topics from the Gulf of Mexico oil spill in 2010 (Bradshaw 2014) and the Spanish economic crisis beginning in 2008 (Bernal *et al.* 2014), to mention a few.

Consequentially, it can easily be seen that the concept of state-corporate crime has been a useful tool for understanding an aspect of crimes of the powerful, though again, we caution students to recognize that concepts such as this and typologies in general present limitations to our broader understanding of the complexities of crimes of the powerful (see Chapter 5, the first section on "The problem with typologies").

Cases of state-corporate crime

Kramer published the first case study of state-corporate crime in Kip Schlegel and David Weisburd's 1992 anthology *White-Collar Crime Reconsidered* (a book that grew out of the 1990 Sutherland Conference on White-collar crime at Indiana University). At the time, most people viewed the Challenger disaster simply as an accident. In his paper, however, Kramer explained how state and corporate actors (NASA and Morton Thiokol) interacted with one another to produce risky decision-making processes and unsafe actions that resulted in the death of six astronauts and school teacher Christa McAuliffe.

Although the technical cause of the explosion was the failure of the O-ring seal in a field joint of a solid rocket booster, larger structural and organizational factors shaped the decision-making in such a way as to make the disaster more probable (for a later and more comprehensive analysis of the Challenger disaster, see Vaughan 1996). Kramer's case study illustrated the usefulness of a multidimensional empirical analysis, as the case is best understood at points where institutional and organizational forces conjoin with cultural and definitional processes to produce conditions favorable to organizational crime. This interest in the interaction effects of historical, political, and contextual factors is also found in the second published case study of state-corporate crime, authored by Kauzlarich and Kramer (1993).

The Department of Energy (DOE) and the Atomic Energy Commission produced nuclear and atomic weapons for 50 years by contracting with private firms, mostly large, multinational corporations like Westinghouse, DuPont,

General Electric, and Martin Marietta. These corporations were charged with the day-to-day manufacture and production of the weapons. The DOE owned the production equipment, but its real activities involved consulting and supervisory roles over various technical aspects of the weapons building process. The DOE also made sure that production quotas were being met.

Kauzlarich and Kramer (1993) showed how this institutional arrangement, guided by Cold War cultural beliefs and structural forces both propelled and sustained by the desire for continued American capitalist expansion, resulted in massive environmental injury. For example, in 1986, the Savannah facility generated more than 200,000 gallons of waste each day and the Hanford plant in Washington state has dumped more than 200 billion gallons of radioactive and hazardous waste since its inception in 1942. The contamination wrought by nuclear weapons production over the decades is so severe that, in the 1990s, estimates for bringing the complex into compliance with applicable environmental laws approached $400 billion.

Both the Kramer and the Kauzlarich and Kramer papers examined instances of state-initiated, state-corporate crime, as the state in both cases was consciously and explicitly involved in acts of crime commission. The next two published case studies of state-corporate crime focused on state-facilitated crimes.

Like the previously reviewed case studies, Aulette and Michalowski (1993) examined another disastrous conjoining of state and corporate interests. On September 3, 1991, an explosion and fire at the Imperial Food Products chicken processing plant in Hamlet, North Carolina, killed 25 workers and injured another 56. The technical cause of the fire was the rupture of a hydraulic line near a deep fryer that resulted in a fireball that quickly swept through the plant. Why did so many people die and become injured by the fire? Critically, it was because the company routinely locked several of its fire doors, effectively sealing off many potential exits from the flames and smoke. The company later said that it had locked the fire doors to prevent employee theft of chicken and to keep flies out of the factory. But, much more than these physically proximate causes and the larger drive for capital accumulation, the deaths and injuries were a product of a series of local, state, and federal crimes of omission that can be directly tied to the fate of the workers at the plant. For example, the state of North Carolina had refused to support the Occupational Safety and Health Administration (OSHA) endeavors that would have made places like Imperial Foods safer for workers, doing so little that it actually returned nearly a half a million dollars in unspent OSHA money to the federal government just prior to the fire. In addition, a US Department of Agriculture (USDA) inspector admitted that he knew of the company's practice of locking doors (potential fire escapes), but thought that he had no authority to do anything about it. Furthering the tragic irony, another USDA inspector actually approved of the locking of the doors, because he thought that it would prevent flies from contaminating the chicken inside the plant. In these ways and others (for example, the failure of local, regional, and federal polity and assorted regulatory bodies), the worker deaths were facilitated by state inaction and negligence. State-facilitated, state-corporate crimes like those in Hamlet involve elements of both crime commission and omission, and as such are likely to be one of the least recognizable forms of state involvement in crime. Yet, injury that is tacitly allowed or mildly encouraged by the state fills the world with as much injury and suffering as those that are explicitly triggered by conspiring corporate and governmental elites. This observation inspired Matthews and Kauzlarich (2000) to analyze another catastrophic event as a state-facilitated, state-corporate crime.

On May 11, 1996, ValuJet Flight 592 crashed in the Florida Everglades, killing all 105 passengers and five crew members. The technical cause of the crash was a fire that erupted after one or more oxygen generators exploded in a cargo compartment. Government investigations indicated that ValuJet and SabreTech (an airline maintenance company) failed to comply with a host of regulations concerning the presentation, storage, and transportation of hazardous materials by air. More generally, however, the Federal Aviation Administration (FAA) was found to be negligent in its oversight of airlines by not adequately monitoring the general safety of commercial aircrafts, as well as in its refusal to institute safeguards and guidelines that would have protected passengers and crews from crashes like that of Flight 592. Following the lead of the earlier studies reviewed, Matthews and Kauzlarich's (2000) case study of the disaster highlighted the broader structural policies that contributed to the crash (deregulation and unbridled capital accumulation), but also addressed the very specific items marginalized or overlooked by the FAA that can be directly linked to the deaths of those on ValuJet Flight 592. These include ignoring two clear recommendations by the National Transportation Safety Board (NTSB) to (1) place smoke detectors in cargo holds exactly like the area in which the fire started on Flight 592, and (2) reclassify cargo holds so that they would contain a fire and not allow it to spread to the rest of the plane. Had the FAA followed these recommendations, the probability that Flight 592 would have landed safely would have been tremendously increased. Additionally, officials in the FAA also ignored several damning reports about the low quality and maintenance of ValuJet planes, not only from other agencies such as the US Department of Defense but also by FAA field inspectors.

More current cases of state-corporate crime continue to show the collusion between states and corporations. The case study of the BP oil spill by Elizabeth Bradshaw (2014) documents efforts by the state and corporation (a state-corporate "cover-up") to suppress the criminality and the environmental impact that was caused by the Deepwater Horizon spill. This includes the coordinated ways in which the United States government and corporate actors attempted to conceal from the public the scale of the actual damages. A media blackout was implemented in the Gulf of Mexico and clean-up workers and employees were censored and forbidden to discuss the crime, the environmental harm, as well as the clean-up efforts where toxic chemicals were used to disperse the oil.

Another case study by Barak (2015: 373) involves the case of the National Mine, Metal and Steel Workers Union of Mexico, Grupo Mexico, and the Mexican government, where civil, criminal, and extra-legal harms "including the death of 65 miners and the injury of numerous others, police brutality, threats, bribes, forged documents, fraudulent charges and conspiracy" occurred. As Barak notes, "these crimes embody collaboration between the mutual interests of the state and capital ... [and] highlights the ways in which governments and corporations collaboratively commit harm in the interest of shared goals and ideology. As is often the case with many state-corporate crimes, Barak notes that the Miners' case involved a number of state-facilitated corporate and corporate-initiated state crimes. "However, the case also involves many related crimes that fall outside traditional interpretations of state-corporate crime" (ibid.: 378).

Box 8.2 State-corporate crime: war profiteering

The intersection of state and corporate interests during times of war is a fundamental part of the war-making process. Every capitalist country must rely on private-sector production to produce the weapons of war. In the United States, for example, major auto manufacturers such as Chrysler, Ford, and Chevrolet retooled to produce tanks, guns, and missiles instead of cars during World War II, while many other companies refocused some or all of their production to serve the war effort. With the introduction of a permanent wartime economy after the end of World War II, amid concerns that the United States was coming to be dominated by a military-industrial complex ... major providers of weapons and logistical support such as General Electric, Boeing, Bechtel Group, and Lockheed Martin became regular recipients of government contracts. They were also repeatedly at the center of controversies concerning cost overruns and questionable charges ... The close alignment of corporate and government interests in the production and procurement of the weapons of war is a vivid example of the "revolving door" effect as described by C. Wright Mills ... in the Power Elite. As executives from major military contractors fill elected or appointed government positions, the interests of the state become increasingly entangled with prior corporate loyalties. In recent years, the integration of state interests with those of the private corporation has intensified. This integration began with efforts to adapt to a downsized military through increased reliance on "just on time" privatized logistic contracts. The move to an active war footing following the attacks of 9/11, including the wars in Afghanistan and Iraq and the permanent "war on terror," further cemented the private–public strategy for war-making in the United States (Rothe 2006). The controversy surrounding links between Vice-President Dick Cheney and Halliburton, the company he formerly headed, provides a demonstration of the potential for state-corporate crime embedded in this new policy of war by subcontract. There have been claims that the association between Cheney and Halliburton resulted in no-bid, cost-plus contractual work without competitive pricing or oversight. According to some, the affiliation between Cheney and Halliburton has established war profiteering as an acceptable and systematic practice within the Bush Administration by rewarding "corporations for who they know rather than what they know, and a system in which cronyism is more important than competence" … Although the relationship between Cheney and Halliburton appeared to be a major factor in awarding contracts to Halliburton … Cheney denied any involvement in the contracts contracting process. On [NBC's] "Meet the Press" he said, "As Vice President, I have absolutely no influence of, involvement of, knowledge of in any way, shape, or form of contracts led by the Army Corps of Engineers or anybody else in the Federal Government" … Private memos, however, proved otherwise. An internal Pentagon e-mail (March 5, 2003) sent by an Army Corps of Engineer official, claimed that Douglas Feith, Defense Department's undersecretary for policy, approved arrangements for a multi-billion dollar contract for Halliburton "contingent on informing the WH tomorrow. We anticipate no issues since action has been coordinated w VP office" … Within three days Halliburton received one of the first State Department contracts for Iraq worth as much as $7 billion … Not only did Halliburton receive billions of dollars from the State through competitive and non-competitive contracts, most of them were cost-plus contracts. Cost-plus contracts are essentially blank checks that ensure whatever Halliburton bills for services is reimbursed for those costs as well as an additional percentage (between 2 and 7 percent) for the company's profits (fees). These types of open-ended contracts are incentives to maximize expenditures to increase the total value of the contract and profits. Moreover, the larger the contract, the more valuable becomes Halliburton's stock. For example, October 2002, Halliburton's stock was $12.62 a share; however, when the KBR (Kellogg, Brown, and Root) Iraq restructure contract was awarded, Halliburton's stock rose to $23.90 a share … According to Henry Bunting's (2004) testimony to the Democratic Policy Committee, the Halliburton motto in Iraq is "don't worry about it, it's cost plus" … In essence, no one questioned pricing. "The comment by both Halliburton buyers and management was "it's cost plus, don't waste time finding another supplier" … By 2005, KBR had earned contracts worth over $2.2 billion from work in Iraq. Overall, it has been estimated that Halliburton has received more than $8 billion in contracts since Cheney became V.P. The close relationship between the Administration and Halliburton constitutes a form of state-initiated war profiteering. While Halliburton may be guilty of inflating total contract values through overcharges and/or charges for services not provided, the opportunities for profiteering were the products of the cozy relationship between the company and a sitting administration whose vice-president was Halliburton's former CEO. Thus, the economic gain was both personal and political.

(From Rothe 2006.)

Another article by Bernal, Forero, and Rivera (2014) examines the collusion between state and corporate sector in Spain with the financial crisis. They note that, since 2008, Spain has continued to face a deep economic and financial crisis, leading to significant levels of harm for the general citizenry. Here, Bernal *et al.* (2014: 233) find that the criminal symbiosis between private banking and politics, in the contexts of the state's financial crisis and the participation of private banking in financing the Spanish military industry, led to destructive relations between private banking and the state that facilitated a variety of state-corporate crimes, "including internal economic frauds and external deaths in the participation in wars, and massive social harms as a result of the response to the country's economic crisis—not least evictions, suicides, unemployment, pauperization and so on."

Rawlinson (2014) uses the concept of state-corporate crime to scrutinize the relationships between the state, the medical and pharmaceutical industry by examining the violence "behind the beneficent arm of the state in its role as health provider, and how the collaboration with medical science and the pharmaceutical industry have resulted in laboratories of human suffering involving society's most vulnerable" (ibid.: 84). Rawlinson locates the abuse of human subjects in contemporary times, most notably in the Global South, within the paradigm of state-corporate crime (the state, public health, and corporate triumvirate), highlighting the growing propensity for serious harm and abuse to test new commoditized medicines, medications, and medical procedures. Rawlinson then illustrates how, when such "experiments" go awry, they are diluted by the term "unethical" rather than "criminal."

The criminogenic culture embedded in the pharmaceutical industry has been well documented (Slapper and Tombs 1999; Braithwaite 1984). "As pharmaceutical companies continue to survey the global terrain for the expansion of the legal drugs and vaccine market, they are simultaneously seeking new jurisdictions for clinical trials" (Tombs 2012: 182). Tombs continues in a recent article to show how the Private Finance Initiative (PFI) in the United Kingdom generated long-term public debt to a consortium of private contractors "effectively privatizing profits while socializing financial risks in areas previously untouched by private sector involvement" (Tombs 2012: 182).

The PFI is a form of public private partnership (PPP) that marries a public procurement programme, where the public sector purchases capital items from the private sector, to an extension of contracting-out, where public services are contracted from the private sector. PFI differs from privatisation in that the public sector retains a substantial role in PFI projects, either as the main purchaser of services or as an essential enabler of the project. It differs from contracting-out in that the private sector provides the capital asset as well as the services. The PFI differs from other PPPs in that the private sector contractor also arranges finance for the project.

(Allen 2001: 10)

From the few case studies noted above, researchers of the crimes of the powerful continue to note the symbiotic and dangerous relationships between states and the corporate sector from manufacturing to services; the toxic nature is often not noticed until significant harm, death, violence become evident. Even then, such relationships tend to be minimalized as a necessary part of our capitalistic system.

In sum, these cases of state-corporate crime show how state and corporate interests can join to produce profound social and personal injury and death. Sometimes, as with state-initiated, state-corporate crime, the state is actively and explicitly involved in crime commission. Other times, the state is complicit because it or one of its agencies has failed to protect people vulnerable to potentially harmful organizational practices.

Summary

There are many examples of state-corporate crime in history and in the modern period, and many of these can be classified as violent crimes. State-corporate crimes can be facilitated by the state or actively committed by a government or governmental entity in direct concert with corporations. Business and government are connected to one another in fundamental ways and the potential for harmful consequences because of this relationship can be even greater than with state or corporate crime as separate entities. As noted by Tombs (2012: 172), "the state is a capitalist state, one that is necessarily if complexly committed to prioritizing the practices and values of profit accumulation above social values." Having said this, we return to our previous discussions of the falseness of typologies and the reductionism that can occur rather than seeing the symbiotic relations within the broader system. As Barak (2015: 384) states:

[T]hese categorizations overlook large-scale patterns of collaborative state and corporate crime occurring across time and space, reducing these patterns to singular events precipitated by singular actors from either government or business rather than by patterns driven by neoliberal ideology, socio-historical and cultural contexts, and powerful elite networks that are deeply embedded within government and business alike.

Activities and discussion questions

1. Research corporate involvement in the Holocaust and compare this with more current forms of state-corporate crime.
2. Discuss how state-facilitated state-corporate crime differs from state-initiated state-corporate crime. Are there similarities?
3. Research how the Federal Aviation Administration (FAA) regulates airline safety. Which airlines have the worst and best safety records?

References

Allen, G. (2001). The Private Finance Initiative. Research Paper 07/117, December 18. House of Commons Library, United Kingdom. Available at: www.parliament.uk/briefing-papers/RP01-117.pdf (accessed onSeptember 4, 2015).

Aulette J., and Michalowski, R. (1993). Fire in Hamlet: A Case Study of State-Corporate Crime. In K. Tunnel (ed.), *Political Crime in Contemporary America*, 171–206. New York: Garland.

Barak, M. (2015). Collaborate State and Corporate Crime: Fraud, Unions and Elite Power in Mexico. In G. Barak (ed.), *The Routledge International Handbook of the Crimes of the Powerful*, 373–385. New York: Routledge.

Bernal, C., Forero, A., and Rivera, I. (2014). State-Corporate Crime and Social Harm in the Spanish Crisis. *State Crime Journal*, 3(2): 220–236.

Bradshaw, E. (2014). "Obviously, We're All Oil Industry": The Criminogenic Structure of the Offshore Oil Industry. *Theoretical Criminology*, 19: 376–395. First published online, October 10: doi:10.1177/1362480614553521.

Braithwaite, J. (1984). *Corporate Crime in the Pharmaceutical Industry*. London: Routledge.

Bruce, A., and Becker, P. (2007). State-Corporate Crime and the Paducah Gaseous Diffusion Plant. *Western Criminology Review*, 8(2): 29–43.

Friedrichs, D., and Rothe, D.L. (2014). State-Corporate Crime and Major Financial Institutions: Interrogating an Absence. *State Crime*, 3(2): 146–162.

Griffin, O., and Miller, B. (2011). OxyContin and a Regulation Deficiency of the Pharmaceutical Industry: Rethinking State-Corporate Crime. *Critical Criminology*, 19(3): 213.

Kauzlarich, D., and Kramer, R. (1993). State-Corporate Crime in the U.S. Nuclear Weapons Production Complex. *The Journal of Human Justice*, 5(1): 1–26.

Kramer, R. (1990). State-Corporate Crime: A Case Study of the Space Shuttle Challenger Explosion. Paper presented at the American Society of Criminology, Baltimore, MD, November.

Kramer, R. (1992). The Space Shuttle Challenger Explosion: A Case Study of State-Corporate Crime. In K. Schlegel and D. Weisburd (eds.), *White Collar Crime Reconsidered*, 212–241. Boston, MA: Northeastern University Press.

Kramer, R., and Michalowski, R. (1990). Toward an Integrated Theory of State-Corporate Crime. Presented at the American Society of Criminology, Baltimore, MD, November.

Kramer, R., and Michalowski, R. (2006). Introduction: The Critique of Power. In Raymond Michalowski and Ronald Kramer (eds.), *State-Corporate Crime: Wrongdoing at the Intersection of Business and Government, 14.* Piscataway, NJ: Rutgers University Press.

Kramer, R., and Michalowski, R. (2012). Is Global Warming a State-Corporate Crime? In R. White (ed.), *Climate Change from a Criminological Perspective*, 71–88. New York: Springer.

Kramer, R., Michalowski, R., and Kauzlarich, D. (2000). The Origins and Development of the Concept and Theory of State-Corporate Crime. *Crime and Delinquency*, 48(2): 263–282.

Lynch, M., Burns, R., and Stretesky, P. (2010). Global Warming and State-Corporate Crime: The Politicization of Global Warming under the Bush Administration. *Crime, Law and Social Change*, 54: 213–239.

Matthews, R. A., and Kauzlarich, D. (2000). The Crash of ValuJet Flight 592: A Case Study in State-Corporate Crime. *Sociological Focus*, 3: 281–298.

Michalowski, R., and Kramer, R. (2006). *State-Corporate Crime: Wrongdoing at the Intersection of Business and Government.* Piscataway, NJ: Rutgers University Press.

Mills, C. W. (1956). *The Power Elite.* New York: Oxford University Press.

Mullins, C., and Rothe, D.L. (2008). International State-Corporate Crime in the Democratic Republic of the Congo. *Contemporary Justice Review*, 11(2): 81–99.

O'Reilly, C. (2010). The Transnational Security Consultancy Industry: A Case of State-Corporate Symbiosis. *Theoretical Criminology*, 14(2): 183–210.

Rawlinson, P. (2015). Foreign Bodies: The New Victims of Unethical Experimentation. *The Howard Journal*, 54(1): 8–24.

Rothe, D. L. (2006). State-Corporate Crime: War Profiteering and the Ali Babba. In Raymond Michalowski and Ronald Kramer (eds.), *State-Corporate Crime: Wrongdoing at the Intersection of Business and Government*, 215–238. Piscataway, NJ: Rutgers University Press.

Slapper, G., and Tombs, S. (1999). *Corporate Crime.* Harlow, Essex: Pearson Educational Ltd.

Smandych, R., and Kueneman, R. (2010). The Canadian-Alberta Tar Sands: A Case Study of State-Corporate Environmental Crime. In R. White (ed.), *Global Environmental Harm: Criminological Perspectives*, 87–109. Cullompton: Willan.

Tombs, S. (2012). State-Corporate Symbiosis in the Production of Crime and Harm. *State Crime Journal*, 1(2): 170–195.

van den Heuvel, G. (2005). The Parliamentary Enquiry on Fraud in the Dutch Construction Industry Collusion as Concept Between Corruption and State-Corporate Crime. *Crime, Law and Social Change*, 44(2): 133–151.

Vaughan, D. (1996). *The Challenger Launch Decision: Risky Technology, Culture, and Deviance at NASA.* Chicago: Chicago University Press.

Welch, M. (2010). Detained in Occupied Iraq: Deciphering the Narratives for Neocolonial Internment. *Punishment & Society: The International Journal of Penology*, 12(2): 123–146.

Chapter 9

Power, organized crime networks, and the elite

While crimes of the powerful are generally thought of as those covered in the previous chapters, one should not discount the power of organized crime and the symbiotic relationships with corporations, states, and, in some cases, international financial institutions. People have probably heard of Al Capone, John Gotti, Joe Valachi, and Charlie "Lucky" Luciano. Most may also have heard of Eliot Ness, head of the "Untouchables," assigned to break up Capone's bootlegging operations during Prohibition. It is common knowledge that Chicago and the New York–Philadelphia–New Jersey area were major centers of organized crime activities. What most people have learned about organized crime, however, has come from the mass media. Apart from periodic news items, which are usually colorful and designed to demonstrate some special kind of inside knowledge, the entertainment industry has been a major window on organized crime. The enduring popularity of films such as *Goodfellas* and *The Godfather* (Image 9.1) as well as the television show *The Sopranos* is evidence of the strong appeal of organized crime as entertainment, where stereotypes of the "criminal syndicate" are Hollywoodized into the mainstream consciousness. At best, the information available to the public via the mass media is fragmentary, superficial, and misleading; at worst, it is patently false and purely titillating.

But, what exactly do we mean when we use the term "organized crime"? After all, the concept has been challenged and, at times, is used alternately with transnational crime. However, organized crime need not be "transnational" in character, though in many cases it is in some form or other. For our purposes, we define organized crime as an organization that is involved in illicit activities, that has a division of labor, a hierarchy, and codes or an ethos, and that remains regardless of changes within the network or syndicate. As noted by Felson and Kalaitzidis (2005: 6):

> It is clear that the degree of organization of criminal activity can vary dramatically, with some groups possessing hierarchical structures and other criminals operating within loosely structured, flexible

Image 9.1 A scene from *The Godfather* (Credit: Paramount Pictures/The Kobal Collection)

networks ... Consequently, critics argue that the term *organized crime* merely simplifies and mystifies the complexities of criminal activities and functions.

We agree that organized crime operates within a market-like structure and that, as Friedrichs notes (2009: 193), "business crime and organized crime can be seen as ways of conducting business illegally, and both reflect political processes that dictate that certain forms of entrepreneurship must be constrained and prohibited." Organized crime, then, is a "product of and an important ongoing element of a capitalist political economy" (ibid.).

Given the interdependent nature of organized crime with the general political economy, one could argue that organized crime is an innovative approach playing within the same field and, at times, same rules as "legitimate" actors. While not the orthodox view of organized crime, it is one that should not be discounted.

Box 9.1 James "Whitey" Bulger and the United States government

Whitey is an Irish-American mob boss of the Winter Hill gang that ruled Boston for nearly three decades and was recently charged in a racketeering indictment that included "19 killings; extorting drug dealers, bookmakers, and businessmen; money laundering; and building an illegal arsenal of guns." The case revealed heavy government corruption and Whitey's protection from the FBI as a deal for his informant status: informant 1544, a file over 700 pages long noting information he provided to the FBI in return for his protection and information. FBI agents routinely provided him tips that he used to kill rivals. FBI agents who were accused of taking bribes from Whitey were never charged, though Whitey himself was found guilty of 31 out of the 32 counts he was charged with, including 11 of 19 murders.

Box 9.2 Kenya and organized crime

A report by Peter Gastrow (2011) states that Kenya has rampant corruption within the Police force, the judiciary and other state institutions, including the parliament, that are linked to organized crime networks dealing in heroin, human smuggling and arms trafficking to mention a few. The report notes that "top politicians are involved" and "senior government officials work with criminal networks and shield them" (ibid.: 18). The report also notes that one of the cartels includes former members of parliament, an elite business woman, and customs officers who have been linked to drug smuggling, receiving counterfeit and other illicit commodities. Additionally, government staff at the Dadaab refugee camp have been linked to human trafficking of women and young girls, using the refugee camp as a hub for migrants and others to be trafficked.

Unlike many of the other forms of crimes of the powerful that are legitimated through law or portrayed as the rare accident, "crimes" of organized crime groups are demonized and pursued through social control mechanisms. But, they are also supported by corporations, states, intergovernmental agencies, and international financial institutions, and are legitimated through these relationships or their criminality is ignored, depending upon the relationships of power, politics and the economy, and the threat to the status quo. In some ways, even the efforts of governments to "end," control, or to prosecute organized crime, further legitimates the system. The focus of organized crime returns to the safe terrain of individuality, accountability, and the masquerading of the broader system that perpetuates these intertwined relationships, even though it is known that power, politics, business, and organized crime often intersect.

Returning to a more well-known criminological topic, burglary may serve as a good mechanism for a comparison of sorts when discussing the relationships and networks needed to function (for example, the "criminal," the fence or the middle man, the pawn shop, and the buyer). A burglar needs a tipster, someone to inform him/her of potential goods and opportunities. They need a fence, someone to buy the stolen product. This could be a pawn shop or flea-market seller. Burglars need protection, most notably by attorneys. Most importantly, as Shover notes (1976: 548), "in order to be successful in his crimes the burglar must gain access to and establish trusted relationships with members of deviant social circles. These deviants are very careful about whom they allow in." Organized crime groups also need a market or purchasers. They need consumers and demand. Both of the above include, but are not limited to, accountants, attorneys, notaries, bankers, and real-estate brokers. They need protection (for example, in the case of Whitey Bulger; see Box 9.1) and they must gain access to and establish relationships with members of "elite" social circles. While simplistic in comparison, the point is that organized crime groups cannot operate without the complicit and implicit support of corporations, consumers, states, and other entities, most notably the powerful in many cases.

Examples of the synergetic relationship of organized crime with corporations, states, and international financial institutions are highlighted in the following section. Additionally, students should be cognizant of the types of crimes that are carried out within the broader system of relationships of power versus those that we hear of when governments investigate and prosecute organized criminal networks or syndicates (for example, homicide, money laundering, tax evasion, and prostitution).

Cases of organized crime, governments, and corporations

The US government considers organized crimes as a threat to national security. The phenomenon was defined by the Obama administration (National Security Council 2011: 2) as transnational:

> [S]elf-perpetuating associations of individuals who operate transnationally for the purpose of obtaining power, influence, monetary and/or commercial gains, wholly or in part by illegal means, while protecting their activities through a pattern of corruption and/or violence, or while protecting their illegal activities through a transnational organizational structure and the exploitation of transnational commerce or communication mechanisms.

As we noted previously however, a major part of the concern centers on the "Threats to the Economy, U.S. Competitiveness, and Strategic Markets" (ibid.). Australia, like the United States, believes organized crime is a national security threat. Again, the focus is on the economic costs: "[the government] estimates serious and organised crime costs the Australian economy $15 billion each year" (Australian Crime Commission 2014: 1). Likewise, Canada's Public Safety Department (2015) states that "the National Agenda recognizes that the fight against organized crime is a national priority that requires all levels of government, the law enforcement community and other partners to work together."

At the international level, the United Nations states that "organized crime is one of the major threats to development and security … Acting as multinational corporations, criminal groups seek profit through the evaluation of countries' risks, benefits and markets analysis …Organized crime adopts all forms of corruption to infiltrate political, economic and social levels all over the world." Interpol, the international police organization made up of 190 member countries, is also actively pursuing organized crime, though recognizing that "what constitutes organized crime vary widely from country to country" (2014c: 1). The main focus as of this writing is on the Pink Panthers: armed jewelry robberies, Asian organized crime, Eurasian criminal organizations, and the "Thieves in Law" network (see Box 9.3).

Box 9.3 Thieves in Law

"Thieves in Law" or "Thieves professing the code" have been identified by Project Millennium as a priority area of investigation. The influence of the "Thieves in Law" extends across groups engaging in a wide variety of crimes, such as trafficking in drugs, human beings and stolen vehicles. They are of various nationalities including Russian, Georgian, Armenian and Belarusian. They contribute to a common criminal fund—the "Obshak"—which is managed by the most influential and high-ranking "Thieves in Law." This represents billions of dollars and is invested in shares, real estate and companies. Money is invested in legitimate companies—with the "Thieves in Law" often having great influence in activities and control of a particular sector—as well as in shadow companies used for money laundering. In this way, criminal funds are generated and distributed through both legal and illegal channels, with an impact on the global economy.

(From Interpol 2014c: 1.)

While states combat organized crime, they take the same approach as with other forms of crimes of the powerful that are investigated and prosecuted: focusing on individuals, though with much harsher sentences than we

Box 9.4 Yakuza organized crime and Japan

In Japan there was a historic record of 110,000 active Yakuza organized crime members divided into 2,500 families. Currently, 2013, the numbers are respectively around 58,600. The Yakuza's influence is more pervasive within Japanese society and is well entrenched in the corporate world and there is a prevalence of forms of collusion with police. Unlike most organized crime syndicates, "the Japanese mafia is recognized and regulated by the police under the organized crime control laws... [they] have offices and fort-like headquarters, business cards, corporate logos, badges and fan magazines. The Yamaguchi-gumi, Japan's largest group "has their own internal newspaper and has a website in development, perhaps hoping to recruit younger members and shore up PR" (Adelstein and Stucky 2014: 2).

They are involved in real estate, "FX trading, investments, restaurant management, construction, waste disposal, and controlling interests in most of Japan's talent agencies" and "the entertainment business [and] has extensive political connections ... officially 'backing' the Democratic Party of Japan (DPJ) since 2007." For example, Kamei Shizuk, former Minister of Financial Services and current special envoy to Prime Minister Naoto Kan, admitted "to receiving a payment of over roughly 5,000,000 dollars from a Yamaguchi-gumi boss into his own bank account" (Japan Subculture Research Center n. d.: 5).

would see for those committing corporate-state crimes. Yet, there is a clear understanding by governments that these networks require the complicit and implicit support of a host of other organizations (facilitators) to succeed.

The following cases offer several different types of "crimes" in an attempt to highlight some of these relationships and the contradictions between states' "war" on organized crime and the realities of their role or that of leading corporations.

Italy has a long history of organized crime networks, which illustrates quite usefully the connections between them, states, and corporations. First, let us give a brief overview of the main syndicates operating in Italy. The four primary or "strongest" Italian Mafia organizations include the Sicilian Mafia, the Calabrian 'Ndrangheta, the Neapolitan Camorra, and the Apulian organized crime network. Cosa Nostra is said to be the oldest and most "traditional" of the Sicilian Mafia. Their expansion outside of the borders of Italy is primarily in North America. The 'Ndrangheta is believed to be the richest and most powerful organized crime group and mainly operates in Italy, Spain, France, Belgium, the Netherlands, Germany, Switzerland, Canada, the USA, Colombia, and Australia. The Apulian group is composed of the Sacra

---

Box 9.5 Pharmaceutical crime, organized criminal groups

Excerpts from Interpol 2014a:

- In March 2013, Philippine authorities arrested five traffickers attempting to traffic slimming pills, pain relief medication and antibiotics which had been shipped to the Philippines from Singapore.
- Between 2011 and 2013, Azuma-Gumi was running a counterfeit medicine operation selling Viagra, Cialis and Levitra in Osaka, Japan.
- In June 2013, Russian authorities reported that they had dismantled a counterfeiting operation which had been ongoing for several years in Rostov. Fake medicines such as Herceptin, Meronem, Cefobit, Mantera, Sulperason were manufactured and distributed.
- In April 2013, open sources reported that fake medicines were being distributed in New Zealand. The group's leader was operating a sophisticated ring of distributors.
- In June 2013, open sources reported that in Guatemala a group operated from a legitimate pharmaceutical company, which was licensed to produce medicines. However, the organized crime group took advantage of this cover to produce illegal medication in order to increase the company's revenue (7–8).

From Interpol 2014b:

" 'Criminals' are also known to operate the pharmacies themselves, as well as wholesalers, 42 distribution companies and other facilities, leading to the development of criminal rings in which counterfeit and illicit medicines are moved through the legal supply chain. One example from 2012 highlights this issue, with two New York pharmacists found to be involved in purchasing almost USD 274 million worth of illegally obtained HIV and AIDS medication since 2008 through a distribution network run by another suspect. There are also indications that government and law enforcement officials have been corrupted in certain countries. From a few open source cases, government officials are known to have had direct involvement in criminal activities, helping to embezzle government medication as was the case in the Sialkot region of Pakistan in 2010. In a prominent case from a country in South America in 2009, illegally imported, expired and counterfeit medicines were knowingly supplied to a pharmacy and union-run healthcare centre whose deputy director was later arrested for his involvement (15).

Corona Unita, the Società Foggiana, the Camorra Barese, and the Gargano's Mafia. Outside of Italy, this group is primarily present in the Netherlands, Germany, Switzerland, and Albania (Europol 2013).

A *New York Times* article by Yardley, dated April 2014, states that:

> Italy's organized crime groups often operate as shadow states, infiltrating local politics while controlling territory through intimidation and violence … this local dominance explains why the organizations are heavily involved in sectors such as construction, mining, waste management and transportation, where their political influence allows them to steer government contracts to their favored firms.

They are strong enough and so deeply embedded that they are capable of "manipulating elections and installing their men in administrative positions even far away from the territories they control … Exploiting legislative loopholes and using the services of corrupt administrators and professionals, they launder money and manage it through front companies and straw men" (Europol 2013: 3).

The connections to government continue to surface. For example, in 2013 a high-profile trial opened in Sicily with ten accused including Salvatore "Toto" Riina, "one of the most notorious mafia bosses Italy has known," and "Nicolas Mancino, who once served as interior minister" (Roberti 2013: 1). Allegations included collusion and secret agreements between the Mafia and key state players. It is not just the links between these Mafia groups and the state that are omnipresent in Italy, but, as with most other syndicates, they are vested in licit market activities that may or may not be fronts for crimes or illegal doings.

Box 9.6 Russia and organized crime

The Guardian sub-headlines read: Kremlin relies on criminals and rewards them with political patronage, while top officials collect bribes "like a personal taxation system." Based off of leaked Wikileaks documents, the Guardian reports that the United States government has stated that "officials, oligarchs and organized crime are bound together to create a 'virtual mafia state.'" According to Wikileaks documents:

- Russian spies are linked with mafia leaders to carry out arms trafficking.
- The police, state run spy agencies and prosecutors operate "a de facto protection racket for criminal networks."
- Bribery serves as a parallel tax system for self gain of public officials including police, government officials and the federal security service (formerly KGB).

- Investigators have compiled a list of Russian government agents and politicians that have direct and indirect dealings with organized crime syndicates.
- The lead prosecutor in Spain has stated that recent operations included gun-running to the Kurds in an attempt to destabilize Turkey and arms trafficking in the mysterious Arctic Sea cargo ship hijacking in 2009.

(From Harding 2010.)

The words "organized crime" and "Mexico" have recently (September and October 2014) taken over many headlines when 43 students were taken and later found massacred. The links between government and organized crime were not as covert as in many of the previous cases; here there was direct collusion and cooperation. It began with responses to student protests in Iguala when the municipal police "broke up a march and a political demonstration ... Police killed six and then arrested another 43 student protestors ... and then handed the others over to the Guerreros Unidos (United Warriors) gang. The gangsters killed the other 30 or so young men and women, shredded their corpses and burned the remains" (Bay 2014: 1). In October, it was also reported that the response to and actions toward the demonstrators were because "Iguala mayor, Jose Luis Abarca, pressured by his wife, Maria de los Angeles Pineda, ordered municipal police to attack the students. Pineda intended to run for mayor of Iguala ... had scheduled a speech before 3,000 bused-in supporters in the city plaza (Bay 2014: 2)" and did not want the protestors to disrupt her political campaign. Pineda also has direct ties to cartels, as she is the sister of two members of the Beltran-Leyva cartel, and several Guerreros Unidos members were once gunmen in the Beltran-Leyva organization.

A further investigation and evidence from video, however, shows a deeper embedment between organized crime and government, beyond the municipal level. The total number of students involved was 57. An unedited report compiled by the government of Guerrero stated that federal and state security forces had been monitoring the students since they left their college. The report showed that the shootings "were reported to Mexico's Center of Control, Command, Communications and Computation (C4), which both the federal police and the military have access to" (Gurney 2014: 1). The Proseco investigation and report findings undermine the official version given by President Enrique Peña Nieto's administration. Moreover, it showed links with organized crime, corrupt officials, and the level of violence of the militarized state. "Mexican government corruption facilitates organized crime. Organized crime enriches a corrupt political class. Cartel gunmen and crooked cops on the streets, cartel comandantes and corrupt politicos through institutions ensnare the Mexican people" (Bay 2015: 2).

Corporations are also involved with organized crime, in some cases directly, as Box 9.7 highlights, or indirectly, as Box 9.8 demonstrates. During the nineteenth century, organized criminal groups learned that money could be made in the fields of industrial organization and employee relations. Faced with the prospects of strikes and unionization, companies called on criminal gangs to help them combat these threats to their power and profits. The companies paid well for the gangs' muscle, and the gangs, in turn, were happy to oblige. Infiltration of the union movement by organized crime soon followed and with it came money and power for leaders of the fledgling unions. First the building trades and then service industries fell under the influence and domination of corrupt officials backed by gangsters. Money was collected from both employers and employees, organized crime playing each side off against the other. Racketeering is explained not merely by the corruption of union and company officials, nor by the fact that organized crime is in the business of making money any way it can. Rather, the spread of racketeering stems from a combination of conditions; some are economic, for example, excessive entrepreneurial competition and an excess supply of labor.

Box 9.7 Caught on tape: construction bosses meet with the Montreal Mob

Hours of RCMP surveillance video reveal links between Mafia and construction industry

Based on tapes from a 2006 surveillance at Montreal's Consenza Social Club, a headquarter hangout for the Rizutto organized crime group, conversations not used in previous arrests were once again at the front of investigations years later. With over 64,000 conversations and 35,000 hours of video were hours of interactions between the Mafia and some of Montreal's largest construction industry bosses. "Those construction bosses, identified here, were seen on tape at the social club and became a key element of the testimony detailing a kickback scheme involving the Mafia, the construction magnates and city officials" (CBC News 2012). Quebec construction tycoon Tony Accurso has testified that he gave $250,000 to an associate of "Jacques Duchesneau to pay off the former police chief and one-time Montreal mayoral candidate's debt after an election defeat." (ibid.: 1).

Trying to divide out the role of states and corporations with organized crime groups is a moot task as more often than not there is involvement of all these organizational actors.

Box 9.8 New Zealand: a haven for shell companies?

"Another New Zealand shell company has been linked to an alleged fraud worth more than US$150m—this time involving Ukrainian state-owned companies ... The company, Falcona Systems Ltd of Albany ... was used to gain $150m in kickbacks for Ukrainian and Latvian officials" (Field 2012:1).

In another case, the Latvian authorities claimed that Tormex Ltd. of Auckland washed $680 million through a Riga bank account that is believed to be tied to the Russian Mafia (ibid.).

Consider the case of illegal dumping that results in significant environmental harm, often carried out by organized crime groups, corporations, and with state complicity or at worst, implicit support. As noted by the United Nations Interregional Crime and Justice Research Institute (2014: 1),

> Among the various forms and typologies of environmental crimes, the phenomenon of illegal trafficking and dumping of both hazardous and e-waste is steadily growing, and its detrimental effects are increasingly affecting the environment and world population. Though the volume of the waste dumping is hard to assess, it is estimated that around 1.5 million waste-loaded containers are shipped illegally every year, with the market value of illegal waste shipments thought to amount to between 10–12 billion USD.

According to the United Nations Interregional Crime and Justice Research Institute (2014), over the past three decades, Italian Mafia criminal organizations, most notably the Camorra and 'Ndrangheta, have been heavily involved in environmental crimes, including illegal trafficking of waste and toxic dumping. Some of the cases have resulted in prosecution of key Mafia players, though declassified testimony shows that Italian politicians have known about the problem for years, ignoring the crimes and subsequent harms from the environmental damage as local death toll and cancer rates climbed (Mayr 2014). Additionally, members of the Camorra and 'Ndrangheta networks had global reach, dealing with governments across the globe, participating in European funded research projects on nuclear waste disposal and making business agreements with multinational and transnational corporations.

Likewise, the production and disposal of nuclear weaponry and waste may be dumped by illicit organized crime groups, though states are active participants. After all, the dumping of nuclear waste and its removal out of the country is not unmonitored or done within a black market, governments are aware of this process and, in fact, are often seeking out the companies or organized crime groups to remove the toxins from their country to another, as occurred in Somalia after the tsunami of 2004 showed evidence of this massive network of states, corporations, and organized crime groups dumping toxic waste materials.

Summary

The connections between what is illegal and what is legal are not so clear. As previous chapters have shown, states, corporations and international financial institutions have, directly and indirectly, committed a fair share of crimes and harms. Organized crime groups do not operate in a vacuum. They require the complicity of the broader structure and are, in many ways, merely another aspect of the political economy. Often migrating between legal and illegal activities, these syndicates provide services that would not exist without a demand. In other words, organized crime could not survive or continue without the support of consumers, corporations, manufacturers, and states. After all, they need a market, a product, a service, and a means to exist.

Activities and discussion questions

1. Why do you think the media rarely highlights the role of corporations and states in organized crime groups?
2. Do you believe implicit links between states and organized crime groups are enough to say that a state should also be accountable for the crimes and harms? Why or why not?
3. Do you believe corporations should be held accountable when they are active agents for organized crime groups? Why or why not?

References

Adelstein, J., and Stucky, N. (2014). Where have Japan's Yakuza Gone? The Daily Beast, September 3. Available at: www.thedailybeast.com/articles/2014/03/09/where-have-japan-s-yakuza-gone.html (accessed on December 22, 2015).

Australia Crime Commission (2014). Organised Crime. Available at: www.crimecommission.gov.au/organised-crime (accessed on September 3, 2015).

Bay, A. (2014). Mexico's Iguala Massacre: Criminal Gangs and Government. *Statesman Journal*, November 12. Available at: www.statesmanjournal.com/story/opinion/2014/11/12/mexicos-iguala-massacre-criminal-gangs-government/18942367/ (accessed on September 3, 2015).

Bay, A. (2015). Mexico Iguala Massacre: Criminal Gangs and Government. Creators.com. Available at: www.creators.com/conservative/austin-bay/mexicos-iguala-massacre-criminal-gangs-and-criminal-government.html (accessed on December 11, 2015).

Canada Government Public Safety (2015). Working Together to Combat Organized Crime. Available at: www.publicsafety.gc.ca/cnt/rsrcs/pblctns/cmbtng-rgnzd-crm/index-eng.aspx#a1 (accessed on September 3, 2015).

CBC News (2012). Quebec Construction Tycoons Caught on Tape Meeting Mob. September 26. Available at: www.cbc.ca/news/canada/montreal/quebec-construction-tycoons-caught-on-tape-meeting-mob-1.1143218 (accessed on December 11, 2015).

Europol (2013). Europol Public Information: Threat Assessment Italian Organised Crime. The Hague, June. File No. EDOC#667574v8. Available at: www.europol.europa.eu/sites/default/files/publications/italian_organised_crime_threat_assessment_0.pdf (accessed on September 3, 2015).

Felson, D., and Kalaitzidis, A. (2005). A Historical Overview of Transnational Crime in Handbook of Transnational Crime and Justice. Thousand Oaks, CA: SAGE Publications.

Field, M. (2012). NZ Shell Company Linked to Alleged $150 m Fraud. Stuff, May 24. Available at: www.stuff.co.nz/business/world/6976306/NZ-shell-company-linked-to-alleged-150m- (accessed December 11, 2015).

Friedrichs, D. (2009). Trusted Criminals: White Collar Crime in Contemporary Society. Cengage Learning. 4th edition. Belmont, CA: Wadsworth Publishing.

Gastrow, P. (2011). Termites at Work: A Report on Transnational Organized Crime and State Erosion in Kenya. Global Observatory, November. Available at: http://theglobalobservatory.org/wpcontent/uploads/2011/10/pdfs_toc_kenya_comp_proof.pdf (accessed on September 10, 2015).

Gurney, K. (2014). Mexico Tortured "Perpetrators" of Student Massacre: Report. InSight Crime, December 16. Available at: www.insightcrime.org/news-briefs/mexico-tortured-perpetrators-iguala-student-massacre (accessed on September 3, 2015).

Harding, L. (2010). Wikileaks Cables Condemn Russia as "Mafia State." The Guardian, December 1. Available at: www.theguardian.com/world/2010/dec/01/wikileaks-cable-spain-russian-mafia (accessed on January 25, 2014).

Interpol (2014a). Countering Illicit Trade in Goods: A Guide for Policy-Makers. June. Available at: www.interpol.int/en/News-and-media/Publications/Guides-manuals/Countering-Illicit-Trade-in-Goods-A-Guide-for-Policy-Makers-June-2014 (accessed on December 22, 2015).

Interpol (2014b). Pharmaceutical Crime, Organized Criminal Groups. Available at: www.interpol.int/Media/Files/Crime-areas/Pharmaceutical-crime/Pharmaceutical-Crime-and-Organized-Criminal-Groups (accessed on September 10, 2015).

Interpol (2014c) Project Millennium. Available at: www.interpol.int/es/Crime-areas/Organized-crime/Project-Millennium (accessed on September 10, 2015).

Japan Subculture Research Center (n. d.). Yakuza Organisations. Available at: www.japansubculture.com/resources/yakuza-organisations/ (September 10, 2015).

Mayr, W. (2014). The Mafia's Deadly Garbage: Italy's Growing Toxic Waste Scandal. Spiegel Online International, January 16. Available at: www.spiegel.de/international/europe/anger-rises-in-italy-over-toxic-waste-dumps-from-the-mafia-a-943630.html (accessed on September 3, 2015).

National Security Council (2011). Strategy to Combat Transnational Crime. Available at: www.whitehouse.gov/sites/default/files/Strategy_to_Combat_Transnational_Organized_Crime_July_2011.pdf (accessed on September 3, 2015).

Roberti, F. (2013). Mafia Hold Over Italy Growing Stronger. *The Hindu*, June 6. Available at: www.thehindu.com/opinion/interview/mafia-hold-over-italy-growing-stronger/article4785260.ece (accessed on September 3, 2015).

Shover, N. (1976). Structures and Careers in Burglary. *Journal of Criminal Law and Criminology*, 63(4): 540–549. Available at: http://scholarlycommons.law.northwestern.edu/cgi/viewcontent.cgi?article=5825&context=jclc (accessed on September 3, 2015).

United Nations Interregional Crime and Justice Research Institute (2014). Environmental Crimes. Available at: www.unicri.it/topics/environmental/research/ (accessed on September 3 2015).

Yardley, J. (2014). Italy's Mob Extends Reach in Europe. *The New York Times*, April 24. Available at: www.nytimes.com/2014/04/25/world/europe/seizing-on-economic-woes-italys-mob-spreads-reach-in-europe.html?_r=0 (accessed on September 3, 2015).

Crimes of international financial institutions

The crimes of international financial institutions[1] are unique in that they involve organizations that are not corporations or states, they are unique international institutions that operate in a vacuum of accountability, save to themselves. Crimes of international financial institutions can be considered organizational crimes where the harms and crimes are intrinsically linked to economic (neoliberal) globalization that translates into social, cultural, and technological globalization (Rothe and Friedrichs 2014b). The crimes and harms that have both historically and currently resulted from the complicit and implicit policies, partnerships, projects, and loans of these financial institutions—the World Bank and the International Monetary Fund—have been referred to as "crimes of globalization" (Friedrichs and Friedrichs 2002; Friedrichs and Rothe 2013; Rothe and Friedrichs 2014b). In a rapidly changing global economy, the roles of the international financial institutions have been increasingly questioned.

At the onset, the focus of the international financial institutions was to maintain growth of the world economies and provide currency stabilization loans to alleviate any major economic crisis, and development loans to foster and promote a neoliberal laissez-faire economic system (Jackson 2012; Woods 2006; Zweifel 2006). The International Monetary Fund came into formal existence at the Bretton Woods Conference in 1944, when 29 member countries signed its Articles of Agreement. Its first official operations began in 1947 with France as the first borrowing country. During the late 1950s and 1960s, membership of the International Monetary Fund began to expand as many colonized territories gained their independence. Since the International Monetary Fund was first established, its stated purposes have remained largely unchanged, but its operations such as surveillance, financial assistance, and technical assistance have changed in focus somewhat throughout its history. In 1986, the institution created a loan program, the Structural Adjustment Facility, which was then succeeded by the Enhanced Structural Adjustment Facility (1987). Since these changes, it has expanded to include programs such as the Poverty Reduction and Growth Facility. Today, it is an organization of 188 member countries and claims to "foster global monetary cooperation, secure financial stability, facilitate international trade, promote high employment and sustainable economic growth, and reduce poverty around the world" (International Monetary Fund 2013a: 1). It "encourages" countries to adopt what it believes to be "sound economic policies or reforms," or what most commentators refer to as neoliberal economics. Such economic reforms are imposed on borrowing states supposedly to create socio-economic conditions more conducive to economic health and growth. These can include, but are not limited to, opening government-owned industries to privatization, the removal of tariffs and healthcare fees, and the acceptance of currency re-evaluations and reductions in social or other governmental spending programs in ways determined by the lenders. In most cases, there has been "a strong focus on fiscal thrift to which most other concerns are subordinated" (Torrance and Lochery 2008: 3). This leads to a broad range of harms for citizens of Global South countries (Rothe and Friedrichs 2014b).

The World Bank, formally the International Bank for Reconstruction and Development (IBRD), was established at the Bretton Woods Conference in 1944 to help stabilize and rebuild economies ravaged by World War II. Eventually it shifted its focus to an emphasis on aiding Global South countries. The World Bank is not a "bank" in the commonly used sense of the term. Rather, it is a specialized financial agency, composed of 184 member countries. Conceived during World War II, it initially helped to rebuild postwar Europe. In 1947, its first loan of $250 million went to France for reconstruction. Once its original mission of postwar European reconstruction was finished, the World Bank turned its lending practices to "development" issues. Its rhetoric was often focused on human rights, human dignity, and infrastructure development, but its operational concerns strongly focused on producing returns for investors. Through the 1970s and 1980s, Global South countries were frequently unable to meet repayment demands. Therefore, during the 1980s the Bank went through an extensive period that focused on issues related to macroeconomics and debt rescheduling. In return for debt reallocation or admission into forgiveness programs, it demanded that macrostructural political and economic changes occur within the debtor nations. In many cases, the World Bank also required recipient countries to adopt certain political measures, such as policies that would foster "democracy," by which it meant opening state holdings to private ownership (Rothe and Friedrichs 2014b).

More recently, the World Bank became a group, encompassing five closely associated development institutions: the International Bank for Reconstruction and Development (IBRD), the International Development Association (IDA), the International Finance Corporation (IFC), the Multilateral Investment Guarantee Agency (MIGA), and the International Centre for Settlement of Investment Disputes (ICSID). Since the mid- to late 1990s, the World Bank has utilized private sector development (PSD) as its strategy to promote privatization in the Global South, wherein other strategies must be coordinated with the push toward privatization. The Bank makes low-interest loans to governments of its member states and to private "development" projects backed by those governments with the stated aim to benefit the citizens of those countries. Today the World Bank is a large, international operation with more than 10,000 employees, 184 member states, and annual loans of $170 billion (Strom 2011). For the World Bank's fiscal years 2013 and 2014, the commitments for the IDA—the Bank's fund for the "poorest" countries—and the IFC—the arm of the Bank promoting private business ventures in Global South countries—were at an all-time high (Rothe and Friedrichs 2014a, 2014b).

Given that the World Bank and the International Monetary Fund were created at the behest of dominant Western states, with little input from non-economic or non-politically empowered countries, the inequalities and structural focus has remained on the interests of the Global North. It is disproportionately influenced by or manipulated by elite economic institutions and entities—for example, transnational mining companies—and has been characterized as an agent of global capital. In most of the Global South countries, World Bank officials deal primarily with the political and economic elites of those countries with little direct attention to the perspectives and needs of indigenous peoples (Babb 2009; Goldman 2005; Weaver 2008). It has loaned money to ruthless military dictatorships engaged in murder and torture and denied loans to democratic governments subsequently overthrown by the military. It has favored strong dictatorships over struggling democracies, because it believes that the former are more able to introduce and see through the unpopular reforms their loan payments require. The World Bank and the International Monetary Fund borrowers are typically the political elites of Global South countries and their cronies, although repaying the debt becomes the responsibility of the countries' citizens, most of whom do not benefit from the loans (Rothe and Friedrichs 2014b).

The World Bank and the International Monetary Fund have been targets of much criticism, especially in the recent era. They have been characterized as paternalistic, secretive, and counterproductive in terms of their claimed goals of improving people's lives. They have been called fundamentally hypocritical due to the gap between the professed objectives for the projects they support and the actual outcomes (Weaver 2008).

They have been charged with complicity in policies with genocidal consequences, with exacerbating ethnic conflict, with increasing the gap between rich and poor, with fostering immense ecological and environmental damage, with neglecting agriculture crucial to survival in many of the Global South countries, and with the callous displacement of vast numbers of indigenous people in these countries from their original homes and communities (Rothe and Friedrichs 2014b). White (2003: 498) notes that,

Undeveloped	Underdeveloped	Developing	Developed

Figure 10.1 Development terms

The activities of international financial institutions like the World Bank (as well as individual firms and companies) are re-dressed in ways that convey the message that "sustainable development" is happening, and that global power-brokers are doing what needs to be done to protect the environment. This belies actual environmental harms perpetrated by many of these institutions and by specific businesses that, cumulatively, are doing great damage to the global environment.

In the wake of these widespread criticisms of the ineffectiveness and harmful consequences of the structural adjustment programs and other programs imposed on Global South countries by the World Bank and the International Monetary Fund, a shift to poverty reduction was announced as a new goal in the more recent period (Abouharb and Cingarelli 2006; Brady 2010). However, since the global economic crisis of 2008, it has been estimated that an additional 50 million people will be locked into poverty at least through 2015 (Chan 2010).

Key terms

Students should first understand that we do not believe these international financial institutions enact policies or programs that they believe are overall detrimental. Rather, we feel that those involved within these organizations and programs fully believe and are committed to the ideology that undergirds their overarching economic policies and programs—namely, neoliberalism, to achieve "development" and "alleviate poverty" by relying on fully open, privatized markets and the laissez-faire dogma. As such, we consider it is necessary to first engage students into critically thinking about the terms that undergird the discourse, policies, and practices.

Development discourse

The term "development" is widely invoked as though it is manifestly obvious that it is a positive phenomenon. Of course, to have development, one needs to assume there is a counter to it: "undeveloped" or "underdeveloped." These terms assume a lower ranking, if you will, as "under" implies beneath and "un" implies not. Development is also seen as an innate, natural linear process like the one in Figure 10.1.

Development is a concept and ideology that undergirds policy and is generally understood in terms of "growth" and advancement. The question really is what is "real" advancement and growth, and for whom? Development can refer to other factors such as life happiness, health, the metaphysical, the intellectual, relationships, and a host of other non-economic factors known as "social development." Which form of "developing" should be prioritized?

Box 10.1 "World Happiness Report wins award for the betterment of the human condition," Sustainable Development Solutions Network, September 18, 2014

The *World Happiness Report* makes the case that well-being should be a critical component of how the world measures development. Here, the measures of happiness include GDP, education, mental health care, perceived freedom, levels of government legitimacy and other factors. The Report (Helliwell *et al.* 2013: 92) found that "The ethos of hyper-commercialism has prevailed the United States for around one century. It remains the dominant US ethos today. Yet there are growing counter-currents, both religious and secular, that insist on social justice, redistribution, ecological sustainability, social capital, and psychological detachment from consumerism. Hyper-commercialism has failed to lift average US happiness for more than half a century, even as per capita income has tripled. In ... this report, the US ranks just 17th in happiness, though it has a higher income per capita than the 16 countries ahead of it, with the exception of Norway."

The happiest ranked top 24 countries include:

1. Denmark
2. Norway
3. Switzerland
4. Netherlands
5. Sweden
6. Canada
7. Finland
8. Austria
9. Iceland
10. Australia
11. Israel
12. Costa Rica
13. New Zealand
14. United Arab Emirates
15. Panama
16. Mexico
17. United States

18. Ireland
19. Luxembourg
20. Venezuela
21. Belgium
22. United Kingdom
23. Oman
24. Brazil

(From Helliwell *et al.* 2013.)

The fundamental belief in a linear progression and development has been around for over a century, as the following quote illustrates:

> If unsettled and sparsely scattered tribes of hunters and fishermen show no disposition or capacity to emerge from the savage to the agricultural and civilized state of man, their right to keep some of the fairest portions of the earth a mere wildness, filled with wild beasts, for the sake of hunting, becomes utterly inconsistent with the civilization and moral improvement of mankind.
>
> (American jurist James Kent, 1866)

In the context of hegemonic discourse, the Global North and international financial institutions, growth and development always infer economic conditions that align with neoliberal market ideology: open markets, privatization, and little to no subsidies and reduced social support systems. The World Bank states that it uses Gross National Income (GNI per capita) to summarize a "country's level of development or measure welfare, [as] it has proved to be a useful and easily available indicator that is closely correlated with other, nonmonetary measures of the quality of life" (World Bank 2015: 1). Terms used to denote low GNI expectancy include developing, underdeveloped, and Third World, all of which imply hierarchy and are riddled with value-laden dogma. Additionally, development and growth are promoted in a profoundly skewed way, so that the interests of wealthy countries and benefits for the multinational corporations and well-connected Global South businessmen/women, and for corrupt politicians, are privileged over long-term benefits for the people of these countries. Accordingly, "development" is a concept that is contested, theoretically and politically, and is ambiguous at best. We suggest that development is not an objective "thing"; rather, it is a value-laden discourse that shapes, frames, and reifies the reality of power relations and global economic positions.

Growth is seen as a result of development or developing. Here again, it is shown in absolute economic terms and understanding. International financial institutions are firmly grounded in the belief that, through growth and development, in a trickle-down aspect, the worst poverty will be reduced or abolished. This is deeply rooted in the belief in the laissez-faire market ideology and neoliberalism which guide their policies and practices (see Box 10.2).

Box 10.2 Organizations, ideology, and goals

There is, undoubtedly, a genuine belief in the neoliberal policies that guide mandated restructuring policies. As such, this ideology serves to undergird the ways in which development is portrayed and understood and becomes the "truth," the authoritative correctness to which discussions of development occur and subsequent measures of implementing policy become institutionalized within the organizational culture. When an organization truly believes in its cause, it is indeed difficult to see the negative ramifications that may be associated with the actions that are guided by a deep-seated belief system that is instilled within the institution/organization, appearing as common sense and as if consensually accepted. This, of course, does not imply the organization is monolithic; however, as organizational theorists point out, there are overarching cultures and goals that remain intact as interchangeable employees and appointees change.

In summary, the policies and practices of international financial institutions are deeply embedded within neoliberalism and, as such, are believed to be the appropriate path to what has come to be the commonsense understanding of development. The political economy of "development" produces a system in which poverty is, in a counterintuitive sense, not reduced but embedded and reproduced. As the following section highlights, regardless of the intent, the harms and crimes associated with these institutions are common occurrences and will continue for as long as the international financial institutions continue with the current mindset.

Criminology, crimes of international financial institutions, or "crimes of globalization"

Over the last 20 years, researchers of globalization have linked the policies of international financial institutions to the production of grave human rights violations; however, criminologists had given this topic little attention until 2002, when Friedrichs and Friedrichs, in an article titled "The World Bank and Crimes of Globalization: A Case Study," suggested that harms caused by the policies and practices of international financial institutions could be operationalized as "crimes of globalization." Informed by Falk's observation that globalization is driven by the interests of capital over people, the term "crimes of globalization" refers to mass social harms that occur as latent consequences of the development and expansion of global capital. Friedrichs and Friedrichs highlighted the role of international financial institutions, with a particular focus on the World Bank, transnational corporations, and states in the context of criminogenic tendencies within globalization. Specifically, they drew on the Pak Mun dam case, where the World Bank helped finance the building of the dam in eastern Thailand in the early 1990s. The construction of the dam had a detrimental effect on the environment, flooding the adjacent forests. This effect violated the World Bank's own policies on cultural property destruction. Many edible plants upon which locals were dependent for their sustenance and for income were lost. Villagers who used the river for drinking, bathing, and laundry developed skin rashes. Most importantly, a severe decline in the fish population occurred. As a consequence, the way of life of indigenous fishermen dependent upon abundant fish for food and income was annihilated. The resettlement of the fishermen and compensation for their losses were wholly inadequate. Traditional communities began to disintegrate. Many of those affected by these developments organized protest villages and engaged in other actions calling for the Thai government and the World Bank to take responsibility for the devastation they caused by building the dam, which cost far more than expected and generated far less electricity than had been anticipated.

Following the Friedrichs and Friedrichs (2002) article, a number of criminologists have applied the concept of crimes of globalization to other circumstances. In 2006, Rothe, Mullins, and Muzzatti conducted research that explored the interrelations between the International Monetary Fund and the World Bank, and the legacies of colonialism, along with foreign policies that set the stage for large-scale atrocities and crimes of states. Exploring the circumstances leading to the sinking of the ferry *Le Joola*, the authors suggested that international financial institutions bore some culpability for the disaster. In response to structural adjustment programs (SAPs) imposed by the International Monetary Fund, the Senegalese government had been forced to cut spending in many areas. These spending cuts extended to ferry programs central to transportation in Senegal, especially in relation to its geographic location. This had a direct impact on the upkeep and return of the *Le Joola* to open waters. The ferry capsized with only one of its two engines functioning, resulting in the deaths of 1,863 passengers.

An article by Rothe, Mullins, and Sandstrom (2009) took a parallel approach, exploring the role of international financial institution policies in the conditions leading to the Rwandan genocide in 1994. While the World Bank and the International Monetary Fund did not seek to instigate economic collapse or to promote genocide, their policies and their systematic inattention in Rwanda set the stage for political and economic disaster as well as the genocide itself. The authors suggested that these international financial institutions had knowingly violated their own standards, as well as international human rights principles. Through the imposition of harsh conditions tied to their financial aid, they facilitated criminal activities on a massive scale.

In an article, Ezeonu and Koku (2008) also adopted the crimes of globalization concept. They demonstrated the key contributing role played by the neoliberal policies of international financial institutions in sub-Saharan Africa, in expanding the vulnerability of people in this region to HIV infection. They called for more systematic criminological attention to the victimization of people in developing countries as a consequence of the promotion of neoliberal policies and practices in an increasingly globalized world (see also Ezeonu 2008).

In a similar vein, Rothe (2010a, 2010b) has provided an analysis of the complicity of international financial institutions in heightened levels of corruption and the suppression or violation of human rights in many of the Global South countries. Analyzing such complicity seems especially important given that these institutions claim to be engaged in combating corruption in developing countries, including those linked to transnational and multinational corporations. Rothe has also illustrated the specific role of the international financial institutions in the illegal expropriation of the rich natural resources of the Democratic Republic of Congo by the neighboring countries of Uganda and Rwanda. Beyond theft on a grand scale, Rwandan and Ugandan state forces and militias also engaged in especially atrocious human rights violations conducted against civilian populations, including forced labor, systematic rape, and widespread killing. Through their funding of African states engaged in crimes against both their own citizens and those of neighboring countries, the international financial institutions bear some responsibility for these crimes.

Parallel circumstances have arisen in other parts of the world. Stanley (2009) analyzed the role of the international financial institutions in Indonesia. They directed some $30 billion to the Suharto regime, despite its known record of massive corruption, false accounting, and a militaristic appropriation of aid funds. As the World Bank's focus was on supporting Indonesia, the state was able to use funds supposedly intended to reduce poverty in its brutal campaign against civilians in the state of Timor-Leste. This campaign had as its purpose terrorizing people to deter them from voting for independence from Indonesia.

Maureen Cain (2011) addresses the notion of a global state, and in this context adopts the term "global crime" for the harms caused by international financial institutions. Drawing on the case of Trinidad and Tobago, Cain attributes increases in instrumental crimes (for example, property crimes) and self-assertive crimes (for example, crimes of violence) to policies mandated by international financial institutions. More generally, Cain suggests that on a global scale the policies of these institutions in highly indebted countries have many criminogenic effects, including heightened levels of poverty, privatization of natural resources, reduced social services, and other recognized structurally negative mandated outcomes.

More recently, Rothe and Friedrichs (2014b) published a book titled *Crimes of Globalization*, expanding on their previous publications and research on the international financial institutions (see also Friedrichs and Rothe 2014; Friedrichs and Rothe 2013). After presenting an overview of crimes of globalization, they offer a chapter covering contemporary cases of international financial institutions violating indigenous rights to supporting environmentally and socially harmful projects from intervention detention centers to villagization projects to mineral resource extraction, funding pipeline and dam projects, to the push for privatization of water. Drawing from Friedrichs' previous analysis of the economic crisis and the role of international financial institutions, the authors include a discussion of debt and the impact on countries in the Global South as a direct result of the policies and mandates of these economic institutions (see Box 10.3).

Box 10.3 Debt as a result of the relationship with the international financial institutions

The core decisions relating to debt are made by the international financial institutions, other Western governmental entities (e.g., the US Department of Treasury), and consortia of big banks in these countries (i.e., the Paris Club and the London Club, as they are known). It is their priorities—to insure debt repayment, to open up borders to capitalist enterprises, and to extend to political allies privileged treatment—that guide these decisions … In one recent year over half a trillion dollars was paid by debtor countries to service their external and private debt, with some $800 billion annually repaid each year by public authorities in these countries.

Altogether, debt has risen sharply in the Global South countries since the mid-1990s, with the international financial institutions playing a key role in this situation … These debt obligations have a crippling and devastating impact on the economies of the Global South countries and on the ordinary citizens of these countries. In the words of one commentator: "The long history of economic exploitation and domination by foreign capital has impoverished much of the African continent. The capitalists have extracted billions in profits and managed to leave the exploited nations hundreds of billions in debt" … Such systemic exploitation is surely increasingly visible and a source of festering resentment and anger within the exploited nations.

The international financial institutions have contributed in a fundamental way to the debt crisis that has crippled the economies of many Global South countries since the early 1980s. Yes, corruption, megalomania and the lack of democracy within these countries has contributed substantially to the state of their economies, but there is much reason to believe that international financial institutions based in the West triggered the debt crisis in the Global South countries ... The huge burden of paying off debt imposed by the international financial institutions and other Global North entities has fallen very disproportionately on the shoulders of ordinary citizens of most of the Global South countries, despite the fact that they have not benefited or profited—for the most part—from this debt. By some estimations, even though repayments on such debts may exceed three or four times the amount of the original debt, due to these repayments being directed almost entirely to interests payments, the principal [sic] of the original debt remains in place ... Furthermore, "the International Monetary Fund basically acted as the world's debt enforcers—"You might say, the high-finance equivalent of the guys who come to break your legs." ... The International Monetary Fund works in cooperation with the World Bank and such entities as the Paris Club and the London Club to insure that repayment of debt takes priority over other concerns and that the Global South countries adopt policies that favor their interests and those of rich Western and Global North countries overall ... These policies include deregulation of the market in line with the promotion of the Western neoliberal economic agenda, and such deregulation has also contributed to an enormous increase in the internal public debt of countries in the global South ... On multiple different levels, then, citizens of these countries are adversely affected by the policies of the international financial institutions.

(From Rothe and Friedrichs 2014b.)

Rothe and Collins (2016) note that, over the past decade, international financial institutions have actively promoted and financed the liberalization of the hydrocarbon and mining sectors of national economies across the globe. They suggest that states' influences and pressures play a role in motivating international financial institutions to continue to push, promote, and finance resource extraction at the behest of corporate and state interests. Moreover states' priorities are directed toward private ownership policies for companies within their own territories. They point out the connection between international financial institutions and the United Nations Framework Convention on Climate Change that established the Green Climate Fund (hereafter referred to as the Fund) in 2010 and the potential impact on resource extraction and environmental harms. The Fund was created to promote low-emission, climate resilient development projects. The World Bank is heavily intertwined with the Fund in that it is the interim trustee, managing the Fund's financial assets, and is being considered as the long-term trustee, accredited to be the implanting entity of the Fund, meaning it would determine the allocation of resources and activities. Even at the initial stages of the Fund's development, the World Bank Group's staff has played a central role in guiding the decisions that the Fund board should make and the structure of the votes allocated. "The World Bank has been at the forefront of financing fossil-fuel projects that have exacerbated the climate crisis. It is now an ironic contradiction that this same institution that has greatly contributed to the climate crisis is to be entrusted with funds that promise to address the very same problem it helped to create in the first place" (Nacpil, quoted in Rothe and Collins 2016). Rothe and Collins conclude by suggesting that the demand for gold (and other natural resources) by governments and general consumers continues to support the broader economic drives, reifying rather than contesting the policies of international financial institutions. See Box 10.4 on IFC funding.

Box 10.4 IFC funding

The majority of resource extraction projects are funded through the International Finance Corporation (IFC), the World Bank Group arm that is the largest global development institution focused exclusively on the private sector. Rothe and Collins (2016) note that this includes projects such as the Ahafo mine, Ghana, which included a $75 million investment loan (A equity loan) and a $10 million secured loan (B loan) to Newmont. Likewise, the Simandou mine, Guinea, included an investment of $35 million loan to Rio Tinto and a $15 million equity loan to Nyota for the Tulu Kapi mine, Ethiopia (International Monetary Fund 2013a). Another current project is a $12 billion investment to develop a copper and gold mine at Oyu Tolgi, in the southern region of Mongolia. The latter project is said to be "a cornerstone of Mongolia's economic development as the country strives to eradicate poverty and emerge as a middle-income country" ... In May 2013, the IFC announced a 5 million Canadian dollar investment in Unigold Incorporated for gold and base metal exploration for the Neita project in the Dominican Republic for a "future development plan," stating that the "IFC will work with the company to ensure that exploration and any subsequent mine development is carried out in an environmentally and socially sustainable manner" (International Monetary Fund 2013a, in Rothe and Friedrichs 2014b).

There is also "widespread recognition that structural adjustment and external debt force many developing nations to increase their natural resources exports to developed nations" (Bello *et al.* 1999; Downey *et al.* 2010). As noted by

Downey, Bonds, and Clark (2010: 2), "One set of institutions that facilitate resource extraction activities are international trade and finance institutions such as the World Bank, International Monetary Fund (IMF), and World Trade Organization (WTO)." They also acknowledge that international financial institutions have multiple negative impacts on individuals, societies, and the environment (Bello *et al.* 1999; Wallach and Woodall 2004).

White (2003: 498) notes:

> The activities of international financial institutions like the World Bank (as well as individual firms and companies) are re-dressed in ways that convey the message that "sustainable development" is happening, and that global power-brokers are doing what needs to be done to protect the environment. This belies actual environmental harms perpetrated by many of these institutions and by specific businesses that, cumulatively, are doing great damage to the global environment.

As White (2003: 497) suggests, the links between capital and a state are manifested in coinciding ideological and financial agendas "regarding the privatization and commodification of nature"; the same can be said of international financial institutions and global capital interests.

Beyond the existing research on crimes of globalization, one need only to take a perusal of the daily news to hear about recent harms and crimes caused by international financial institutions. For example, in September 2014, *The Guardian* ran a story titled "World Bank accuses itself of failing to protect Kenya forest dwellers" (Vidal 2014: 1). The story continues: "Thousands of homes belonging to hunter-gatherer Sengwer people living in the Embobut forest in the Cherangani hills were burned down earlier this year by Kenya forest service guards who had been ordered to clear the forest as part of a carbon offset project that aimed to reduce emissions from deforestation" (ibid.). These forced relocations have resulted in more than 1,000 people becoming squatters and victims of state harassment, intimidation, and arrests. Reports of the harms and crimes of international financial institutions may not appear to occur as often or as blatantly titled as in *The Guardian* report. Recall our previous discussion regarding state crime: the details are often omitted and headlines may make it appear as a necessary or positive act. The same is true for the crimes and harms committed by the international financial institutions. For example, on December 6, 2014, a headline read, "World Bank to help stabilise Ghana's economy" (Brown 2014). Sounds great, right? The report let us know that the World Bank president had assured Ghana "that the Bretton Woods institution will advance the necessary financial support to help stabilise Ghana's troubled economy" (ibid.: 1) Another report hints that Ghana must first meet certain conditions, but the Bank was certain that would happen quickly to disperse funds: stated in one brief sentence "Vice President of the Bank, Makhtar

Diop said there still are some conditions that Government must first meet for the World Bank support to come" (SIC Financial Services Ltd. 2014: 1). Through more research, we find out that the conditions for Ghana include the typical mandated freeze on hiring for the public sector, reducing the current public sector and spending, and the selling off of state assets such as the Agricultural Development Bank (ADB), Ghana Commercial Bank, Tema Oil Refinery (TOR), or Volta River Authority (VRA), which is a similar mandate to that of five years previous when a condition of a former loan required the sale of Ghana Telecom to Vodafone, and for the end of electricity subsidies for citizens.

One need only recall the role of the International Monetary Fund and the World Bank during the economic crisis of 2008 (respectively, 2008 and 2013) and the negative outcome for many countries due to the stipulations imposed as part of the bailout agreement:

> Greece, Spain, Ireland and Portugal all went to the IMF/World Bank to seek financial bail-outs. As a result of these countries ... have all faced severe austerity measures, that has led to public sector wages freeze ... severe public sector wage cuts, mass unemployment, hunger crisis and massive cuts in public services.
>
> (Osei 2014: 2)

As noted by Elliott and Smith (2013: 1), the International Monetary Fund admits "that it has made serious mistakes in the handling of the sovereign debt crisis in Greece, according to internal reports." Beyond Greece, the International Monetary Fund's Independent Evaluation Office (IEO) (2014) released its report on the institution's response to the economic crisis, assessing the years of 2008 to 2013, stating it tailored its actions to more powerful members' needs.

Summary

In summary, crimes and harms of the international financial institutions are the result of their deeply embedded ideology and subsequent policies, which are symbolic of the system that drives crimes of the powerful in general: reproducing the global power and economic arrangement and replicating current power structures and inequalities. After all, one cannot easily separate the crimes of globalization from corporations, states, and other elite actors, as it does take the complicit and implicit actions of all of these for the commission and realization of policies of these financial institutions. Harms caused by international finance are often under-studied by criminologists and overlooked by the public, though they may well represent one of the worst forms of crimes by the powerful in the long run.

Activities and discussion questions

1. Why do you think the international financial institutions continue with policies and practices that have been proven to be harmful to vast populations?
2. How do you think the voting rights of states in the World Bank and the International Monetary Fund impact the loans, grantees, and practices of these institutions? Why?
3. Do you think these financial institutions are for the betterment of the global economic situation or a hindrance? Why?
4. Consider why the Global North is the primary beneficiary of the policies and involvements of international financial institutions.

Resources

See the film *Life and Debt* (2001) by Stephanie Black: www.lifeanddebt.org/about. html.

See the film *Bamako* (2006) by Abderrahmane Sissako: http://artthreat.net/2007/04/ bamako-film-puts-the-world-bank-on-trial-and-wins/.

Note

This chapter draws from the previous research of one of the authors, as well as from new material: see D. L. Rothe and David Friedrichs (2014). *Crimes of Globalization*. London: Routledge; D. Friedrichs and Dawn L. Rothe (2014). State-Corporate Crime and Major Financial Institutions: Interrogating an Absence. *State Crime*, 3(2): 146–162; D. Friedrichs and Dawn L. Rothe (2013). Crimes of Globalization as a Criminological Project: The Case of International Financial Institutions. In F. Packes (ed.), *Globalization and the Challenge to* Criminology, 45–63. New York: Routledge; D. L. Rothe and David Friedrichs (2014). Controlling Crimes of Globalization: A Challenge for International Criminal Justice. In Willem de Lint, Marinella Marmo, and Nerida Chazal (eds.), *Crime and Justice in International Society*, 246–266. London: Routledge; D. L. Rothe and Victoria Collins (2016). International Financial Institutions as Facilitators of Environmental Crimes. In Emanuela Orlando and Tiffany Bergin (eds.), *Forging a Socio-Legal Approach to Environmental Harms: Global Perspectives*. Routledge (in press).

References

Abouharb, M. R., and Cingarelli, D. L. (2006). The Human Rights Effects of World Bank Structural Adjustment, 1981–2000. *International Studies Quarterly*, 50: 233–262.

Babb, S. (2009). *Behind the Development Banks: Washington Politics, World Poverty, and the Wealth of Nations*. Chicago: University of Chicago Press.

Bello, W. F., Cunningham, S., and Rau, B. (1999). *Dark Victory: The United States and Global Poverty*. Oakland, CA: Pluto Press.

Brady, D. (2010). Common Ground for Sociology and the World Bank?. *Contemporary Sociology*, 39: 530–532.

Brown, A. (2014). World Bank To Help Stabilise Ghana's Economy. AFK Insider, December 6. Available at: http://afkinsider.com/80942/world-bank-help-stabilise-ghanas-economy/ (accessed on September 3, 2015).

Cain, M. (2011). Crimes of the Global State. In F. Brookman, M. Maguire, H. Pierpoint, and T. Bennett (eds.), *Handbook on Crime*, 801–824. Devon: Willan Publishing.?

Chan, S. (2010). Poorer Nations Get Larger Role in World Bank. *New York Times*, April 26: B3.

Downey, L., Bonds, E., and Clark, K. (2010). Natural Resource Extraction, Armed Violence, and Environmental Degradation. *Organization and Environment*, 23: 417–445.

Elliott, L., and Smith, H. (2013). IMF "to Admit Mistakes" in Handling Greek Debt Crisis and Bailout. *The Guardian*, June 5. Available at: www.theguardian.com/business/2013/jun/05/imf-admit-mistakes-greek-crisis-austerity (accessed on September 3, 2015).

Ezeonu, I. (2008). Crimes of Globalization: Health Care, HIV and the Poverty of Neo-Liberalism in Sub-Saharan Africa. *International Journal of Social Inquiry*, 1(2): 113–134.

Ezeonu, I., and Koku, E. (2008). Crimes of Globalization: The Feminization of HIV Pandemic in Sub-Saharan Africa. *The Global South*, 2(2): 112–129.

Friedrichs, D. O., and Friedrichs, J. (2002). The World Bank and Crimes of Globalization: A Case Study. *Social Justice*, 29(1–2): 1–12.

Friedrichs, D., and Rothe, Dawn L. (2013). Crimes of Globalization as a Criminological Project: The Case of International Financial Institutions. In F. Packes (ed.), *Globalization and the Challenge to Criminology*, 45–63. New York: Routledge.

Friedrichs, D., and Rothe, Dawn L. (2014). State-Corporate Crime and Major Financial Institutions: Interrogating an Absence. *State Crime*, 3(2): 146–162.

Goldman, M. (2005). *Imperial Nature: The World Bank and Struggles for Justice in the Age of Globalization*. New Haven, CT: Yale University Press.

Guttall, S. (2006). Fuelling Discontent: The World Bank and International Monetary Fund in Singapore. Available at: http://alainet.org/active/13945 (accessed May 1, 2009).

Helliwell, J., Layard, R., and Sachs, J. (2013). The World Happiness Report. United Nations Sustainable Development Solutions Network. Available at: http://world-happiness.report/ed/2013/ (accessed December 13, 2015).

International Monetary Fund (2013a). About the IMF. Available at: www.imf.org/external/about.htm (accessed on September 4, 2013).

International Monetary Fund (2013b). Overview. Available at: www.imf.org/external/about/overview.htm (accessed on February 1, 2013).

International Monetary Fund Independent Evaluation Office (IEO) (2014). IMF Response to the Financial and Economic Crisis. Available at: www.ieo-imf.org/ieo/pages/EvaluationImages227.aspx and www.ieo-imf.org/ieo/files/completedevaluations/FULL%20REPORT%20final.pdf (accessed on September 3, 2015).

Jackson, R. (2012). *Occupy World Street: A Global Roadmap for Radical Economic and Political Reform*. White River Junction, VT: Chelsea Green Publishing.

Kent, James (1866). Commentaries on American Law. 11th edition. Edited by G. F. Comstock. Boston, MA: Little Brown, Vol. III, sect. 387.

Osei, K. (2014). Why the IMF/World Bank Bailout Will be Bad for Ghanaians. News Ghana, August 11. Available at: www.spyghana.com/imfworld-bank-bailout-will-bad-ghanaians/ (accessed on September 3, 2015).

Rothe, D. L. (2010a). International Financial Institutions, Corruption and Human Rights. In Martine Boersma and Hans Nelen (eds.), *Corruption and Human Rights*, 177–197. Antwerp: Intersentia.

Rothe, D. L. (2010b). Facilitating Corruption and Human Rights Violations: The Role of International Financial Institutions. *Crime, Law and Social Change*, 53(5): 457–476.

Rothe, D. L., and Collins, Victoria (2016). International Financial Institutions as Facilitators of Environmental Crimes. In Emanuela Orlando and Tiffany Bergin (eds.), *Forging a Socio-Legal Approach to Environmental Harms: Global Perspectives*. Routledge (in press).

Rothe, D. L., and Friedrichs, David (2014a). Controlling Crimes of Globalization: A Challenge for International Criminal Justice. In Willem de Lint, Marinella Marmo, and Nerida Chazal (eds.), *Crime and Justice in International Society*, 246–266. London: Routledge.

Rothe, D. L. and Friedrichs, D. O. (2014b). *Crimes of Globalization*. London: Routledge.

Rothe, D. L., Mullins, C. W., and Muzzatti, S. (2006). Crime on the High Seas: Crimes Globalization and the Sinking of the Senegalese Ferry Le Joola. *Critical Criminology: An International Journal*, 14(2): 159–180.

Rothe, D. L., Mullins, C. W., and Sandstrom, K. (2009). The Rawandan Genocide: International Finance Policies and Human Rights. *Social Justice*, 35(3): 66–86.

SIC Financial Services Ltd. (2014). World Bank Assumes Support to Stabilize Ghana's Economy. December 8. Available at: www.sic-fsl.com/7/37/402/world-bank-assures-support-to-stabilize-ghana's-economy (accessed on December 13, 2015).

Stanley, E. (2009). *Torture, Truth and Justice: The Case of Timor-Leste*. Abingdon: Routledge.

Strom, S. (2011). Cracking Open the World Bank. *New York Times*, July 3: B.1.

Torrance, M., and Lochery, E. (2008). An Analysis of the IFIs' Fiscal Policy Recommendations. The Oxford Council on Good Governance. Available at: http://ocgg.org/fileadmin/Publications/EY008.pdf (accessed on June 27, 2009).

Vidal, J. (2014). World Bank Accuses Itself of Failing to Protect Kenya Forest Dwellers. *The Guardian*, September 29. Available at: www.theguardian.com/global-development/2014/sep/29/world-bank-kenya-forest-dwellers (accessed on September 3, 2015).

Wallach, L., and Woodall, P. (2004). *Whose Trade Organization: A Comprehensive Guide to the WTO*. New York: New Press.

Weaver, C. (2008). *Hypocrisy Trap: The World Bank and the Poverty of Reform*. Ithaca, NY: Cornell University Press.

White, R. (2003). Environmental Issues and the Criminological Imagination, *Theoretical Criminology*, 7(4): 483–506.

World Bank (2015). Why Use GNI Per Capita to Classify Economies into Income Groupings?. Available at: https://datahelpdesk.worldbank.org/knowledgebase/articl es/378831-why-use-gni-per-capita-to-classify-economies-into (accessed on December 22, 2015).

Zweifel, T. D. (2006). *International Organizations and Democracy: Accountability, Politics, and Power*. Boulder: Lynne Rienner Publishers.

Chapter 11

Victims of crimes of the powerful

When we think of victimization, we should be cognizant that this is a both subjective and objective concept. As noted by Lamb (1996: 5), when a crime is committed we "search for representatives of two extremes, perpetrator and victim, two archetypes who will represent for us evil and innocence, a hero and an antihero, for our modern day saga of woes." The reality is not that simple. As a citizen, a consumer, employee, even an agent of a corporation or state, we have experienced some form of victimization by the powerful. In some cases we may be actively participating in our own victimization and in other cases we may be victimized merely through our existence and being present at a certain moment, in a specific place, under certain circumstances that result in our harm.

When we are talking about victims of crimes of the powerful, we should think about the types of victimization. We suggest these can be conceptually separated as direct victims, indirect victims, and unknowing victims. Each of these categories or labeling thereof, can be contested and manipulated by the powerful as well as accepted, denied, or claimed by those that are victimized. In other words, the process of labeling is complex: from self-labeling to external labels that are applied informally and formally by audiences, researchers, the media, politicians, and institutions of social control. Each of these has an impact on whether an individual is recognized as a victim and/or able to receive any recourse to their victimization. With victims of the powerful, these issues are significant. Consider that in cases of state crimes of omission or the broader category of social harm (for example, institutionalized classism and racism that impact everything from due process to immigration policies) victims may not even recognize they have been victimized. Do you believe you are being victimized as the state monitors your social media or hovers over you with constant 24-hour surveillance? Or when we buy and consume a tainted food product, we generally do not think we have been victimized, even if the corporation took shortcuts or knew there was a problem but did not pull the product for days or weeks. Or imagine walking down the market street and a jet or drone flies overhead sending out a missile bomb headed your way, given there are a host of conflict areas and target assassinations occurring at this minute across the globe.

Further, given the resources of the powerful, discourse can change the public's view of a victim to one of a criminal. This is especially so in cases of whistleblowers who threaten the legitimacy or power of states, corporations, or international financial institutions. The discourse surrounding a situation leading to victims may be altered, presenting the victims as unworthy and undeserving of sympathy and/or the label. For example, consider the victims of illegal dumping in Somalia, where fishermen began protesting through piracy or the war on Iraq, those of the "shock and awe" invasion, or those swept up in mass raids seeking "terrorists" who end up in a black hole such as Guantanamo or Abu Ghraib, or the Edward Snowdens of the world. One can think of the many indigenous groups that are supposed to relocate because of a project funded through the World Bank and refuse, making them the non-compliant citizen rather than the victim, even though they are about to lose their homes and livelihoods. These victims become the criminals, masking the realities of the victimization.

> **Box 11.1 President Ahmed Hussen of the Canadian Somali Congress in an interview with CBC News (2009)**
>
> When you see the coverage of piracy, you don't hear much about the $300 million annually that's lost by Somali fisherman in illegal fishing done by foreign interests. You also never hear about the cost that cannot be estimated, the negative costs of toxic waste … What is hard to comprehend is why the outside world [is] turning a blind eye to foreigners fishing illegally in Somali waters and poisoning them with toxic waste …The attacks on foreign ships, Somalis say, started as a reaction to foreign pillages trying to put their fishermen out of business.

Furthermore, victims may or may not be recognized as such by formal institutions of control. Likewise, domestic, intergovernmental, and international institutions of control remain selective over whom they define and label as a victim. This has serious ramifications for victim recourse as well as victim healing and for accurate accounts of the facts and subsequent history of their victimization. In many cases, the processes of labeling or lack thereof can result in new forms of victimization and/or revictimization. The complexities and multiple layers of seeing oneself as a victim, accepting such a label, being given the label of victim by others, exclusion or inclusion as a victim are additional aspects to understanding victimization as a result of the crimes and harms of the powerful. The following section offers some insight and examples, drawing from the crimes described in previous chapters and more, into the three main types of victim proposed here: direct, indirect, and unknowing.

Direct victims

A direct victim can be thought of in the same way as victimization from interpersonal street crime. There is an immediate harm or impact. This includes violent acts such as torture, rape, death, disappearances, as well as those that impact victims' livelihoods including displacement, environmental degradation of land, removal of subsistence, and removal of humanitarian aid. One need only recall the many pictures of torture that the general public saw when the case of Abu Ghraib came to light or the war on Iraq to immediately think of violent acts, though the "victims" may not be considered the same: is it possible to consider "terrorists" as victims, or the hundreds of thousands of insurgency fighters, or only the civilians? We would suggest yes, given the label of "terrorist" and "insurgency" are socially constructed and applied for political reasons and interests.

Box 11.2 United States war on terrorism: the number of direct victims/deaths, the consequences of war, and indirect victimization

Documented civilian deaths from violence as of December 20, 2014: 133,482–150,494; total violent deaths including combatants: 202,000.

Consider that in one day, on December 20, the following occurred:

137 killed; Baghdad: 6 by IEDs, mortars, stabbing, Madaen: 4 by IED, Taji: 3 by IED, Babil: 20 bodies found in mass grave, Hardan: 70 bodies found in mass grave, Albu Ayfan: 21 by IEDs; 2 in clashes, Mosul: 5 Yazidi women executed, Baquba: 1 tribal leader by gunfire, Falluja: 1 in clashes, Muqdadiya: 2 by mortars, Tikrit: 2 by IED. 891 civilians killed so far in December, 16; 774 civilians killed so far this year (Iraq Body Count 2014).

The decade-long war in Afghanistan continues to take lives. *The Guardian* reports that, as of "February 2014, at least 21,000 civilians are estimated to have died violent deaths as a result of the war. The total number of civilians killed in Pakistan may be as high or higher than the toll in Afghanistan, with NGO estimates ranging widely between 20,000 and 50,000 recorded deaths." In addition to the direct violence, thousands upon thousands more "Iraqis, Afghans and Pakistanis are falling victim to the dangers of a battered infrastructure and poor health conditions arising from wars" (Rogers and Chalabi 2013).

The direct victims of crimes of the powerful are much easier to identify. One need only recall the examples and mini cases of crimes of the powerful included in previous chapters, from the students in Mexico to Kenyans resisting an international financial institutions project, to the targeted assassinations that have claimed hundreds of civilian lives.

Box 11.3 Syria, torture, disappearance, and death

The Human Rights Watch (2012) report, "Torture Archipelago: Arbitrary Arrests, Torture and Enforced Disappearances in Syria's Underground Prisons since March 2011," stated that "interrogators, guards, and officers used a broad range of torture methods, including prolonged beatings, often with objects such as batons and cables, holding the detainees in painful stress positions for prolonged periods of time, the use of electricity, burning with acid, sexual assault and humiliation, the pulling of fingernails, and mock execution" (ibid.: 1). Additionally, in May 2012, 49 children were among the 108 civilians killed by Syrian military forces in the village of Houla, 15 miles from the central city of Homs.

Though we generally do not associate direct victimization with the corporate sector, there are a host of recent examples to draw from that show victims impacted by corporate decisions and products. There is also the link to inaction or government crimes of omission in some cases.

Box 11.4 Tainted food

A lawsuit has been filed in December 2014 over the death of an eight-year-old child on July 7, 2014, after eating contaminated beef purchased at a Whole Foods. Andrew Kaye told New England Cable News that federal agents had been investigating an "*E. coli* cluster" in June that involved Whole Foods, "far before Joshua was identified as sick" (Sonfist 2014: 1). Two other individuals were also hospitalized from consuming the tainted beef in July. It was not until August, 2014, when Whole Foods issued a recall of "ground beef products due to possible E. coli contamination after the state Department of Public Health, Centers for Disease Control and Prevention and federal Food Safety and Inspection Service determined the link" (Goodison 2014).

Box 11.5 Contaminated caramel apples

On December 20, 2014, a Fox News headline reads: "Contaminated caramel apples linked to four deaths, dozens of illnesses in 10 states."

The story states that "health officials are warning consumers to avoid prepackaged caramel apples because they are linked to four deaths and more than two dozen illnesses in 10 states." Though the story is dated in December, it should be noted that the outbreak began in mid-October, leaving two months of unreported danger. The Centers for Disease Control and Prevention stated that in 28 cases people were sickened with the bacterial illness listeria. Of those, five died and three cases of meningitis were linked to the listeria as well (Fox News 2014).

It is not just people who are directly impacted. Consider the case in Box 11.6.

Box 11.6 The following is from the United States Food and Drug Administration 2014

As of May 1, 2014, FDA has received approximately 4,800 reports of pet illnesses which may be related to consumption of the jerky treats (these include 1,800 complaints received since FDA's last update in October 2013). Most of the reports involve jerky products sourced from China. The majority of the complaints involve dogs, but cats also have been affected. The reports involve more than 5,600 dogs, 24 cats, and three people. (Food and Drug Administration 2014: 1.)

There can never be any estimations of the total numbers of direct victimization of crimes of the powerful. This is because the scope is far too vast and covers a range of actors, from states to corporations to the implicit non-actions that result in these types of interpersonal victimization. Given this, when we consider the indirect victims and those who are "unknowing" victims, it is overwhelming and rather unimaginable that such harms and crimes are able to continue and, as we present in our conclusion in Chapter 14, with our own complicity and legitimation of the system that reifies the conditions and victimization of so many across the globe.

Indirect victims

Indirect victimization may seem "less important" than direct victimization, as a "worthy" victim is not readily identifiable. Yet, we argue that this is far from the case and merits as much attention as we give to the non-obscure or directly violent forms of victimization. Why?, students may ask. Because this level of victimization is broader and has victimized, or has the potential to continue to victimize, for generations. Additionally, this form of victimization generally impacts the most vulnerable populations: the poor, the minorities, the mentally ill—in other words, those with low social status. Having said this, it should be noted that many times, while having a more direct impact on the groups noted above, in the end this form of victimization impacts everyone and all societies. Consider global warming as an example of the extended and immediate impact, victimization, and inequalities of the distribution of harm and crime.

Box 11.7 Global warming

According to scientists, global warming is "speeding up the cycling of water between the ocean, atmosphere and land, resulting in more intense rainfall and droughts at the same time across the globe" (NASA 2014: 1). This is causing a surge in wildfires, increased flooding, rise in sea levels, increased drought, food crisis, heat waves, increased hurricanes and tornadoes, and poses a threat to human health, and worsening of air quality. The latter two will inevitably see a rise in asthma and deaths from insect borne diseases and other viral conditions. According to NASA (2014):

Global climate change has already had observable effects on the environment. Glaciers have shrunk, ice on rivers and lakes is breaking up earlier, plant and animal ranges have shifted and trees are flowering sooner.

In the United States:

Northeast. Heat waves, heavy downpours, and sea-level rise pose growing challenges to many aspects of life in the Northeast. Infrastructure, agriculture, fisheries, and ecosystems will be increasingly compromised. Many states and cities are beginning to incorporate climate change into their planning.

Northwest. Changes in the timing of streamflow reduce water supplies for competing demands. Sea-level rise, erosion, inundation, risks to infrastructure, and increasing ocean acidity pose major threats. Increasing wildfire, insect outbreaks, and tree diseases are causing widespread tree die-off.

Southeast. Sea-level rise poses widespread and continuing threats to the region's economy and environment. Extreme heat will affect health, energy, agriculture, and more. Decreased water availability will have economic and environmental impacts.

Midwest. Extreme heat, heavy downpours, and flooding will affect infrastructure, health, agriculture, forestry, transportation, air and water quality, and more. Climate change will also exacerbate a range of risks to the Great Lakes.

Southwest. Increased heat, drought, and insect outbreaks, all linked to climate change, have increased wildfires. Declining water supplies, reduced agricultural yields, health impacts in cities due to heat, and flooding and erosion in coastal areas are additional concerns.

Yet, the impact of global warming will not be generalized across the globe. Rather, the most vulnerable populations will be impacted the most. As the World Bank rightly notes (2014: 2), "a changing climate affects the poorest people in developing countries the most. Droughts or heavy rains that lead to floods are disastrous to people with no buffers or savings. A changing climate may cause major migrations of displaced peoples which will affect all countries." This is reaffirmed in a report by Deustche Welel (2014: 1): "It is very clear from the last IPCC report, and confirmed again by recent scientific literature, that the main losers, or first losers, of climate change will be poor people both in developing countries and in developed or industrialized countries."

As Robert Agnew (2012) argues, the "crimes of climate change" are globally positioning the human species for serious risks of extinction. "Hyperbolic or not, the potential harm and victimization from environmental crimes to the earth's ecosystems may ultimately dwarf the combined harm and victimization from all the other crimes of the powerful" (Barak 2015: 11).

Box 11.8 Indirect victimization: Ebola and international financial institutions?

An article in *The Lancet*'s Global Health section by Kentikelenis, King, McKee, and Stuckler (2014) examined the links between the International Monetary Fund and the Ebola outbreak in West Africa. They state that the programs of the international financial institution imposed heavy constraints on the health systems in Guinea, Liberia, and Sierra Leone—the hub of the Ebola outbreak that, at the time of writing, had resulted in roughly 6,800 deaths since March 2014—created the conditions for the outbreak and the inability to properly address and control it. The policy reforms mandated by the International Monetary Fund undermined the health-care sector. By analyzing the lending programs between 1990 and 2014, the researchers identified three main factors that were at heart of the weakened health-care system and health/hygiene conditions within the countries. As we noted in the chapter on crimes of globalization, these mandates more often than not result in dire conditions for the populations of these countries. Regarding the case at hand, Kentikelenis *et al.* state that the required economic reforms reduced government spending, including on health care, imposed caps on public sector wage bills that impacted the capacity to hire and properly pay health-care workers—leading to a general shortage of personnel within the health industry—and that the decentralization of the health-care system all contributed to the conditions of a weak health-care system that was inadequate to address or respond to the Ebola outbreak. As such, the International Monetary Fund, along with the state governments, were complicit in the indirect victimization of those who contracted Ebola and died.

While we begin with the broad examples of global warming (Box 11.7) and Ebola (Box 11.8) as a consequence of the demands and policies of international financial institutions, consider the indirect (and direct) victimization of the homeless and the mentally ill; in the United States, this surplus population is treated by the state, relatively speaking, as being equivalent to "trash" and as a "disposable" population. Consider the many programs the police have carried out to remove these populations from one jurisdiction to another: at times, being denied even basic hospital treatment or put in a cab to another care center down the road. In many cases, the mentally ill end up in our jails, denied basic medications, psychiatric care, bedding, or other humane basics. The failure to provide treatment and services to people suffering from a mental illness results in overburdened emergency rooms, crowded state and local jails, or them ending up on the streets, where their chance of revictimization is much greater than it is for the non-mentally ill population. Regretfully, the United States, a supposed champion of human rights, routinely and systematically fails to provide the most basic services for people with mental illness. On December 22, 2014, *The Daily Mail* newspaper ran the following headline: "Mentally ill inmate died after seven days alone in New York prison cell with toilet overflowing and without medication." He had been denied medication for his mental health and diabetes and he was found naked, covered in his own feces with his genitals badly infected and swollen. This case is not an exception. As the USA news reports:

> Stigma against the mentally ill is so powerful that it's been codified for 50 years into federal law, and few outside the mental health system even realize it. This systemic discrimination, embedded in Medicaid and Medicare laws, has accelerated the emptying of state psychiatric hospitals, leaving many of the sickest and most vulnerable patients with nowhere to turn.
>
> (Szabo 2014: 1)

Other examples of indirect victimization that are rarely discussed in these terms are the redaction, removal, or even denial of civil rights. As in the previous chapters, we have seen states deny basic civil rights to immigrants, indigenous groups, and others. From a historical perspective, this is most clearly seen when the United States was committed to slavery or in the case of South Africa and Apartheid. In less glaring terms, consider the victimization caused by lack of due process and the inability to get redress for your victimization (see, for example, the International Criminal Court and issues over the selectivity of victims). More recently (as well as historically), consider the lack of rights for those who identify as LGBTQIA across the globe, from discrimination and inability to marry to the use of the death penalty in some countries. Think of the inequalities and discrimination for females across the globe, from lower wages and general harassment to being considered an object with no legal standing.

When we think of indirect victimization and corporations, the economic crisis may come to mind, where financial frauds, the selling off of bad debt, and toxic securities masquerading as Triple-A certified investments created the housing bubble and economic crash, and a subsequent global recession that resulted in the "loss of trillions of dollars in capital and the victimization of hundreds of millions of people worldwide" (Barak 2015: 12). Yet, as Dodge and Steele (2015) rightly note, victimization extends beyond the fiscal and emotional impacts of the frauds and crimes of banks and Wall Street to the difficulties of establishing a standing or being recognized as a victim, allowing potential for some relief or recourse.

The chance that each of you has been victimized by price fixing is quite high (see Box 11.9).

Box 11.9 Price fixing

On December 18, 2014, *The Guardian* ran the story "France Fines 13 Consumer Goods Firms €951m for Price-Fixing":

> Some of the world's biggest consumer products companies, including Unilever, Reckitt Benckiser, Procter & Gamble and Gillette, have been fined a combined €951m (£748m) by the French competition watchdog for price fixing in supermarkets. The regulator said the 13 companies including Colgate-Palmolive, Henkel, L'Oréal, Beiersdorf and Johnson & Johnson's Laboratoires, vVendôme, had colluded on price increases between 2003 and 2006.

(Kollewe 2014)

We may not think of this as victimization, though these actions do indeed victimize consumers. However, it is not just consumers who are victimized by price fixing. One need only recall the Libor case (see Box 11.10), where victimization impacted daily lives.

The examples of indirect victimization could go on and on for pages, though we do wish to briefly introduce you to what we see as unknowing victims. Having said this, it should be noted that just as with types of crimes of the powerful, these typologies are not so easily demarcated. Furthermore, when discussing unknowing victims, we recognize the subjectivity of our claims/labels.

Box 11.10 The Libor case

The Libor scandal involved between 16 and 20 major banks that manipulated global interest rates, with the price of estimated $500 trillion worth of financial instruments, making this one of the biggest financial scandals ever. Banks were inflating or deflating their interest rates to profit from trades or appear more creditworthy. The interest rate determines the prices that we as global citizens pay for loans or receive for our savings. This impacted things including mortgage repayments, debts, interest rates, and a host of other factors that affect citizens. Yet, not only is the victimization masked, but "THE most memorable incidents in earth-changing events are sometimes the most banal" (*The Economist* 2014: 1).

Unknowing victims

The victims we call the "unknowing" ones are those who are victimized during the normality of the political administration and governance of the "modern" state. In many cases, these victims, aka us, are also indirect facilitators of their own victimization through compliance, support, consumption, and complacency. Across the globe, citizens' rights and freedoms have been limited or retracted in the name of national security and "for our own protection." We have willingly accepted these limitations and victimization, or, at best, have normalized them and the violence and harm of the crimes of the powerful (see Box 11.11).

Box 11.11 Banality of violence

It is much easier to sleep comfortably if you make yourself believe that the prison you are committing others to for your entitlement to a particular piece of land needs to exist because those people are all potential terrorists. It is much easier not to think about the terror of ghettoizing people, of shoving guns in children's faces, of demolishing people's homes and displacing them from their land, of humiliating people at checkpoints, of starving people by making their local economies nearly impossible to sustain … It is much easier not to think about the production of violence. The comfortable lives Ardi and Batya [2 interviewees] lead in their West Bank settlement depend every day [on the production of violence]. They remain in complete denial of this relationship, however, as their role in the production of this violence is quite banal. (From Lucas 2007.)

Image 11.1 Austerity for some: power and capital (Noonan 2014: 5)

Indirect and unknowing victimization, through the normality of life, includes what Giroux (2014: 5) suggests as the plight of youth as disposable populations. "It is evident in the fact that millions of them in countries such as England, Greece, and the United States have been unemployed and denied long term benefits. The unemployment rate for young people in many countries such as Spain, Italy, Portugal, and Greece hovers between 40 and 50 per cent." Likewise, citizens born and raised in countries that deny the rights of women, subjugate its own citizens, and rule with general oppression may not claim their victimization, given the normalcy of everyday life and conditions, yet does this make it not so? Similarly, if one sees only one perspective, it appears as "the" reality, leaving no alternative. Yet, does this disallow their victimization? Is it the self-label of victim that is *more* important or *as* important as an external label or even necessary?

Of course, the concept of unknowing victims can be interpreted as ethnocentric or Westernized dogma in itself, given the subjective nature of claims making and victimology. After all, one can ask what right we have to label a population as victims merely because they are denied what we perceive to be an innate right, or practice what we consider to be a draconian tradition. The same can be said with our claims that homelessness in the land of the world's superpower and economic empire is a crime and they are victims. We accept this criticism. While we do not believe our assertions or claims are anything but our own, we do understand the discourse is grounded in a critical understanding of crimes of the powerful and their victims.

Victimized in the name of what?

The elephant in the room, if you will, that undergirds all of the victimization of crimes of the powerful is *power*. Having said this, power cannot be separated from the capital it affords: economic, social, and political. "It is all of one fabric, this web of life" (Quinney 2006). All of this currently operates within the neoliberal agenda and ideology that perpetuates the types of victims discussed here (as well as the crimes of the powerful).

This is not to say, as we stated before, that neoliberalism or capitalism is *the* problem. Indeed, it has its problems, though this has more to do with the enactment and practice of it than the theoretical premise of capitalism. In short, crimes of the powerful were surely committed on vast scales under different modes of economic production (for example, communism and feudalism). Yet, we must understand victimization of the powerful in today's terms: a hyper-capitalistic system where enough is never enough, where consumption is sold and used to perpetuate crime and victimization, where power begets power.

Summary

Victimization is a more complex phenomenon than most people recognize as there are several types inducing direct, indirect, and unknowing. At the heart of victimization is a power imbalance between those harmed and those doing the harming. One can be victimized in an obvious sort of way, as in having civil rights violated, but more people are victims of larger normative state policies such as domestic spying, corporate activities such as fraud and price fixing, and the obvious harms resulting from global warming and climate change.

Activities and discussion questions

1.   Research what organizations are most responsible for climate change and identify how much power they have in domestic and international affairs.
2.   Ask friends how they would define a "victim." Are their responses consistent with how scholars think about victimization?
3.   Research how victims of the Enron crimes attempted to procure reparations. Was justice ultimately served to the victims?

References

Agnew, R. (2012). Dire Forecast: A Theoretical Model of the Impact of Climate Change on Crime. *Theoretical Criminology*, 16(February): 21–42.
Barak, G. (2015). *The Routledge International Handbook of the Crimes of the Powerful*. Abingdon, Oxon: Routledge.
The Daily Mail (2014). Mentally Ill Inmate Died After Seven Days Alone in New York Prison Cell with Toilet Overflowing and Without Medication. 22 December. Available at: www.dailymail.co.uk/news/article-2636364/Mentally-ill-inmate-died-seven-days-New-York-prison-cell-toilet-overflowing-no-medication.html (accessed on September 10, 2015).
Deustche Welel (2014). Climate Change Affects the Poor Most, Scientist Says in DW, Change for Minds. Available at: www.dw.de/climate-change-affects-the-poor-most-scientist-says/a-4694648 (accessed on September 10, 2015).
Dodge, M., and Steele, S. (2015). Transnational Institutional Torturers: State Crime, Ideology and the Role of France's Savoir-Faire in Argentina's Dirty War. In G. Barak (ed.), *The Routledge International Handbook of the Crimes of the Powerful*, 289–302. Abingdon, Oxon: Routledge.
The Economist (2014). The Rotten Heart of Finance. July 5. Available at: www.economist.com/node/21558281 (accessed on September 10, 2015).
Food and Drug Administration (2014). Questions and Answers Regarding Jerky Pet Treats. Available at: www.fda.gov/AnimalVeterinary/SafetyHealth/ProductSafetyInformation/ucm295445.htm (accessed on September 10, 2015).
Fox News (2014). Contaminated Caramel Apples Linked to Four Deaths, Dozens of Illnesses in 10 States. December 20. Available at: www.foxnews.com/health/2014/12/20/minnesota-links-caramel-apples-2-listeria-deaths/ (accessed on September 10, 2015).

Giroux, H. (2014). Protesting Youth in an Age of Neoliberal Savagery. Philosophers for Change, June 3. Available at: http://philosophersforchange.org/2014/06/03/protesting-youth-in-an-age-of-neoliberal-savagery/ (accessed on September 10, 2015).

Goodison, D. (2014). Couple Sues Whole Foods in Son's Death. *Boston Herald*, December 14. Available at: www.bostonherald.com/business/business_markets/2014/12/couple_sues_whole_foods_in_son_s_death (accessed on September 10, 2015).

Human Rights Watch (2012). Syria Torture Centers Revealed. March 7. Available at: www.hrw.org/news/2012/07/03/syria-torture-centers-revealed (accessed on September 11, 2015).

Hussen, A. (2009). President Ahmed Hussen of the Canadian Somali Congress in an interview with CBC News. YouTube video, uploaded April 14. Available at: www.youtube.com/watch?v=_jCBy09zKZ0 (accessed on September 10, 2015).

Iraq Body Count (2014). Available at: www.iraqbodycount.org/ (accessed on September 10, 2015).

Kentikelenis, A., King, L., McKee, M., and Stuckler, D. (2014). The International Monetary Fund and the Ebola Outbreak. *The Lancet* Global Health, December 21. Available at: www.thelancet.com/journals/langlo/article/PIIS2214-109X%2814%2970377-8/fulltext (accessed on September 10, 2015).

Kollewe, J. (2014). France Fines 13 Consumer Goods Firms €951m for Price-Fixing. *The Guardian*, December 18. Available at: www.theguardian.com/business/2014/dec/18/france-fines-unilever-reckitt-benckiser-procter-and-gamble-gillette-price-fixing (accessed on September 10, 2015).

Lamb, L. (1996). *The Trouble with Blaming*. Cambridge, MA: Harvard University Press.

Lucas, C. (2007). Banality of Violence. Common Dreams, September 24. Available at: www.commondreams.org/views/2007/09/24/banality-violence (accessed on September 10, 2015).

NASA (2014). The Current and Future Consequences of Global Change. Available at: http://climate.nasa.gov/effects/ (accessed on September 10, 2015).

Noonan, J. (2014). Preservative Struggles in the Age of Austerity. Philosophers for Change, December 2. Available at: http://philosophersforchange.org/2014/12/02/preservative-struggles-in-the-age-of-austerity/ (accessed on December 22, 2015).

Quinney, R. (2006). The Life Inside. *Contemporary Justice Review* 9(3): 269–275.

Rogers, S., and Chalabi, M. (2013). Afghanistan Civilian Casualties. *The Guardian*, August 10. Available at: www.theguardian.com/news/datablog/2010/aug/10/afghanistan-civilian-casualties-statistics (accessed on December 22, 2015).

Sonfist, A. (2014). Whole Foods Sued in Boys Death: Eight-year-old Died After Allegedly Eating Ground Beef Contaminated with E. coli. NECN, December 17. Available at: www.necn.com/news/new-england/Whole-Foods-Sued-In-Boys-Death--286088641.html (accessed on September 10, 2015).

Szabo, L. (2014). Cost of Not Caring: Stigma Set in Stone. USA Today, June 25. Available at: www.usatoday.com/story/news/nation/2014/06/25/stigma-of-mental-illness/9875351/ (accessed on September 10, 2015).

World Bank (2014). Climate Change Affects the Poorest in Developing Countries. March 3. Available at: www.worldbank.org/en/news/feature/2014/03/03/climate-change-affects-poorest-developing-countries (accessed on September 10, 2015).

Part III

The master's tools and beyond

Chapter 12

Regulating crimes of the powerful

This chapter introduces students to what are commonly thought of and referred to as systems of control that address or respond to crimes of the powerful. These include domestic controls such as civil, regulatory, and criminal laws, as well as international institutions and international law. Students are also introduced to other forms of addressing or responding to crimes of the powerful including non-governmental organizations, as civilians, and other forms including resistance movements that take on many shapes in our everyday lives.

Domestic

Applicable to states/regimes/high-ranking officials

Most governments have similar laws that govern traditional street crimes such as murder, kidnapping, and larceny, and many of them treat any offender from any country as the same as one of their citizens. As such, these laws act in a way to allow a citizen of another country to seek redress in the offenders' state(s) of citizenship. For example, in the United States there is the Alien Tort Claims Act (ATCA), the origins of which date back to the first Judiciary Act of 1789, which created the US court system. It provides that "the district courts shall have original jurisdiction of any civil action by an alien for a tort only, committed in violation of the law of nations or a treaty of the United States." The ATCA grants US courts jurisdiction in any dispute where it is alleged that the "law of nations," or international laws, are broken (Rothe 2006). This would ideally include being able to sue corporations whose employees took part in crimes or harms covered under the ATCA. Such is the case with CACI International and Titan, who are named as defendants in a suit filed in the Federal District Court in Washington, DC, under the Alien Tort Claims Act, on behalf of four Abu Ghraib detainees for torture and cruel and unusual punishment. The Center for Constitutional Rights (CCR) and the Philadelphia law firm of Montgomery, McCracken, Walker and Rhoads filed a second lawsuit (a class action suit) on June 9,

2004, in the federal court in San Diego. This action also utilizes the Alien Tort Claims Act (ATCA), along with the 5th, 8th, and 14th Amendments to the US Constitution (Rothe 2006).

Many other countries with civil law systems (for example, France, Spain, and Sweden) have alternative methods of bringing civil suits where the civil claim is attached to a criminal prosecution. In France, under the French Code of Criminal Procedure, the prosecution and any civil claims "must be a direct result of the criminal act of which the defendant is accused" (Mostajelean 2008: 511). On the other hand, the United Kingdom's system does not have an ATCA equivalent for civil suits against aliens who have committed acts covered under a tort claim. There are avenues that can be taken, but they are burdensome and rarely able to fit within the regulations of jurisdiction, save for having a location in UK territory.

Similar to the French Code of Criminal Procedure, most countries have an aspect within their domestic laws to try non-citizens for crimes committed within their territory or, in some cases, committed in one country by a national of another country—enforcement by third countries. For example, the Belgian parliament empowered Belgian courts to exercise jurisdiction over war crimes and breaches of the Geneva Conventions committed anywhere in the world by a citizen of any country (Hitchens 2001).

Beyond this, there are generally laws within each state's legal system that prohibit these types of behaviors, some stronger than others, especially given the position of a state to legitimate or even decriminalize its actions. Again, at this point we are talking about the presence of laws, not the enforcement of them. Additionally, due to the vast array of domestic laws, it would be beyond the scope of this chapter to identify and discuss them in detail. Nonetheless, as an example, consider the following: Sweden criminalized genocide with a special domestic law in 1964 and war crimes are penalized through a legal norm. On the other hand, Finland and Poland cover genocide and war crimes within the general Finnish and Polish penal codes. In Finland and Sweden, crimes against humanity can be punished only as ordinary offenses. In order to prosecute war crimes in Finland, Poland, and Sweden, a reference to an international treaty and customary law is deemed necessary. Austria has a special national provision covering only the crime of genocide. Croatia, Serbia, and Montenegro penalize not only genocide but also war crimes as special offenses; yet, crimes against humanity are not codified separately and are prosecuted as ordinary criminal offenses. When looking at domestic laws in Spain, Côte d'Ivoire, France, and Italy, national prosecution systems also differ. Heterogeneity is the key word regarding "national prosecution of international crimes." Canada, on the other hand, has enacted an independent Crimes Against Humanity and War Crimes Act, which penalizes the worst of the worst state crimes—acts of genocide, crimes against humanity, and war crimes—and relies on customary international law. In Israel and the United States, crimes against humanity can be punished only as an ordinary criminal offense, while acts of genocide are explicitly covered. In China, violations of international criminal law can be prosecuted only as ordinary offenses. The legal situation in domestic jurisdictions is quite heterogeneous and the prosecution of international crimes is very limited in many countries' legal systems (Ambos and Stegmiller 2008). Yet, we can safely say that such "controls" are available and could ideally be implemented against crimes covering *other* heads of state, high-ranking officials, or foreign diplomats.

On a different level, temporary special courts have also been convened to address violations of international criminal law by agents of the state (or post heads of state administrators). The use of these special courts can provide an alternative to, or act as a complement to, international tribunals (for example, East Timor, Kosovo, Bosnia, Serbia, and Croatia). These local justice mechanisms operate under state law, although there can be an international component. Nonetheless, they are considered domestic courts and differ from other hybrid forms of domestic/international systems, as in the case of Sierra Leone that will be discussed later in this chapter. For example, there has been a transfer of cases from the ICTY (International Criminal Tribunal for the former Yugoslavia) to local Bosnian courts. In this case, the temporary or ad hoc court serves as an "internationalized" war crimes chamber of the Bosnian State Court system. The War Crimes Chamber, established in Sarajevo in March 2005, handles cases of serious war crimes that were transferred from the ICTY, as well as war crimes cases initiated locally (Human Rights Watch 2006). Additionally, it will continue to handle war crimes cases after international involvement has been phased out.

In response to the atrocities committed in the Kosovo conflict during 1999, panels known as "Regulation 64 Panels" were instituted to adjudicate war crimes cases. At the time of this writing (2014–2015), the Regulation 64 Panels have conducted more than two dozen war crimes trials, which resulted in the indictments of Milos Jokic and Dragan Nikolic for genocide. Additionally, the trial for Milorad Trbic began in November 2007, in which he was being charged with genocide. In March 2000, the UN Transitional Authority for East Timor created a judicial system of district courts for East Timor, which included "Serious Crimes Panels." In the case of East Timor, the Dili District Court has exclusive jurisdiction over genocide, war crimes, crimes against humanity, murder, sexual offenses, and torture, for crimes committed between January and October 1999 (UN Office for the Coordination of Humanitarian Affairs 2008). Similarly, "Extraordinary Chambers" were created in Cambodia to address the crimes committed by the Khmer Rouge between 1975 and 1979.

In response to the 1994 genocide, the Rwandan government wanted to hold accountable the massive numbers of genocidaires through prosecution in an effort to end the impunity that had long characterized the Rwandan political culture. To do so, it passed a special domestic legislation, Organic Law No. 08/96 (1996), which established specialized genocide chambers in the

Courts of First Instance, and Organic Law No. 40/2000 (2001) for the creation and implementation of the *gacaca* (Amnesty International 2002). The *gacaca* is a hybrid system that merges customary practice with a Western, formal court structure. Historically, the *gacaca* was a customary system of community hearings that were used to resolve community disputes such as land or inheritance rights, or marital disputes. These were informal, ad hoc in nature and led by community elders (*inyangamugayo*). By creating approximately 10,000 *gacaca*s throughout the country, the Rwandan government transformed this traditional mode of conflict resolution in order to try the more than 800,000–1,000,000 genocide suspects that are overfilling the country's prisons. Thus, the new tribunals are formal legal judicial bodies that hear three of the four categories of genocide and crimes against humanity.

Moving on to impeachment, this is a process of removing heads of state who hold security of tenure; the official cannot be removed from his or her office except in exceptional and specified circumstances. It is a formal process that is governed by nearly every country's constitution or laws and is equivalent to a criminal indictment. Typically, impeachment serves to remove the person(s) from office; however, this may not always be the case. While all laws, regulations, and other systems of controls are politicized, impeachments are particularly vulnerable to misuse and manipulation by other or competing party members. Nonetheless, it is a control mechanism that can be used to address crimes committed by a regime and/or parts of an administration.

Impeachments are not a new phenomenon, though they are rather rare. The United States has had two presidents impeached: Andrew Johnson (for violating the Tenure of Office Act) and Bill Clinton (for perjury and suborning perjury), though neither was removed from office. The process of impeachment against Richard Nixon by the House Judiciary Committee was ended when he resigned before the house voted. In 1992, the Peruvian Congress voted to impeach President Fujimori and to remove him from office, naming the Second Vice-President as the new head of state. Fujimori's impeachment was in response to a general fear of dictatorship rule due to his attempt to dissolve Peru's Congress, to suspend the constitution, and to detain lawmakers who were primarily from the opposition Apra Party. During 2004, South Korea experienced the country's first presidential impeachment when President Roh Moo-hyun was removed from office on the grounds of illegal electioneering and incompetence. Other examples include President Banisadr of Iran, who was impeached during 1981 by the Iranian parliament, Brazil's President Collor de Mello in 1992, President Pérez of Venezuela in 1993, and President Grau of Paraguay in 1999.

Having noted some of the domestic means to address crimes of the powerful holding high-ranking state positions, we should take note that these are not commonly used, are selective in nature, and are impacted by power, politics, economics, and intervening states' interests that more often than not come to bear on the effectiveness or implementation of these mechanisms.

Additionally, no mechanism of "control" can serve as a form of "justice" for all. In other words, there will always be underlying factors to each system that can be easily critiqued.

Corporate domestic laws and regulations

Each country has its own set of domestic systems of regulation or controls for corporations, some varying greatly between countries. In addition, while not exercised owing to the capitalistic system, any corporation that violates international or domestic law could have its charter pulled, rendering "the death penalty" for that specific corporation. While the number of domestic laws and regulations from country to country is far too vast to cover in this chapter, we do provide some current examples.

In some cases, depending on the crime and harm, the Alien Tort Claims Act similarly applies to corporations as it applies to states (see the examples in Box 12.1).

Box 12.1 The Alien Tort Claims Act

"Chiquita Bananas to face Colombia torture claim" (March 30, 2012)

Chiquita, the global banana producer, has directly funded military groups in Colombia that were known to have killed and tortured many villagers. EarthRights International and Cohen Milstein filed a lawsuit against Chiquita on behalf of victims. Originally the case was based on the Alien Tort Claims Act (ATCA), though ATCA is currently under scrutiny in *Kiobel* v. *Royal Dutch Petroleum*. However, a US federal judge allowed the lawsuit to proceed when the prosecutor claimed that Chiquita had violated Colombian law (Chatterjee 2012: 1).

"General Motors concedes to Khulumani in Apartheid reparations case" (March 1, 2012)

In 2002, the Khulumani Support Group for victims of Apartheid brought a suit against five corporations for providing infrastructure to South Africa's Apartheid regime. The case also used the Alien Tort Claims Act that allows non-US citizens to charge offenders of human rights. Again, the ATCA has been criticized by corporations, and the Act's relevance is now under review in the United States Supreme Court. The South African President Zuma approved of the lawsuit, "hoping that reparations would help South Africa come to terms with the apartheid's legacy" (Global Policy Forum 2015).

Generally speaking, corporate crimes are dealt with through regulatory agencies that vary by country. Ironically, corporations have legal recognition and status as individuals, with the rights conferred upon all citizens, though when it comes to the commission of crimes, the corporation itself is rarely brought up on criminal charges. Rather, a few individuals may be brought up on charges, though this is more common in those crimes we consider as occupational rather than organizational. For example, in the United States, when it comes to corporate crimes of the environment, even though "more than 64,000 facilities are currently listed in agency databases as being in violation of federal environmental laws … fewer than one-half of one percent of violations trigger criminal investigations" (Biron 2014: 1). If criminal charges are brought forth, corporations have the ability to negotiate guilt through non-prosecution, deferred prosecution and *nolo contendere* agreements, which is unique to corporations.

Box 12.2 Department of Justice, Office of Public Affairs, Wednesday, March 19, 2014

"Justice Department announces criminal charge against Toyota Motor Corporation and deferred prosecution agreement with $1.2 Billion financial penalty"

The Department of Justice announced a deferred prosecution agreement with TOYOTA ("the agreement") under which the company admits that it misled US consumers by concealing and making deceptive statements about two safety issues affecting its vehicles, each of which caused a type of unintended acceleration. The admissions are contained in a detailed statement of facts attached to the agreement. The agreement, which is subject to judicial review, requires TOYOTA to pay a $1.2 billion financial penalty—the largest penalty of its kind ever imposed on an automotive company, and imposes on TOYOTA an independent monitor to review and assess policies, practices and procedures relating to TOYOTA's safety-related public statements and reporting obligations. TOYOTA agrees to pay the penalty under a Final Order of Forfeiture in a parallel civil action also filed today in the Southern District of New York.
(From Department of Justice 2014.)

You may be asking why is this the case? Here again, we note the symbiotic relationship between the state and corporations grounded within the neoliberal capitalistic agenda and prioritization of the economy. For example, in the United States, the Department of Justice claims that corporate criminality is a priority, though, as Box 12.3 suggests, the number one priority is the threat to the economic system.

> ### Box 12.3 Department of Justice 2008
>
> #### Title 9, Chapter 9–28.000 Corporate Charging Guidelines
>
> The prosecution of corporate crime is a high priority for the Department of Justice. By investigating allegations of wrongdoing and by bringing charges where appropriate for criminal misconduct, the Department promotes critical public interests. These interests include, to take just a few examples: (1) protecting the integrity of our free economic and capital markets; (2) protecting consumers, investors, and business entities that compete only through lawful means; and (3) protecting the American people from misconduct that would violate criminal laws safeguarding the environment.

With this in mind, the following contains an example list of some of the primary regulatory agencies in several countries.

- **Australia:**

    Australian Competition and Consumer Commission (ACCC) is responsible for the promotion of competition and fair trading and the protection of consumers, with the power to take legal action in respect of consumer protection matters and matters involving anti-competitive behavior.

    Australian Securities & Investments Commission (ASIC) is an independent government body that regulates companies, financial markets, and financial service providers and "enforces" the Corporations Act and the Financial Services Reform Act 2001.

- **Canada:**

    The Canadian Food Inspection Agency (CFIA) is responsible for the enforcement and regulation of products related to food production under the authority of Acts including, but not limited to, the Agriculture and Agri-Food Administrative Monetary Penalties Act, the Canadian Food Inspection Agency Act, the Consumer Packaging and Labelling Act, Food and Drug Acts, Meat Inspection and Plant Protection Acts.

    The Environmental Protection Review Canada (EPRC) is charged with providing a platform for individuals, government, and corporations under the Canadian Environmental Protection Act, 1999 (CEPA, 1999) to request reviews of Environmental Protection Compliance Orders (EPCOs).

The **Financial Consumer Agency of Canada (FCA)** is charged with overseeing and protecting Canadian financial consumers and to promoting responsible financial market conduct.

- **New Zealand:**

The **Electricity Authority (EA)** is responsible for regulating the electricity industry and markets under the authority of the Electricity Act and the government's energy policy.
The **Environmental Protection Authority (EPA)** is charged with safeguarding people and the environment under the Hazardous Substances and New Organisms (HSNO) Act.
The **Financial Markets Authority (FMA)**, under the 2011 Financial Markets Authority Act, replaced the Government Actuary and has regulatory authority over financial institutions and the market.
Work Safe New Zealand is charged with overseeing compliance in the workplace including health and safety issues for workers.

- **The United States:**

Consumer Product Safety Commission (CPSC) is responsible for enforcing federal safety standards that apply to products.
Environmental Protection Agency (EPA) enforces pollution standards and other related infractions in the protection of the environment.
Federal Deposit Insurance Corporation (FDIC), along with the **Federal Reserve System (the FED)**, oversees the financial banking sector with routine audits of banking practices, mergers, and money supply.
Federal Trade Commission (FTC), while promoting market priorities, ideally protects consumers from unfair or deceptive corporate practices.
Occupational Safety and Health Administration (OSHA) enforces federal standards and regulations ensuring safe working conditions.

The regulatory agencies noted above are the primary domestic "controls" for corporate forms of crimes of the powerful. Though, as we noted above, these agencies are often underfunded and understaffed and do not have the power and authority of a prosecutor or court to penalize corporate harms beyond tickets, fines, and non-compliance orders.

Domestic laws pertaining to organized crime

As with any other form of crimes of the powerful, domestic laws governing organized crimes vary widely between countries and legal systems. They can be charged under the existing criminal offenses including murder, embezzlement, fraud, trafficking, assault, illegal firearms possession, and the possession or sale and distribution of drugs.

Box 12.4 James "Whitey" Bulger

(CNN) – Reputed mob boss James "Whitey" Bulger is charged with "19 counts of murder after the FBI found him hiding out in a Santa Monica apartment with his girlfriend in 2011. He was on the lam for 16 years after allegedly being tipped off to a 1995 indictment by his rogue handler, former FBI agent John Connolly, who is now behind bars." During trial, Bulger "slouched uncharacteristically in his chair Monday, muttering 'I'm not (a) f***ing informant.'" But his 700-page FBI file and informant card with his ID number BS1455 OC [the OC stands for "organized crime"] show otherwise. Bulger provided information on murders, drug deals, armed robberies, and criminal fugitives including La Cosa Nostra, rival gangs, though always keeping quiet about those in his immediate circle, the Winter Hill gang. According to entries in his informant file, Bulger knew he could get away with it. Documents also expose that Bulger met with more than one FBI agent, including the former FBI supervisor John Morris who pled guilty to accepting bribes from Bulger for information. Morris is set to testify against Bulger in exchange for immunity (Feyerick and Sguelia 2013: 1).

In some countries, there are other means to charge and prosecute organized crime syndicates and members. For example, the United States has the Racketeer Influenced and Corrupt Organizations Act (RICO Act) that was legislated in 1970 to address organized crime, though it has since been used more broadly. Under the RICO Act, prosecution and civil action can be taken against an individual accused of at least two offenses such as illegal gambling, bribery, kidnapping, murder, counterfeiting, slavery, and money laundering as part of an ongoing criminal enterprise that affects interstate or foreign commerce. There are also joint efforts by domestic agencies to combat organized crime that include national, regional, and local enforcement agencies.

Each country has its own definitions of what constitutes organized crime, some taking from the United Nations Convention on Transnational Organized Crime. For example, the United Kingdom does not have a legal definition of organized crime. Rather, the United Kingdom uses characteristics that roughly define it:

> [O]rganised crime is serious crime planned, coordinated and conducted by people working together on a continuing basis. Their motivation is often, but not always, financial gain. Organised crime is characterised by violence or the threat of violence and by the use of bribery and corruption: organised criminals very often depend on the assistance of corrupt,

Box 12.5 Operation Archimedes

Europol, The Hague, Netherlands, September 24, 2014.

Law enforcement officers from 34 countries take part in the largest ever coordinated operation against organized crime in the EU – 1027 individuals arrested

Between 15 and 23 September, law enforcement authorities from 34 countries, coordinated and supported by Europol from its headquarters in The Hague, joined forces in Operation Archimedes. The operation targeted organized crime groups and their infrastructures across the European Union (EU) in a series of actions in hundreds of locations, with the cooperation of Eurojust, Frontex and Interpol.

"Operation Archimedes is a milestone in attempts by the law enforcement community to deliver concerted action against organised crime groups in Europe. The scale of the operation is unprecedented and the outcome, with over 1000 arrests made across Europe, a reminder to even the most serious criminal groups that the international law enforcement community is determined to combat their illegal activities," says Rob Wainwright, Director of Europol. "This week, as EU police chiefs gather at Europol for the 2014 European Police Chiefs Convention, our focus will be on how our combined strengths can best be applied to bringing down even more of the organised criminal groups that threaten the safety and wellbeing of our society."

Focused on disrupting the activities of the most threatening criminal groups and top targets active in key crime hotspots across Europe, the intelligence-led Operation Archimedes saw the participation of law enforcement officers from all 28 EU Member States as well as Australia, Colombia, Norway, Serbia, Switzerland and the USA (ICE and CBP).

In the largest period of joint action days held so far in the EU, raids and other interventions took place between 15 and 23 September 2014 in hundreds of locations including airports, border-crossing points, ports and specific crime hot spots in towns and cities all of which had featured variously in Europol's SOCTA, criminal intelligence reports from EU Member States and third countries and analytical products drawn from Europol's criminal databases.

Results from the operational actions include:

- 1,027 individuals arrested
- 599 kg of cocaine and 200 kg of heroin seized
- 1.3 tonnes of cannabis seized
- 30 children saved from trafficking.

complicit or negligent professionals, notably lawyers, accountants and bankers. Organised crime also uses sophisticated technology to conduct operations, maintain security and evade justice.

(Home Department 2013: 14, 2.5–2.6)

Generally speaking, prosecuting organized crime is a vast operation that, not unlike all other crimes of the powerful, is impacted by politics, power, and economic interests.

As we noted, the potential to use "street" crime indexes to prosecute individuals within organized groups is an alternative and does provide an avenue to address this type of harm. Of all forms of crimes of the powerful, the broadest ability to prosecute and punish offenders is for those who can be charged under existing domestic criminal laws at the state, federal, or union level.

International

International law and systems of control for states/regimes/high-ranking officials

International law does indeed have a long history; however, it is only in recent years (relatively speaking) that it has become a regular feature of modern political life. The second half of the twentieth century marked significant developments within the codification of public law (including the codification of criminal liability for individuals who violate public law). International rules now codified as criminal law provide a framework for judging and prosecuting individual behavior and state actions.

The laws of the sea are one of the oldest disciplines in international law. The League of Nations Conference for the Codification of International Law (1930, The Hague) dealt with the breadth of the territorial sea. Parts of treaties or conventions also guide the laws of sea (Geneva Convention for the Amelioration of the Condition of Wounded, Sick, and Shipwrecked Members of the Sea). Nonetheless, the next directly related significant developments occurred with the United Nations Conferences on the Law of the Sea (1958 and 1960, Geneva), which accentuated a need for a generally acceptable convention on the law of the sea. This resulted in the United Nations Convention on the Law of the Sea (UNCLOS) (1982). The UNCLOS states the area of the seabed, ocean floor, subsoil, and its resources are the common heritage of mankind, irrespective of the geographical location of states. The Convention includes the banning of pollution and dumping: (1) the introduction by man, directly or indirectly, of substances or energy into the marine environment, including estuaries, which results or is likely to result in such deleterious effects as harm to living resources and marine life, hazards to human health, hindrance to marine activities, including fishing and other legitimate uses of the sea, impairment of quality for use of sea water and reduction of amenities; (2) any deliberate disposal of wastes or other matter from vessels, aircraft, platforms, or other man-made structures at sea.

The law of space started with the United Nations Committee on the Peaceful Uses of Outer Space (COPUOS) in 1958. The Outer Space Treaty (1967) was later elaborated on, resulting in the 1979 Moon Agreement wherein the international use of the Moon and the exploration of its resources are addressed. There are other treaties that cover both space and sea, for example, the Treaty Banning Nuclear Weapons Tests in the Atmosphere, in Outer Space and Under Water (1963). The public international air laws relate primarily to laws and agreements governing aviation. These include the Treaty on Open Skies (1992, Helsinki), the Protection of Civilian Populations against Bombing from the Air in Case of War (1938), the Warsaw Convention (1929), the Montreal Convention (1999), and the historical Hague Rules of Aerial Warfare (1923). These laws, unlike the criminal laws discussed previously, are for states and as such would have a different institution of control and handling violations.

Contemporary international humanitarian law (IHL) (*jus in bello*) is split into international armed conflict (IAC) and non-international armed conflict (NIAC). Treaties include The Hague Conventions of 1899 and 1907, the Geneva Conventions I and II, relating to the treatment of the wounded and sick, Convention III that addresses the treatment of prisoners of war, and Convention IV that is meant to protect civilians. There are also the two Additional Protocols of 1977 that relate to protecting victims of international armed conflicts, and the third Additional Protocol of 2005 and the United Nations Charter of 1945. More recently, the statutes for the International Criminal Tribunal for the former Yugoslavia (ICTY), the International Criminal Tribunal for Rwanda (ICTR), and the 1998 Rome Statute of the International Criminal Court (ICC) serve as foundations of humanitarian law, in this case specifying what is considered prosecutable at the international level: war crimes, crimes against humanity, and genocide. The crime of aggression, while listed, is currently not defined by the ICC, however, making prosecution for this particular form of state crime impossible at the international level.

International human rights law (IHRL) is primarily for peacetime and applies to every human being. These laws are based on international rules versus international treaties or customs and are viewed as inherent entitlements based solely on being human. Their principal goal is to protect individuals from arbitrary acts by their own governments that infringe upon their rights; thus, they primarily protect people against state violations of internationally recognized (customary) civil, political, economic, social, and cultural rights committed against a state's own citizens. Human rights law does not deal with the conduct of hostilities. States are bound (if or when they have accepted these international rules or principles—the soft laws) by IHRL to bring together their domestic law with international obligations. These include the Universal

Declaration of Human Rights, adopted by the UN General Assembly in 1948; the Convention on the Prevention and Punishment of the Crime of Genocide of 1948; the International Covenant on Civil and Political Rights of 1966; the International Covenant on Social and Economic Rights of 1966; the Convention on the Elimination of All Forms of Discrimination against Women of 1981; the Convention against Torture and Other Cruel, Inhuman, or Degrading Treatment or Punishment of 1984; and the Convention on the Rights of the Child of 1989. Criminal prosecution can occur for these violations; however, they must fall under violations of international crimes such as crimes against humanity, genocide, or torture.

Exploring the issue of the ability of intergovernmental bodies to act as control agents is important, even if these agencies have had a historically poor record of enacting control. The International Court of Justice (ICJ), formerly the World Court of Justice, seated in The Hague, is the principal judicial organ of the United Nations. It was established in June 1945 by the Charter of the United Nations and began work in April 1946. The sources of law that the Court can apply include international treaties and conventions in force, international customs, general principles of law, and judicial decisions (or precedent decisions). The Court has two functions: (1) to settle legal disputes submitted by states, and (2) to give advisory opinions on legal questions. The settlement of legal disputes can occur through mediation, the intervention of a third party to allow states to resolve their dispute, and arbitration; the dispute is submitted to the decision or award of an impartial third party resulting in a binding settlement. Mediation and arbitration precede judicial settlement. Simply, the ICJ is a court for state arbitration, not for addressing individual criminality.

International tribunals have been used to address past atrocities, including those committed by the German Nazis and Japan during World War II. Yet, it was nearly a half-century later before key international tribunals were used again: the ICTY and the ICTR. Due to the costs and many weaknesses of these ad hoc tribunals, it is highly unlikely they will be used in the future.

Rather, it is more likely the ICC will address crimes that violate international law by heads of state, high-ranking military, and those in charge or control of insurgency or militia groups that commit any of the three major crimes covered under the jurisdiction of the Court. While these crimes are now considered to be both customary and criminal offenses, the ability of the ICC to penalize all who offend is limited. For example, the ICC is limited in its investigative reach, making it unable to subpoena any state or its records. While the Court may request a warrant or subpoena, the Prosecutor and the Court lack an empowered policing agency to ensure the enforcement of either request (Articles 54–58). However, on December 22, 2004, a cooperation agreement between the Office of the Prosecutor (OP) and the International Criminal Police Organization (Interpol) was signed establishing a framework for cooperation between the two agencies. The agreement enables the OP and

Interpol to exchange police information and criminal analysis and to cooperate in the search for fugitives and suspects. The agreement also gives the OP access to Interpol's telecommunications network and databases (Rothe and Mullins 2006).

The ICC has several other barriers to its potential and real effectiveness, including issues of opting in or out of the Court's jurisdiction. In order for a case to fall under its jurisdiction, one of three conditions must be met in terms of location of the crimes (Article 12). The first geographic criterion is that the crimes in question must have occurred within the territory (or territory controlled by), vessel, or aircraft of a state party, or have been committed by nationals of a state party (namely, uniformed military). Second, a state may agree to accept the jurisdiction of the Court, without being a state party. Third, the United Nations Security Council can recommend a case to the Court and authorize the its jurisdiction in the matter if neither of the above conditions is met (for example, the situation in the Sudan-Darfur case).

Other issues include prosecutorial selectivity and the fact that it is grounded in the assumption that deterrence works. Many actors within the field of international criminal justice have heralded the deterrent power of the international criminal justice system and its ability to remove impunity for violations of international criminal law. Nearly all extant criminological research on deterrence has been at national levels and on "street" crime in general. This body of research has shown mixed results, at best, for a deterrent effect. One of the major issues highlighted in the literature is the assumption that actors are rational (including bounded rationality) in their decision-making prior to and during crime commission. Such a strict assumption of human nature as rational beings ignores the structural and contextual factors of individual decision-making (for example, organizational or cultural pressures) (Michalowski and Kramer 2006; Smeulers 2008; Rothe and Kauzlarich 2010).

Factors that have had empirical support for a deterrent effect include certainty and legitimacy of the law, both of which are tied to the most important variable, individual perception. Simply, when offenders do not perceive a punishment as likely to be imposed, then there will be little disincentive toward offending, no matter the celerity or the proportionality of the punishment in question. This relates to certainty of being both caught and punished, as well as to legitimacy. If an offender has absolute knowledge that someone else who committed the same act was not "caught" or punished, there is a disjuncture and certainty is lost—this is the case at the international level for nearly all crimes of the powerful, transnational organizations, and others. Additionally, the issue of legitimacy is highly relevant for international criminal law and criminal justice, as both the law and the institution of social control must be perceived as legitimate.

As noted, individual perception is central to a deterrent effect. Given the ongoing resistance to the legitimacy of international criminal law and the ICC by several states, insurgency groups, and militaries, the Court is further weakened in its ability to serve as a general deterrent. Consider the case of Libya, where the ICC issued arrest warrants for Muammar Gaddafi, the second sitting head of state to be indicted by the ICC, his son Saif al-Islam, and his military intelligence chief General Abdullah al-Sanoussi. The issue of the perceived lack of legitimacy of the law was reflected in a statement by Gaddafi's spokesperson, Moussa Ibrahim: "The ICC has no legitimacy whatsoever. We will deal with it" (Walt 2011: 2). Whether a symbolic or defiant statement, it does reflect an ongoing issue with the Court's perceived legitimacy.

Furthermore, scholars have noted that mass violence and conflicts give rise to situations where individuals behave differently from what is seen in street crime contexts. In situations of conflict, the law can be seen as necessarily negotiable and its meaning is seen as invalid given the circumstances. This is especially the case when individual morality is influenced by the ongoing situation or the individual ideology guiding their behavior. Here, the fighting and subsequent crimes committed can be believed as legitimate, just, or as the only means available to defend or advance the interests of the group or the individual's situation or status, making the crimes necessary, if they are even viewed as "crimes." This can be impacted further by the greater sense of fear an individual feels in terms of the potential loss if they do not choose the behavior that is cast as "illegal" under international law (for example, liberation movements or actions taken to depose a regime). Simply, environments affect the moral choices made by individuals where behavior is contextual.

To summarize, international law and institutions of social control do exist and have been used to punish certain crimes of the powerful, though with the caveat that they have been used in relation to power, politics, and economic interests.

Corporations, international financial institutions, organized crime, and international law and controls

There are many debates as to the applicability of criminal liability for corporations through applying international criminal law or the international mechanisms of control such as the ICC, or ad hoc or military-type tribunals. Generally speaking, given the atomistic nature and foundation of sovereignty that guides international law and relations, corporate crimes, as with other forms of crimes including organized crime, transnational crime, or any other type of harm or crime by the powerful, require states to address the behavior through domestic law and institutions of social control. This is complicated further due to the symbiotic nature of relations, power, and the interests of states with corporations and organized crime networks including, most importantly, economic interests followed by "national security" interests.

Image 12.1 Who gets labeled criminal?

Box 12.6 Arms trafficking and complicity of other governments: system criminality

The most widely known recent case of arms trafficking involves Charles Taylor, Liberia and the RUF (Revolutionary United Front, Sierra Leone). Less known is the involvement and criminality of a host of other countries involved in the trafficking of small arms to Liberia that would then be supplied to the RUF. Sources of the trafficked small arms include Russia and other former USSR states, the United States, Israel, France, Italy, and the United Kingdom to name a few. Additionally, arms were diverted to the RUF through Liberia due to the covert activities of the United States in support of former President Samuel Doe and the UK support of Sandline (a private military corporation), and through their airlines and linkages with the UK government. States which sold arms to Liberia included Burkina Faso, China, the Democratic Republic of Congo, Nigeria, the Ukraine, and Russia, to name a few. Likewise, Bulgaria used Nice as a diversion destination to then ship the small arms to Liberia and from there to the RUF. Other diversion states included Burkina Faso through Côte d'Ivoire to Liberia; Russia direct to Liberia, as well as through Côte d'Ivoire to Liberia; China to Nigeria to Ghana to Liberia. Uganda used Slovakia as a diversion where the small arms were then resold to Guinea and then shipped to Liberia, where Taylor and his network provided them to the RUF. The RUF also purchased small arms directly from Guinea.

- In 1997, actors in the British government encouraged Sandline International, a private security firm and non-state entity, to supply arms and ammunitions to the loyal forces of the exiled government of President Kabbah ... Sandline signed a contract with Ahmed Tejan Kabbah, the then exiled President of Sierra Leone to provide a 35-ton arms shipment from Bulgaria.
- Britain shipped arms to the RUF directly: two British firms owned and operated by retired British military generals who had strong connections with the former British foreign secretary Robin Cook: Sky Air Cargo of London and Occidental Airlines, partly owned by a British pilot, were at the center of supplying arms to the AFRC/RUF rebels.
- The United Nations Security Council Report on Liberia (2001) stated that Sharif al-Masri was contracted to deliver arms from Uganda to Slovakia in 2000. These arms were rerouted to a company in Guinea, a front company for the Liberian government. When the weapons arrived in Slovakia, the military refused delivery as they did not meet specifications on the contract. Instead of arranging for the guns to be shipped back to Slovakia, al-Masri sold them to Pecos, New Guinea. Pecos then diverted the sub-machine guns to Liberia through an elaborate "bait-and-switch" scheme.
- Toward the end of the Doe regime, the United States was using Robertsfield Airport in Liberia to supply arms to UNITA (National Union for the Total Independence of Angola). These would later be used in the trade of diamonds-for-arms with the RUF.
- Approximately 200 tons of illegal arms were shipped from Belgrade to Monrovia between May and August 2002 with the aid of Mr. Slobodan Tezic, director of the Belgrade-based Temex company. Temex organized the contracts to send mainly old military equipment from Yugoslavian army stocks. The cargo documents, shown to the United Nations Expert Panel Report on Liberia (October, 2002) as part of its investigation, had stamps from the Nigerian receiver, Aruna Import, yet the two Nigerian End User Certifications were false.
- The government of Côte d'Ivoire played a role in the November 2000 diversion of a large shipment of ammunition to Liberia, providing the necessary cover story, documentation, and staging ground for the diversion.
  - On February 16, 2003, an arms shipment arrived at Liberian International Airport from Kinshasa in the Democratic Republic of Congo and was subsequently transferred to the RUF.

- The President of Burkina Faso, Blaise Compaore, in Abidjan directly facilitated Liberia's arms-for-diamonds trade, to the benefit of the RUF in Sierra Leone through its sales of small arms to Liberia.
- In May and July 2002, 45 tons of weapons shipments were delivered to Harper Port, Liberia, having originated in Bulgaria with a stop in Nice.
- Shipments of arms from Nigeria regularly made their way to Buchanan Port, Liberia, under the guise of shipping food and non-sanctioned supplies after the UN arms embargoes were implemented.
- South Africa labeled small arms were sent to Liberia.
- Ukraine sold weapons directly to Taylor, who then traded with the RUF the weapons for diamonds.
- China shipped arms to Nigeria as a diversion state, from Nigeria to Ghana and from Ghana to Liberia.
- Burkina Faso soldiers accompanied a shipment of small arms to Côte d'Ivoire, where Taylor met with them and loaded the arms onto trucks to return to Liberia and which were later provided to the RUF.
- On over a dozen occasions, Russian planes transported Russian arms directly to Liberia, at times using Côte d'Ivoire as a diversion state.
- Small arms shipments to Taylor also came from Burkina Faso, America, and Europe. Some of these shipments were rerouted through Côte d'Ivoire.

Consider also the crimes of arms trafficking. Small arms trafficking is complex and involves a host of actors (see an example in Box 12.6). As numerous court documents, transcripts, United Nations and NGO reports have revealed, many state institutions play a prominent role in the facilitation of, complicity in, and implicit involvement in black and grey arms trafficking. Yet, prosecutions for this crime involve only the rogue individual, even though they most likely worked with members of corporations and governments.

International controls for these types of crimes of the powerful are not laws per se, or hard laws, rather they come in the form of the conventions and resolutions that states agree with and sign on to, which bind the state to supporting domestic prosecution and the control of certain crimes. For example, the United Nations Convention against Transnational Organized Crime, adopted in November 2000 and entered into force on September 29, 2003, is the main international instrument for addressing transnational organized crime. The Convention is supplemented by three protocols: the Protocol to Prevent, Suppress and Punish Trafficking in Persons; the Protocol against the Smuggling of Migrants by Land, Sea and Air; and the Protocol against the Illicit Manufacturing of and Trafficking in Firearms, their Parts and Components and Ammunition. The Convention also establishes the potential for criminal liability of corporations in addition to individual liability of persons acting on behalf of the corporation. However, there is a far stretch between a convention and its enforcement.

When it comes to the crimes of international financial institutions, there are even fewer avenues to address the crimes and harms perpetrated by them. No international institution or tribunal has specific jurisdiction over international financial institutions to take complaints on or to adjudicate the broad range of harmful activities engaged in by them. These financial institutions are currently not included as actors that fall under the jurisdiction of these laws and treaties or any controlling agency at the international or domestic levels, as they are seen as intergovernmental organizations. The powerful countries that dominate these institutions—notably the United States and Western European countries—are highly unlikely to call them to account or create a venue for their harmful activities to be addressed, since their policies and practices are aligned with and advance their own economic interests. Unlike most organizations, where there are checks and balances or a populace to which they answer, international financial institutions have no formal external monitoring system (Rothe and Friedrichs 2014a). The idea of making international financial institutions formally accountable at this time may be unrealistic and potentially counterproductive. It is highly unlikely that international financial institutions will be willing to self-regulate and comply with extant human rights standards or to end their support and facilitation of corrupt regimes and practices, given the geopolitical environment within which they operate. These institutions typically claim that human rights concerns are outside their scope. However, Rachael Kyte (2011), Vice-President for Sustainable Development of the World Bank Group, conceded that these institutions were often blighted by corruption, environmental degradations, and a general disregard for local communities. The human rights obligations of the World Bank were conceded by its own General Counsel, but the legal opinion circulated by this officer was largely greeted with silence (Sarfaty 2012: 63–70). The Bank's board resists adopting human rights initiatives if there is opposition from one of its member countries, which is what happens.

In summary then, any control of corporate crime, transnational crime, organized crime and rogue crimes of the powerful remains at the domestic level. This, of course, is complicated, as we have stated, by power, politics, and economic interests that more often than not take primacy over "punishment."

Resistance to crimes of the powerful

> The real political task in a society such as ours is to criticize the workings of institutions that appear to be both neutral and independent, to criticize and attack them in such a manner that the political violence that has always exercised itself obscurely through them will be unmasked, so that one can fight against them.
>
> (Chomsky *et al.* 2006)

Resistance can be thought of as a form or context of opposition to a host of situations including oppression, domination, control, violence, policies, and actions that are perceived to be harmful. The famous French thinker Michel Foucault (1990) observed that resistance is contained in all oppression and all forms of power results in other forms of power and resistance. Simply, "Where there is power, there is resistance." In many cases, when the term resistance is used, it is with the image of non-profit organizations or massive social movements or even large demonstrations against a particular issue. Yet, resistance is not always so overt; it can be subtle, private, or internal forms of dissenting behavior, taking on everyday life forms. As Goffman (1961: 181) noted, resistance can refer to small acts of living and the everyday forms of communication expressing resistance, often found in song lyrics, jokes, art, novels, or poems. In this chapter, we touch upon each of these types and forms of resistance followed by some concluding thoughts about how even these forms of resistance can legitimate the very system, policy, exercise of power, oppression, harm, or violence.

The role of non-governmental agencies

There are non-governmental agencies that operate at the international, national, and local levels (far too many for us to cover in this chapter), yet we do need to recognize the value of these organizations in contributing to the awareness of and accountability for crimes of the powerful. The host of non-profit organizations range in their focus from monitoring state behavior to corporate crime watch lists and transnational/organized crime groups, some of which cover more than one type of harm and crime. For example, Human Rights Watch, Amnesty International, and Doctors Without Borders monitor human rights violations, state oppression and suppression across the globe. Monitoring freedom of speech and journalists' right to cover crimes of the powerful include organizations such as Journalists Without Borders, the Reporters Committee for Freedom of the Press, and Press Freedom. Corporate Crime Watch, Corporate Crime Reporter, Global Exchange, Corp Watch, and Third World Traveler all report on crimes of corporations, both domestic and transnational in nature.

There are also agencies that develop in response to specific situations, as have been discussed throughout this text; recall the various non-profit groups that organized to protect indigenous populations in relation to World Bank or International Monetary Fund projects. The local levels should not be overlooked in showing awareness of "everyday" crimes by states and corporations, including those that disclose the disparities of income and the growing homeless populations, to the level of censorship in education.

There is no doubt in our minds that such organizations, while ideologically driven with specific agendas, do help to contribute to our awareness, and some of the large groups have indeed managed to pressure states and corporations to address some of their harms. Nonetheless, such movements also help legitimize the very systems that create and facilitate the harms and crimes they are fighting against. This will be discussed in more detail later in this chapter.

Civil society and social movements

We need only to recall the Arab Spring uprising or to read the current news to see examples of protests to state oppression, violence, and harms generated by policies not in the interest of citizens.

Box 12.7 Arab Spring resistance

Many Arab citizens have endured years of state repression and violence. December 2010 was a tipping point. The onset of the Arab Spring is generally attributed to the self-immolation of Mohamed Bouazizi after police took away his livelihood in Sidi Bouzid, Tunisia. In Egypt, it was photos of the deformed face of Khaled Said after the police had beaten him to death. In Syria, it was the torture of teenagers for scribbling anti-regime graffiti. In Libya, it was the arrest of Fathi Terbil, the lawyer of the victims of the 1996 Abu Salim prison massacre ... Yet movements had begun in several countries years before. In Egypt, the Kefaya (Enough) movement emerged in 2004 to oppose a new term for President Hosni Mubarak. Labor strife in Egypt continued to intensify and in April 2008, police repression of a textile workers strike in Mahalla al-Kubra, in which four people were killed, sparked the creation of the April 6 Youth Movement. The movement quickly grew to tens of thousands of members through Facebook and was key to the organization of the Tahrir Square protests that began on January 25, 2011. Mass demonstrations in Cairo, Alexandria, and other cities and the occupation of Tahrir Square lasted 18 days before Mubarak and the National Democratic Party were removed from power. The protesters were met with violence in many cases, and the government ordered to shut down the Internet and cell phone services to quell the social

media force that facilitated the growth of protests. Protesters were not dissuaded by Mubarak's symbolic efforts to address the growing uprising, including appointing Omar Suleiman as vice president, installing a new cabinet, and promising not to run for office again. On February 11, 2011, Mubarak stepped down and handed power over to the army council. The legislature was dissolved and the constitution was suspended ... Protests over the slow progress of political change continued, though the scale was much smaller. In June 2012, the Muslim Brotherhood's candidate, Mohammed Morsi, became the first democratically elected president in decades, replacing the national unity government headed by the new Prime Minister Kamal al-Ganzouri. Morsi then sought to lessen the power of the Egyptian army, including stripping the military of its say in legislation and the drafting of the new constitution. In December 2012, a new constitution was approved, boosting the role of Islam and restricting certain freedoms of speech and assembly. Protests continued into 2013. With the economy still in shambles, little changed socially or economically. Given Morsi's continued lack of inclusion, protestors began to call for his resignation. On July 1, 2013, the Egyptian army issued an ultimatum calling on Morsi to resolve the political deadlock and make the political process more inclusive. Morsi was given 48 hours to do so or he would be removed from power. Mass protests continued, including clashes between Morsi supporters and those calling for his resignation. July 3, 2013, Morsi was forced to step down. The military stepped in and installed the head of the country's highest court as an interim leader.
(From Collins and Rothe 2014; see for a broader discussion including the role of states in supporting the Mubarak and Morsi regimes.)

In October 2014, protests continued in Hong Kong, where protesters had blocked major highways in several main districts for a week, calling for democracy. Activists accused Beijing, China, of having too much influence on Hong Kong, its politics, and policies that impact the citizens, and demanded the right to choose political candidates for elected office—rather than the current policy that provides a veto power over eligible candidates to the candidates chosen by the population (Mullen *et al.* 2014). In the same vein,

As many as one million public sector workers on Thursday began a mass demonstration against austerity cuts in the UK ... protesters from a variety of unions—health workers, trash collectors, firefighters, office employees, and other civil servants—against low wages, poor working conditions, and pension changes that some public worker groups are calling punitive.

(Prupis 2014)

Protests against the state are not the only ones that occur, however. To date, global justice (or anti-globalization) activists have been the principal entities protesting international financial institutions' harmful policies and practices. Local resistance has also increased in areas directly affected by international financial institutions' policies and investments, some with success and others not. For example, in November 2011, 20,000 citizens in the Peruvian state of Cajamarca demonstrated against a Conga mine proposed by Minera Yanacoch, a mining company owned by Newmont, a large US multinational mining corporation (Bretton Woods Project 2013). The demonstrators included 8,000 local farmers blockading a town amidst concerns that the state was pressuring locals to sign agreements without consultation with the locals who would be harmed by these agreements. In response, the government suspended the construction of the mine and announced it would seek international consultants to evaluate the impact of the mine project.

Other protests by local communities include the April 2013 demonstrations in Bhubaneswar, New Delhi, and Bangalore, India, against World Bank policies and projects (Express News Service 2013). There was widespread concern that harmful and corrupt public–private sector activities promoted by the World Bank would occur. More specifically, these World Bank initiatives included illegally closing down various public sector programs relating to education and health, funding environmentally unsustainable projects, and complicity in basic human rights abuses. The protesters stated that thousands of people have been forcibly displaced and the Bank's programs have destroyed parts of the environment, including land aimed at forestry sector development. As one protester stated, "[t]he World Bank Group claims that it has lent around $26 billion to India between 2009 and 2013. However, these funds are spent through different anti-community policies, programmes and projects and has helped the corporate sectors only. Poverty has increased during this period" (Express New Service 2013: 1). Coverage was intense enough that the public outcry by the general population forced the World Bank to respond with an op-ed in the largest newspaper in India.

The most recent World Bank project includes a $58 million Partial Risk Guarantee (PRG) for a proposed Kosovo power project (Mainhardt and Sinani 2012: 1). This project calls for building a new 600 megawatt lignite coal-based power plant, known as Kosova Re Power Project, and expanding open pit coal-mining operations. The project has a huge potential to cause devastating environmental harm to waterways upon which people in this region of Kosovo are wholly dependent. Citizen advocacy groups joined together to protest the Bank's funding of the coal plants (Hitt 2012), releasing public health advertisements and using social media in connection with this protest campaign.

Public protests have occurred in other countries. In Egypt, protests against the former Morsi regime addressed its acceptance of a major $4.8 billion loan from the International Monetary Fund. The loan was conditional on mandated tax increases and subsidy cuts to food and other daily subsistence needs of Egyptian citizens. Such conditions are similar to those accepted by the former regime of Hosni Mubarak, who was forced out of office during the Arab Spring uprising in 2011. Many of the consequences of the International Monetary Fund mandated structural reforms accepted by Mubarak were a central part of the populations' dissatisfaction that contributed to the uprising.

Through the expanded use of social media, activists and local communities are creating websites dedicated to exposing the policies and practices of international financial institutions that have hugely harmful consequences. Such websites receive thousands of "hits" and accordingly contribute to the potential of an expanding global movement against these institutions. For example, the World Development Movement's website states that "[t]he World Bank has a long history of funding projects that are destructive to the environment and undermine human rights, investing in projects regardless of their devastating impacts both on local populations and on our planet" (2013: 1). They provide an interactive map that allows users to follow projects funded by international financial institutions that have caused devastating harm. These projects range from the Guyana–Omai gold mine in Brazil to the Kedung Ombo Multipurpose Dam and Irrigation Project in Indonesia, to the Kumtor Mining Project in Kyrgyzstan. An activist group calling itself "Third World Traveler" uses a website to bring attention to a harmful project in San Marcos, Guatemala. The Glamis Gold mining company, a Canadian company with headquarters in Reno, Nevada, was given a $45 million loan from the World Bank to construct and operate an open pit gold and silver mine there. During the initial phase of construction, over 2,000 indigenous farmers and villagers blocked a convoy traveling on the Pan-American Highway carrying mining equipment from reaching the Marlin site (Mychalejko 2005: 2). The blockade lasted for 40 days. At that point, Guatemala's Interior Ministry deployed the military and security forces to the protest site to protect the interests of investors. While this protest was unsuccessful at stopping the implementation of the mine, monitoring of the Guatemala mine project is ongoing. Canada's Mine Watch is one website viewed by thousands where mine-related damage is reported.

In a more formal sense, local protests have resulted in 20 current cases being filed at the Compliance Advisor/Ombudsman (CAO) office of the World Bank. Local groups have organized and brought forth complaints against various projects that have led to or will lead to serious environmental, social, and cultural harms. Activist complaints about development projects have been broadranging, with the dominant complaints directed at economic and environmental degradation. For example, in 2011, two local communities in the Philippines brought a complaint over the $9.5 million equity investment of the Canadian mining company Mindoro Resource Ltd. They claimed that the project would destroy forest vital to their social, environmental, and cultural well-being. Another case involves two communities in Peru that claim that the Maple Energy Company that received $40 million from the World Bank Group in 2007 to drill for new oil caused mass spillage, resulting in numerous health and environmental problems (Bretton Woods Project 2013). The Comité por la Defensa del Agua y el Páramo de Santurbán, a non-governmental organization, filed its case in June 2012, alleging that the World Bank's private lending arm's $20 million investment in the project, the Greystar mine in Colombia, would result in massive environment, economic, and social harms.

Some Global South countries are also responding to the harmful policies of the international financial institutions by refusing to accept mandated policies and turning to other financial sources, or by paying back their loans in full early and requesting the institutions to remove their oversight agencies. For example, dating back to 2007, the late President Hugo Chavez of Venezuela announced that his country was removing itself as a member of the World Bank Group and the International Monetary Fund. This announcement was made after Venezuela had repaid its debts to the World Bank Group five years in advance of schedule, reducing the interest by $8 million. The formal closing of the regional International Monetary Fund offices then occurred in the latter half of 2007. Following suit, Nicaraguan President Daniel Ortega stated that his country would also "get out of that prison" of the International Monetary Fund debt and began negotiating an exit strategy to leave the Fund. And, in 2007, Ecuadorean President Rafael Correa asked the World Bank's representative to leave his country after it had paid off its debt in advance. Argentina also has paid back billions of dollars to the International Monetary Fund in an effort to reduce the control and impact of the international financial institution's policies. More recently, Latvia, in late December 2012, paid back the entire $9.9 billion 2008 rescue loan to the International Monetary Fund, claiming they wanted to make their own economic policies and decisions and not be held accountable to outside pressures. In January 2013, Ukrainian Prime Minister Mykola Azarov stated that the country would not concede to demands made by the International Monetary Fund to hike gas tariffs and would instead seek funds elsewhere to finance outstanding payments to the Fund (Gorchinskaya 2013). Likewise, in August 2013, Hungary repaid the remainder of its €2.15 billion outstanding debt to the International Monetary Fund to end what Prime Minister Viktor Orban stated as "undue foreign influence over its economic policies" (Dunai and Szakacs 2013: 1). All of these initiatives could be regarded as reflections of growing recognition that Global South countries have been victims of the crimes of the international financial institutions. The leaders of such countries are likely to be under increasing pressure to accede to the perceptions of their citizenries in regard to such crimes (Rothe and Friedrichs 2014b).

Crimes of the powerful that impact the environment are also protested. Consider the demonstrations against a petrochemical plant throughout cities in China's south-eastern Guangdong province. Protesters objected to plans for a "3.5 billion yuan ($563m) paraxylene (PX) plant, a joint venture between the local government and Sinopec, a state-owned oil and gas company ... After several days of protest in Maoming, by April 4th smaller sister demonstrations had broken out in the cities of Shenzhen and Guangzhou" (*The Economist* 2013).

Similarly, the global protests most commonly called "Occupy Wall Street," took to cities across the United States and in many countries across the globe protesting the prioritization of profit and the corporate sector, and on behalf of the remaining population that are the recipients of the harm and social inequalities that result from policies and practices of states supporting the prioritization of neoliberal agendas and hyper-capitalism. In the wake of the 2010 global economic crisis, local protests covered areas across the globe.

It is not just social movements or direct protests that are a form of resistance to the crimes of the powerful. Resistance is a part of the banality and routines of everyday life, from art to poetry to music to graffiti. Music can be viewed as a form of cultural engagement which can take on political or social organizational purposes. Indeed, most research finds that music can be an important component of social movements in a variety of contexts (Bennett and Peterson 2004; Eyerman and Jamison 1998; Roberts and Moore 2009). For example, there is ample evidence to show that the historic work of popular musicians such as Bob Dylan, Woody Guthrie, Pete Seeger, and John Lennon made some impact on more than those already sympathetic to anti-war messages during the Vietnam War era. Resistance music continues to be heard from small local groups to chart-toppers and cover a variety of topics from the subtle to the overt.

Songs have always been an important component to resistance. In 1970s Nigeria, Afrobeat music protested the oil company regime of Nigeria including "Zombie," which denounced Nigeria's military dictators. In South Africa, the Mbatanga music rang out against Apartheid. In Brazil, the Tropicalia movement was created as a form of protest against the military junta. In Australia and New Zealand, songs written by the indigenous populations sparked an indigenous land reclamation movement (Martin 2013). Further, labor organizations, civil rights groups, and the like have been found to benefit from the galvanizing power of words put to music (Eyerman and Jamison 1998).

As Ferrell (2001, 2006) found in his ethnographic studies of urban graffiti artists, dumpster divers, and others on the street, "crimes of style" are partly developed out of the desire to share creativity with others and to perform individual artistic expression (which is often quashed in schools, jobs, and home life). At the same time, this drive often produces various forms of resistance to agencies of social control such as the police, schools, and government. Research on punk rock musicians (Kauzlarich and Awsumb 2011; Kauzlarich 2012) has demonstrated that while complex, art can serve as a key part of resisting state and corporate crimes but is most powerful when situated within other nested contexts of protest.

One of the ironies of protests, however, from large-scale social movements to dozens demonstrating on the streets, is that it can be interpreted as a sign of democracy, legitimating the system that is more often than not being protested. As noted by the President Benigno Aquino III of the Philippines over the use of funds under the Disbursement Acceleration Program, "Iyan po ay senyales ng isang masiglang demokrasya (That is a sign of a healthy democracy)" (Cayabyab 2014). In many situations, the unintended consequence of protests is additional policies aimed at repression or that are symbolic in nature to momentarily appease the group(s) until they have moved on back into the banality of everyday life.

> A million people marched for peace in New York in 1982, but this did not lead to any substantive changes in government policy. Instead, responses to the peace movement were in the form of "arms control initiatives," the "strategic defense initiative," and other symbolic stands which served to convince many people that the government was doing something to promote peace, while the key parts of its military stance were left unaltered.
>
> (Martin 1994)

Likewise, some music, whether sold or listened to at local venues, that aims to be a form of resistance is partaking in the system that is being criticized, generating money for some establishment and encouraging consumption of a product, that of resistance. Protesting capitalism, you can purchase a host of T-shirts, bumper stickers, cups, mugs, or nearly any product reinforcing the legitimacy of the system rather than negating it.

We are not suggesting that protests, resistance, or social movements should be abandoned, or that they cannot make the difference or change that is well overdue. Rather, we encourage and support such efforts, and have ourselves been active participants. What we are suggesting is that some forms of resistance, without thought and precautions, can further legitimate the system they are resisting. The next chapter provides an example of how protests and calls for change can result in an enhanced legal system that legitimates the harm and violence of many of the crimes of the powerful.

Summary

Controlling, resisting, and responding to crimes of the powerful is a multidimensional process that involves several elements. Some control mechanisms are state and government based while others are found in civil society. The popular conception of criminal justice is less relevant to elite crime because everyday policing is focused on traditional street crimes. Thus, many forms of control over states and corporations such as regulatory bodies and international courts are unknown to casual observers. Other forms of action such as music, art, journalism, and social media posts are also considered to be potential forms of control over crimes of the powerful.

Activities and discussion questions

1. Why shouldn't local police and criminal justice systems focus on crimes of the powerful?
2. Go to the US Environmental Protection Agency's website and read about recent criminal enforcement cases. What are the similarities and differences between the cases?
3. Search terms such as "music and political protest" and listen to the lyrics of the songs. What and whom are they resisting?

Resources

A chart of EPA violations: www.thecrimereport.org/news/inside-criminal-justice /2014-07-environmental-crime-the-prosecution-gap.
An interactive map of EPA violations: www.thecrimereport.org/epa-violators.

References

Ambos, K., and Stegmiller, I. (2008). German Research on International Criminal Law. *Criminal Law Forum*, 19(1): 181–198.

Amnesty International (2002). Rwanda: Gacaca: A Question of Justice. December 17. Index No. AFR 47/007/2002. Available at: www.amnesty.org/en/documents/ afr47/007/2002/en/ (accessed on December 14, 2015).

Bennett, A., and Peterson, R. A. (2004). *Music Scenes: Local, Translocal and Virtual*. Nashville, TN: Vanderbilt University Press.

Biron, C. (2014). Criminal Prosecution Rates For Corporate Environmental Crimes Near Zero. Mint Press, July 25. Available at: www.mintpressnews.com/ criminal-prosecution-rates-for-corporate-environmental-crimes-near-zero/194479/ (accessed on October 9, 2015).

Bretton Woods Project (2013). The World Bank and Extractives: A Rich Seam of Controversy. Available at: www.brettonwoodsproject.org/art-569560 (accessed on April 1, 2015).

Cayabyab, M. (2014). Anti-DAP Protests Sign of "Healthy Democracy." INQUIRER.net, July 22. Available at: http://newsinfo.inquirer.net/622275/anti-dap-protests-sign-of-healthy-democracy-palace (accessed on September 11, 2015).

Chatterjee, P. (2012). Chiquita Bananas to Face Columbia Torture Claim. Global Policy Forum, June 30. Available at: www.globalpolicy.org/international-justice/alien-tort-claims-act-6–30/51457-chiquita-bananas-to-face-columbia-torture-claim-. html?itemid=id#654 (accessed on September 11, 2015).

Chomsky, Noam, Foucault, Michel, and Rajchman, John (2006). *The Chomsky–Foucault Debate: On Human Nature*. New York: New Press. [Previously published as *Human Nature: Justice versus Power*, 1974.]

Collins, V., and Rothe, Dawn L. (2014). United States Support for Global Social Justice? Foreign Intervention and Realpolitik in Egypt's Arab Spring. *Social Justice*, 39(4): 1–30.

Department of Justice (2008). Title 9, Chapter 9–28.000 Corporate Charging Guidelines. August 28. Available at: www.justice.gov/sites/default/files/opa/legacy/ 2008/08/28/corp-charging-guidelines.pdf (accessed on September 11, 2015).

Department of Justice (2014). Justice Department Announces Criminal Charge Against Toyota Motor Corporation and Deferred Prosecution Agreement with $1.2 Billion Financial Penalty. Office of Public Affairs, Wednesday, March 19. Available at: www. justice.gov/opa/pr/justice-department-announces-criminal-charge-against-toyota-motor-corporation-and-deferred (accessed on September 11, 2015).

Dunai, M., and Szakacs, G. (2013). Hungary Repays 2008 IMF Loan in Full. Reuters, August 12. Available at: http://uk.reuters.com/article/2013/08/12/uk-hungary-imf-repaid-idUKBRE97B07720130812 (accessed on September 11, 2015).

The Economist (2013). Environmental Protest in China: Volatile Atmosphere. April 1. Available at: www.economist.com/blogs/analects/2014/04/environmental-protest-china (accessed on September 11, 2015).

Express News Service (2013). World Bank Team Faces Protest. April 11. Available at: www.newindianexpress.com/states/odisha/World-Bank-team-faces-protests/2013/04/11/article1539813.ece (accessed on September 10, 2015).

Eyerman, R., and Jamison, A. (1998). *Music and Social Movements: Mobilizing Traditions in the Twentieth Century*. Cambridge: Cambridge University Press.

Ferrell, J. (2001). *Tearing Down the Streets: Adventures in Urban Anarchy*. New York: Palgrave.

Ferrell, J. (2006). *Empire of Scrounge: Inside the Urban Underground of Dumpster Diving, Trash Picking, and Street Scavenging*. New York: New York University Press.

Ferrell, J., Hayward, K., and Young, J. (2008). *Cultural Criminology: An Invitation*. London: SAGE Publications.

Feyerick, D., and Sguelia, K. (2013). "Whitey" Bulger Says He's Not a Snitch, But FBI File Tells a Different Story. CNN, June 25. Available at: www.cnn.com/2013/06/25/justice/whitey-bulger-trial/ (accessed on September 11, 2015).

Foucault, M. (1990). *The Use of Pleasure*. New York: Vintage Books.

Global Policy Forum (2015). Alien Tort Claims Act. June 30. Available at: www.globalpolicy.org/international-justice/alien-tort-claims-act-6–30.html (accessed on September 11, 2015).

Goffman, E. (1961). *Asylums: Essays on the Social Situation of Mental Patients and Other Inmates*. Garden City, NY: Anchor.

Gorchinskaya, K. (2013). Ukraine Can Get EU Cash if it Secures IMF Loan. KyivPost, October 2. Available at: www.kyivpost.com/content/ukraine/ukraine-can-get-eu-cash-if-it-secures-imf-loan-330031.html (accessed on September 11, 2015).

Hitchens, C. (2001). *The Trial of Henry Kissinger*. London: Verso.

Hitt, Mary Anne (2012). "Our Land, Our Decision": Kosovo Protests World Bank and U.S. Plans for New Coal. *Huffington Post*, March 30. Available at: www.huffingtonpost.com/mary-anne-hitt/kosovo-coal-protests_b_1391053.html (accessed on September 10, 2015).

Home Department (2013). Serious and Organised Crime Strategy. The Stationery Office Limited, UK, October.

Human Rights Watch (2006). Looking for Justice: The War Crimes Chamber in Bosnia and Herzegovina [resource document]. February. Available at: www.hrw.org/reports/2006/ij0206/ (accessed on April 1, 2015).

Kauzlarich, D. (2012). Music as Resistance to State Crime and Violence." In E. Stanley and J. McCulloh (eds.), *State Crime and Resistance*, 154–167. London: Routledge.

Kauzlarich, D., and Awsumb, C. M. (2011). Resisting State Violence: The Role of Music. In W. S. DeKeseredy and M. Dragiewicz (eds.), *The Handbook of Critical Criminology*, 501–512. London and New York: Routledge.

Kyte, R. (2011). Profile page for World Bank Vice President and Special Envoy for Climate Change, Rachel Kyte. Available at: www.worldbank.org/en/about/people/vp-rachel-kyte (accessed on April 1, 2015).

Mainhardt, H., and Sinani N. (2012). Draft Country Environmental Analysis Fails to Account for Significant Pollution Costs: Reviewing World Bank's Draft Country Environmental Analysis for Kosovo. Institute for Development Policy, August. Available at: www.bankinformationcenter.org/wp-content/uploads/2012/08/Review+of+WBs+Kosovo+CEA.pdf (accessed on September 10, 2015).

Martin, B. (1994). Protest in a Liberal Democracy. *Philosophy and Social Action*, 20(1–2): 13–24. Available at: www.bmartin.cc/pubs/94psa.html (accessed on September 11, 2015).

Martin, B. (2013). Music and the Politics of Resistance. *Huffington Post*, October 14. Available at: www.huffingtonpost.com/barrett-martin/music-and-the-politics-of_b_4087557.html (accessed on September 11, 2015).

Michalowski, R., and Kramer, R. (2006). *State-Corporate Crime: Wrongdoing at the Intersection of Business and Government*. Piscataway, NJ: Rutgers University Press.

Mostajelean, B. (2008). Foreign Alternatives to the Alien Tort Claims Act: The Success (or Is It Failure) of Bringing Civil Suits against Multinational Corporations that Commit Human Rights Violations. *George Washington International Law Review*, 40: 497–525.

Mullen, J., Hume, T., and Joseph, E. (2014). Hong Kong Protesters Remain on Streets but Allow Government Workers Past. CNN, October 5. Available at: www.cnn.com/2014/10/05/world/asia/china-hong-kong-protests/index.html (accessed on September 10, 2015).

Mychalejko, C. (2005). Indigenous Resistance to Glamis in Guatemala. *Against the Current*, 20(5): 21.

Prupis, N. (2014). UK Workers Stage Mass Protests Against Austerity Measures: Cameron Promises Crackdown on Future Strikes. Common Dreams, July 10. Available at: www.commondreams.org/news/2014/07/10/uk-workers-stage-mass-protests-against-austerity-measures (accessed on September 10, 2015).

Roberts, M., and Moore, R. (2009). Peace Punks and Punks Against Racism: Resource Mobilization and Frame Construction in the Punk Movement. *Music and Arts in Action*, 2: 21–36.

Rothe, D. (2006). Iraq and Halliburton. In R. Michalowski and R. Kramer (eds.), *State-Corporate Crime: Wrongdoing at the Intersection of Business and Government*, 215–238. Piscataway, NJ: Rutgers University Press.

Rothe, D. L., and Friedrichs, D. (2014a). Controlling Crimes of Globalization: A Challenge for International Criminal Justice. In Willem de Lint, Marinella Marmo, and Nerida Chazal (eds.), *Crime and Justice in International Society*, 246–266. London: Routledge.

Rothe, D. L., and Friedrichs, D. O. (2014b). *Crimes of Globalization*. New York: Routledge.

Rothe, D. L. and Kauzlarich, D. (2010). State-Level Crime: Theory and Policy. In Hugh D. Barlow and Scott Decker (eds.), *Crime and Public Policy: Putting Theory to Work*, 166–187. 2nd edition. Philadelphia, PA: Temple University Press.

Rothe, D. L., and Mullins, C. W. (2006). *The International Criminal Court: Symbolic Gestures and the Generation of Global Social Control*. Lanham, MD: Lexington.

Sarfaty, G. (2012). *Values in Translation: Human Rights and the Culture of the World Bank*. Redwood City, CA: Stanford University Press.

Smeulers, A. (2008). Perpetrators of International Crimes: Towards a Typology. In A. Smeulers and R. Haveman (eds.), *Supranational Criminology: Towards a Criminology of International Crimes*, 487–512. Antwerp: Intersentia.

United Nations Office for the Coordination of Humanitarian Affairs (2008). Organization Reports Page Including IRIN Reports [resource document]. Available at: www.unocha.org/what-we-do/policy/thematic-areas/evaluations-of-humanitarian-response/reports#2008 (accessed on April 1, 2015).

Walt, V. (2011). A Gaddafi Arrest Warrant Raises the Stakes in Libya. *Time*, June 27. Available at: http://content.time.com/time/world/article/0,8599,2080052,00.html (accessed on April 1, 2015).

World Development Movement (2013). World Bank Fuelling Dirty Energy. Global Justice Now, March 17. Available at: www.globaljustice.org.uk/news/2010/mar/17/world-bank-fuelling-dirty-energy (accessed on September 11, 2015).

Chapter 13

A counterview

Law as violence and facilitator of crimes of the powerful

The normality of violence and crimes of the powerful

> What may be most difficult to see is that to use law is also to invoke violence, at least the violence that stands behind legal authority ... The reverse is also true—to use violence is also to invoke the law, the law that stands behind war, legitimating and permitting violence.
>
> (Kennedy 2009)

In Chapter 12 we presented the normal criminological discussion of controlling crimes of the powerful, the existing structures, regulations, and laws that are all state created and sanctioned responses to these harms and crimes. In this chapter we propose an alternative view, one which we both hold: law is a system of violence and a tool that legitimates other forms of violence and harm perpetrated by the powerful, as reflected in the opening quote. After all, any debate on controlling crimes of the powerful, on the activities of the world's owners and players is organized by these same entities and individuals where "everything is said about the extensive means at its disposal to ensure that nothing is said about their deployment" or alternatives. Law then, should be seen as reflective of the existing power relations, which are structured, repetitious, and self-reproduced (Hörnqvist 2010) by the "states of domination" (Foucault 1997: 283). Moreover, as discussed in Chapter 14, law and the subsequent domination of populations is further legitimated, reproduced, facilitated and consumed by "the rest of us."

The box of neoliberalism, globalization, and power

If we can accept the above and the previous discussions of the symbiotic nature of these crimes, it should come as no surprise that law and the "systems" of control for crimes of the powerful are situated and confined within the box of laissez-faire "neoliberalism" dominated by the most powerful players and elites, ensuring asymmetrical power relations. After all, we have rules of warfare that dictate levels of acceptable violence, corporate legislation that is lobbied for by corporations to ensure their own protection, and states sponsoring elites that commit horrendous crimes through the casuistry of law. We have organized crime groups committing transnational crimes from arms trafficking to drug distribution that survive and are protected through the support of heads of state, military and high-ranking officials, legitimated through national security interests, temporary legislation, or executive orders. Consider the course of the last century, where political perspectives ranged from communist movements to liberalism to neoconservatist policies; where calls for controls regulation, deregulation, human rights, and international criminal justice systems all were made, retracked or watered down; where international financial institutions went from giving aid and rebuilding countries after World War II to laissez-faire economics and hyper-privatization; in the end, all swung from one ideological perspective to another like a pendulum, but only as far as the box of power and neoliberalism allowed.

The market has become the "organizing principle for all political, social, and economic decisions, neoliberalism wages an incessant attack on democracy, public goods, and non-commodified values" (Giroux 2005: 2). Neoliberalism can be seen in how "corporations have been increasingly freed from social control through deregulation, privatization, and other neoliberal measures" (Tabb 2003: 153), where democracy becomes a word meaning free market. This lends to power being centralized in the hands of the few, those who create, implement, and deny the harms and the need for social control for the crimes of the powerful: where the violence of crimes of the powerful is not separated from the subjective nature of the mediatized and politicized discourse and framing. The following sections provide several examples of how law legitimates and facilitates crimes of the powerful.

The rule of law: to control what?

As we have previously discussed, critical scholars have long noted that law is used in a subjective manner to control some actions, generally those of the surplus population, while legitimating violence sanctioned by the elite. As asserted by Cover (1986: 1601), "[l]egal interpretation takes place in a field of pain and death. This is true in several senses. Legal interpretive acts signal and occasion the imposition of violence upon others ... Neither legal interpretation nor the violence it occasions may be properly understood apart from one another." This includes domestic laws applied to the "street" criminal or those interpreted to legitimate the crimes of the powerful. Let us first consider international and domestic law that legitimates and confers violence in the context of war and peace.

Laws of warfare

If we consider international humanitarian law (IHL), we can see how law legitimates many forms of state violence. To recap on our discussion in the previous chapter, contemporary IHL (*jus in bello*) is split into international armed conflict (IAC) and non-international armed conflict (NIAC). Treaties include The Hague Conventions of 1899 and 1907, the Geneva Conventions I and II, relating to the treatment of the wounded and sick, Convention III that addresses the treatment of prisoners of war, and Convention IV that is meant to protect civilians. There are also the two Additional Protocols of 1977 that relate to protecting victims of international armed conflicts, and the third Additional Protocol of 2005 and the United Nations Charter of 1945. More recently, the statutes for the International Criminal Tribunal for the former Yugoslavia (ICTY), the International Criminal Tribunal for Rwanda (ICTR), and the 1998 Rome Statute of the International Criminal Court (ICC) serve as foundations of humanitarian law, in this case specifying what is considered prosecutable at the international level: war crimes, crimes against humanity, and genocide.

Humanitarian law, the rules governing warfare noted above, confers legitimacy on military action, that is, state violence: it has legitimized it rather than restrained it. It codifies "sovereignty, upholds territorial and border controls, economic, regulatory and tax sovereignty, control over airspace, sea-lanes, natural resources ... The use of law to validate the practices of sovereign states is perhaps most clear with regard to the laws of war." Jochnick and Normand (1994: 56) have also argued that the laws of war provide legitimacy for state violence due to the way states codified an elastic definition of necessity. "Through overly broad and unchallenged conceptions of military necessity and military objectives, international law has legitimized and facilitated state practices" (Kramer 2009).

Consider that the ban on dropping explosives and projectiles from balloons was negotiated at the Hague Conference in 1899. However, due to aircraft programs in Germany, Russia, and the United States, and the advent of the flight in 1903 in the United States, legal curbs on the new technological tool were adamantly opposed, fearing it would hinder the competitive advantage of the new technology (Watt 1979). During World War II, when massive bombing—carpet bombing—existed without the ability to discriminate between civilians and military targets, statutes governing the Nuremberg and Tokyo Tribunals did not criminalize the behavior regardless of the extant humanitarian laws in place, as the victors had fully carried out such practices. "The Hague Conferences were recognisably of our own era. No major power gave away anything that could be of use to it; no weapon was banned if any major power had serious need of it" (Best 1991: 20). Military necessity/desire was the dominant principle undergirding the laws of war, given that submarines were excluded just as air warfare became legitimate without being restrained (Jochnick and Normand 1994).

More recently, we see this with the use of drones and targeted assassinations. As Smith (2002: 356–357) notes, "new military technology invariably has been matched by technical virtuosity in the law. New legal interpretations, diminished ad bellum restraints, and an expansive view of military necessity are coalescing in a regime of legal warfare that licenses" war as long as their actions are deemed to be just. The language woven into the Hague and Geneva laws through to the most recent Rome Statute is that civilians shall not be "the object" of attacks, and that attacks shall not be "directed at" civilians or "calculated" to produce civilian suffering (Smith 2002: 360). While civilians are thought to be protected, there is legal malleability where civilian death, or collateral damage, is legally defensible. Here Thomas Aquinas' doctrine of double effect formulated in the thirteenth century remains, where even foreseen bad consequences are acceptable as long as they are unintended. This general ideology continues to undergird the legal doctrine protecting civilians where they become unintended collateral damage or the "incidental accompaniment" to war (Ford 1944: 289). As stated by the Special Rapporteur on the promotion and protection of human rights and fundamental freedoms while countering terrorism, Ben Emmerson (2013: 6), "while the fact that civilians have been killed or injured does not necessarily point to a violation of international humanitarian law, it undoubtedly raises issues of accountability and transparency." Humanitarian law is ripe with this level of casuistry. Additional Geneva Convention 1977 Protocol I Article 52(2) defines military objectives as "those objects which by their nature, location, purpose or use make an effective contribution to military action and whose total or partial destruction, capture or neutralisation, in the circumstances ruling at the time, offers a definite military advantage."

The law defers to military necessity and it bestows on those same military demands the psychological trappings of legality. "The result has been to legalize and thus to justify in the public mind 'inhumane military methods and their consequences,' as violence against civilians is carried out 'behind the protective veil of justice'" (Jochnick and Normand 1994a: 50). The same can be said with the legal casuistry of states' right to self-defense under international humanitarian law. Related specifically to the use of drones, the United States and other countries claim that the law of self-defense entitles states to "engage in non-consensual military operations on the territory of another State against armed groups that pose a direct and immediate threat of attack, even where those groups have no operational connection with their host State," based on the United Nations Security Council Resolutions 1368 (2001a) and 1373 (2001b).

We must also briefly examine the laws governing (or legitimating) assassinations, as these are relevant to our argument of the normality of state violence through and within the law. The use of "lethal force" and "targeting" are recognized as legal, or not criminalized, in the UN Charter, the Geneva Conventions' other significant law governing warfare, as previously mentioned. Further, as noted by the Special Rapporteur (2013: 6) on the promotion and protection of human rights and fundamental freedoms while countering terrorism, the "meaning and significance" of the term targeted killings "differ according to the legal regime applicable in specific factual circumstances. In a situation qualifying as an armed conflict, the adoption of a pre-identified list of individual military targets is not unlawful; if based upon reliable intelligence it is a paradigm application of the principle of distinction." Additionally, the use of force must be stated as "necessary," comply with notions of proportionality, and minimize civilian casualties.

The notions of necessity and proportionality are left difficult to assess and are ambiguous enough to allow legal casuistry in their application. The legitimation of assassination in war is more easily manipulated by the United States owing to the fact that they have not ratified the Additional Protocols to the Geneva Conventions. The above combine with the concept of military advantage, which is also ambiguous and easily manipulated within the confines of the social constructionism of military objectives and efforts to legitimate actions through the legal discourse and casuistry of lawyers. As noted by Keeva (1991: 59), commanding officers "have come to realize that, as in the relationship of corporate counsel to CEO, the JAG's [Judge Advocate General] role is not to create obstacles, but to find legal ways to achieve his client's goals—even when those goals are to blow things up and kill people." The recent case of the United States' over-encompassing "war on terrorism," the invasion and occupation of Iraq, the legal manipulation of torture, the defining of prisoners of war as "enemy combatants," and the unlimited detention all highlight the role of juridical manipulation to legitimate practices within the parameters of law.

Consider also the crime of assassination and US domestic laws. As with the language of the laws at the international level, the US doctrines of warfare contain the same mechanisms to justify and legitimize the various political administration of violence. Further, when domestic laws are enacted to curb state violence, they are often reversed to allow the continuation of violence when deemed "necessary." Consider the February 18, 1976, Executive Order No. 11905 (2–305) issued by President Gerald Ford that states "no employee of the United States Government shall engage in, or conspire to engage in political assassinations" (United States Foreign Intelligence Activities 1976). This was reaffirmed with Executive Orders No. 12036 (United States Foreign Intelligence Activities 1978) and No. 12333 (United States Foreign Intelligence Activities 1981) by Jimmy Carter and Ronald Reagan respectively. However, as noted by Lotrionte (2003: 75), "nowhere in the executive orders of Ford ... Carter or Reagan that continued the ban on assassination is there a definition for the term. Although this omission may possibly have been a mere oversight in drafting, it was more likely an intentional effort to grant the president flexibility in interpreting the applicability of this order." Furthermore, the Executive Orders were only intended to prohibit the killing of foreign political leaders when the United States was not engaged in armed conflict with those countries. The ban on assassinations was meant to control the activities of the Central Intelligence Agency during a time of peace. Moreover, Executive Order No. 12333 specifically states that assassinations are exempt from any executive order banning assassinations "when the death is incidental to a military action" (Foreign and Military Intelligence 1976: 448). The Terrorist Elimination Act of 2001, while not passed, does set the stage for direct legal sanctioning of state violence: the following provisions of executive orders shall have no further force or effect: (1) Section 5(g) of Executive Order No. 11905; (2) Section 2–305 of Executive Order No. 12036 and; (3) Section 2.11 of Executive Order No. 12333.

The Patriot Acts of 2001 and 2005 and the Intelligence Reform and Terrorism Prevention Act of 2004 are other examples of where state violence is conducted through the law, expanding its powers and reducing those of civilians as well as "alleged or suspected terrorists." It is not the state of emergency that authorizes such actions, or where they are conducted with impunity, rather the state of emergency is another tool that is regularly used by the United States to continue with legal expansionism and casuistry. Consider that, since 2001, the United States continues to declare a state of emergency to ensure legality in its "war on terrorism."

> Because the terrorist threat continues, the national emergency declared on September 14, 2001, and the powers and authorities adopted to deal with that emergency must continue in effect beyond September 14, 2013. Therefore, I am continuing in effect for an additional year the national emergency that was declared on September 14, 2001, with respect to the terrorist threat.
>
> (Obama 2013a: 107)

This continues the "right" to carry on the "war on terrorism" originally granted by the September 18, 2001, Authorization for Use of Military Force:

> [T]he President is authorized to use all necessary and appropriate force against those nations, organizations, or persons he determines planned, authorized, committed, or aided the terrorist attacks that occurred on September 11, 2001, or harbored such organizations or persons, in order to prevent any future acts of international terrorism against the United States by such nations, organizations or persons.
>
> (Obama 2013a: 107)

This expressly permits pre-emptive action against non-state actors (Friedman 2012) and includes the needed legal aspect ensuring the United States "abides" by rules of international law (self-defense):

Whereas, such acts render it both necessary and appropriate that the United States exercise its rights to self-defense and to protect United States citizens both at home and abroad; and Whereas, in light of the threat to the national security and foreign policy of the United States posed by these grave acts of violence; and Whereas, such acts continue to pose an unusual and extraordinary threat to the national security and foreign policy of the United States; and Whereas, the President has authority under the Constitution to take action to deter and prevent acts of international terrorism against the United States.

(Obama 2013a)

The scope of legal powers to carry on the war and the legitimation of state violence in terms of targeted killings are carried out within the confines of law. The US policy for the use of assassinations states that "there must be a legal basis for using lethal force," that it will only use targeted killings "against a target that poses a continuing, imminent threat," and if an "assessment that the relevant governmental authorities in the country where action is contemplated cannot or will not effectively address the threat to U.S. persons" (The White House 2013). It is these doctrines and ideologies that also allow the legal manipulation of the "right" of the United States to conduct military operations in Syria at the time of this writing, covertly and with ground troops, in the name of fighting terrorism—in this case non-Western or non-Global North friendly Islamic insurgencies.

Summary

The examples of international law legitimating violence are but a few of those that could be drawn on to illustrate our point. One need only consider the use of torture and the manipulation of the existing laws that allow some harmful interrogation techniques, while disavowing others—allowing interpretations to be made legitimating harsher methods, as the United States and others have and continue to rely on. It is not a matter of regulating violence or controlling egregious acts, law is legitimating the violence it claims to control or end. It is a paradoxical tool that is held up as an insurance of justice and end of violence, but is played out as a legitimation of such violence. The following section considers other forms of violence, law legitimation, and crimes of the powerful.

Corporate regulation and control?

As we previously noted, law and regulations "controlling" crimes of the powerful are situated within the box of power and neoliberalism. Regulatory bodies, such as the Consumer Product Safety Commission, the Food and Drug Administration of the United States, the Australian Competition and Consumer Commission or the individual State Consumer Affairs agencies, or the United Kingdom's Office of Fair Trading are examples of agencies that are in place to "protect" the consumer and citizens from harmful products and practices. However, in general terms, regulatory bodies such as those noted above have shifted their focus from protecting consumers to protecting industries: neoliberalism is assimilated at all levels of government and economic policies (Makwana 2009). See Box 13.1.

Box 13.1 Personalizing the impersonal: corporations and the Bill of Rights

Between 1989 and 1992 Americans will celebrate the bicentennial of the ratification of the Bill of Rights. Even more than average citizens, however, corporations and their managers are marking this anniversary with approval because they successfully have used the Bill of Rights as a shield against government regulation. Businesses now wield the Bill of Rights in much the same way that the fourteenth amendment was used during the Progressive era when corporations impeded state governmental regulation with constitutional roadblocks. In this sense, the supposedly defunct doctrine of substantive due process—under which the Court imposes its own economic views to strike down regulation—retains surprising vitality. Indeed, the current era can be characterized as one of corporate due process.

Consider, for example, the following recent Supreme Court decisions: a textile corporation successfully invoked the fifth amendment double jeopardy clause to avoid retrial in a criminal antitrust action; a consortium of major corporations, including the First National Bank of Boston, joined in a first amendment lawsuit that overturned state restrictions on corporate spending for political referendums; an electrical and plumbing concern invoked the fourth amendment to thwart federal inspections conducted under the Occupational Safety and Health Act; and a California public utility relied on the first amendment to overturn state regulations designed to lower utility rates.

The corporations' invocation of the first ten amendments symbolizes the transformation of our constitutional system from one of individual freedoms to one of organizational prerogatives.

(From Carl J. Mayer 1991.)

Consider the processes of deregulation of markets, intensifying from the late 1980s to today, and how that supports the corporate sector, not the consumer (see Box 13.2 for an example).

The electricity sector is a prime example of how deregulation led to corporate profit while harming the environment and citizens. Over the course of the past two decades, governments around the world have restructured,

---

Box 13.2 Texas and electricity deregulation

In the first few years after Texas joined the race to deregulate the electricity sector in 2002, the residential rate for electricity increased nearly seven fold. According to a 2014 report by the Texas Coalition for Affordable Power (TCAP), "deregulation cost Texans about $22 billion from 2002 to 2012." Residents that live in areas in Texas that are participating in the deregulation "pay prices that are considerably higher than those who live in parts of the state that are still regulated" (Dyer 2014).

---

deregulated, and privatized electricity systems. As a result, there have been worldwide cases of blackouts, price manipulations, price fixing, bankruptcies, and electricity shortages while the electricity sector profit levels have soared. In the United States, by the end of the 1990s, the increase of technology stocks put pressure on the energy industry to achieve higher rates of return, "as Wall Street threatened to move its capital elsewhere unless energy companies found a way around their tightly controlled profit margins" (Slocum 2001: 2). The end result was heavy lobbying by energy sectors for deregulation, which they got, resulting in power companies significantly increasing prices for profit, leaving consumers to pay higher prices. For example, Enron lobbied the US government very successfully to deregulate the electricity market, the trading of energy futures, and to create a blanket of secrecy of futures contracts that enabled it to trade without revealing any financial details to regulators or the public. This was all part of the conditions that led to the collapse of Enron after huge financial gains had been made by the few at the top of the Enron food chain.

The stories and results are echoed across the globe. For example, in New Zealand, electricity costs to households have continuously been rising since the mid-1980s, when the Electricity Corporation of New Zealand (ECNZ) was set up to operate on a for-profit commercial basis. The process of deregulation has led to blackouts such as the Auckland blackout of 1998, and the manipulation of "shortages" of electricity, spiking profits, and the recent electricity shortages. Australian states began deregulation much later, in 1998, with some of the same stories. Additionally, in 2013, the state's energy watchdog, the Essential Services Commission (ESCOSA), lost its ability to be effective in that it could no longer control the contract price for electricity and gas. Instead, the leading energy corporations, AGL and Origin Energy, set the prices as a result of a compromise where oversight was removed "in return for AGL dropping legal action against the commission" (ABC Australian News 2013: 1).

Other systems of regulation have been watered down including those that protect workers. Consider the case in the United Kingdom where law has been used to decrease workers' protections while strengthening corporations' rights and protections with changes to the Transfer of Undertakings and Protection of Employment (TUPE) legislation. TUPE is supposed to protect employees' pay and conditions of work when a business is transferred from one corporation or entity to another, so that they enjoy the same terms including pay and benefits, roughly estimated to affect 26,000 to 48,000 employees each year. The change made by the government in 2014 substantially weakens these protections and reduces job security. Under the new legislation, all employers can renegotiate even collective agreements after 12 months, including layoffs, cuts to pay, and dismissals. As noted by TUC General Secretary Frances O'Grady (2015: 1), "[w]atering down TUPE law means hundreds of thousands of vulnerable workers around the UK will lose out on vital protections at work. This is a deliberate bid by government to make privatisation cheaper and quicker." As would be expected, the Department for Business, Innovation and Skills consulted on the legislation and has since stated that the "simpler, more flexible employment laws" are designed to "remove unfair legal risks from businesses."

Summary

Law, regulations, and civil retort for corporate crimes are often framed within the context of capitalist systems at the expense of consumers and workers. In the United States, recent decisions by the Supreme Court have been a victory for CEOs and managers of large corporations "against the quaint, old-fashioned claims for fairness and justice brought by mere citizens, states, consumers, workers, company whistle-blowers, doctors, patients, parents, and corporate shareholders" (Raskin 2014: 1). Given the global nature of these corporations, it should not be surprising that we are witness to a host of support systems and protections for corporations including those regulated by the World Trade Organization. As with crimes by governments, law, while said to be present to constrain or control harms and protect civilians, yet legitimated violence and harm; legal regimes for corporations are used to protect the corporation, the vested economic interests of the state at the expense of you and me. Even when corporate or state crimes occur and are revealed, we see that law is used to protect levels of secrecy and the corporate and state form. The following section highlights how whistleblowers are demonized and punished using law, while simultaneous claims are made that protections for them have been strengthened.

Law as a suppressive tool: whistleblowers and crimes of the powerful?

> The greatest rogue in the whole land is, and will remain, the informer.
> (Hoffmann von Fallersleben (1798–1874), author
> of the lyrics of the German national anthem)

The most common response to whistleblowing is to suggest better whistle-blower protection legislation. However, as with all laws that perpetuate or facilitate violence, whistleblower laws are flawed with exemptions, in-built weaknesses, and are rarely helpful, as the terms of political discourse and manipulation of the conditions of whistleblowing are more often than not turned to protect corporations, international financial institutions, and states. While it is claimed that there are now more protections for whistleblowers who divulge information on the crimes, harms, and abuses by governments, corporations, and international financial institutions, the praxis is quite the opposite. Rather, while legislation is occurring across the globe in the name of protecting whistleblowers, governments are following this symbolic appeasement with harsher punishment and the creation or manipulation of existing laws to penalize those whistleblowers from the press and media (*The Guardian*, *New York Times*), agents working within the state (Bradley Manning, Edward Snowden), or in international financial institutions (Karen Hudes and the World Bank). As noted in the opening quote, regardless of rhetoric, more often than not a whistleblower is viewed as being a threat to the system: a rogue.

In the United States, the 2013 National Defense Authorization Act, for example, includes a small, mostly unread, statement that produces ambiguity and room for legal casuistry against whistleblowers. President Barack Obama noted that the bill's whistleblowing protections "could be interpreted in a manner that would interfere with my authority to manage and direct execu-tive branch officials"; as such, if they conflicted with his power to "supervise, control, and correct employees' communications with the Congress in cases where such communications would be unlawful or would reveal information that is properly privileged or otherwise confidential" (Obama 2013b), national security and his authority would take precedence. Here again, the crackdown on whistleblowers, particularly those revealing state crimes and harms, is not unique to the United States (see Box 13.3).

Box 13.3 Whistleblowers and law

The United States has used control mechanisms against individuals and organizations that attempt to whistle-blow and/or disclose government documents deemed to be important to the general public. Consider the landmark 1971 case, New York Times Company vs. US. This was the first effort by the federal government in contemporary times to control the publication of a newspaper. *The New York Times* received and pub-lished articles from a leaked copy of a Rand report (authored by Daniel Ellsberg and later known as the "Pentagon Papers"), on the military sit-uation in Vietnam. The appellate courts' indecisiveness brought the ulti-mate decision to the Supreme Court, which ruled that a prior control of

publication would be allowed only in the most extraordinary cases that threatened grave and immediate danger to the security of the US. This case was central to the March 2006 controversy surrounding the publication of leaked information exposing the National Security Agency's secret surveillance program on US citizens. These cases were taken to court using the 1917 Espionage Act. Likewise, in 2001, former Attorney General John Ashcroft commissioned a group of top intelligence professionals to examine the legal authority to charge government agents who leak unauthorized classified information under the Espionage Act. In a letter to Congress, Ashcroft stated the government needed to "entertain new approaches to deter, identify, and punish those who engage in the practice of unauthorized disclosure of classified information" ... Subsequently, several investigations ensued, including inquiries into the secret war plans leaked to *The New York Times* and *The Washington Post* and the leak of a letter written by Secretary of State Colin Powell to the Pentagon objecting to the Syria Accountability Act. On 30 December 2005, authorities undertook an additional criminal investigation into the circumstances surrounding the disclosed information exposing the National Security Agency's secret eavesdropping program. This case is highly controversial, as it tested the contradiction between the media's ability to report on national security issues of public interest, improperly classified material, and as a constraint against unwarranted government secrecy and/or illegal activities against governmental claims of national defense and issues of security.
(From Ross and Rothe 2008.)

In July 2014, Australia's attorney general proposed a bill that would have whistleblowers face up to ten years in prison for leaks on special intelligence operations. In the end of 2013, in Canada, the House of Commons demanded its employees sign a comprehensive, lifetime "gag order" with draconian sanctions for any breach. Some Canadians believe that, regardless of the Canadian government's "rhetoric, Canadian whistleblowers are actually worse off today than they were 10 years ago. The laws and agencies that are supposed to protect them simply don't work; and even Charter rights are being stripped away by deceptive legislation and perverse codes of conduct" (Hutton 2013: 2).

Summary

While law is used to facilitate or legitimate many crimes of the powerful, as we have highlighted here, it is also used to curb counter forces, checks and balances, and potential risk factors to the existing economic relationships and interests of the powerful. The most well-known case in recent history that may come to mind is Edward Snowden and the politicization and media coverage of his actions that was reflected in the political rhetoric of the left, with the right painting him as a traitor or a whistleblower, while the US political administration used much political clout to ensure the potential to try him as a traitor through law and hegemonic discourse of national security.

We caution students to take a critical look when calls are made to draw on or expand the "rule of law" to address crimes of the powerful, as it is through the law that they are legitimated and in many cases sanctioned. Furthermore, by uncritically thinking that law might bring "justice" or "accountability" to various social injustices we are reproducing the same conditions and are complicit with the liberalism that has ravaged the world, often through law.

Activities and discussion questions

1. Search for anarchist writings on the limits and problems of law and compare those positions with our arguments about law serving the interests of the powerful.
2. Why do people generally think that law is a good way to stop or solve a problem? Why isn't it?
3. To what extent do laws reflect economic versus democratic interests when it comes to addressing crimes of the powerful?

Resource

Students may want to watch the HBO film *Citizenfour* (2014).

References

ABC Australian News (2013). Power Price Deregulation Comes into Effect. February 1. Available at: www.abc.net.au/news/2013-02-01/power-price-deregulation-comes-into-effect/4495348 (accessed on September 4, 2015).

Best, G. (1991). The Restraint of War in Historical and Philosophical Perspective. In J. Astrid, M. Dilissen, and G. J. Tanja (eds.), *Humanitarian Law of Armed Conflict*, 3–26. Challenges Ahead. The Netherlands: Martinus Nijhoff Publishers.

Bowcott, O. (2013). Drone Strikes by US May Violate International Law, Says UN. *The Guardian*, October 18. Available at: www.theguardian.com/world/2013/oct/18/drone-strikes-us-violate-law-un (accessed on September 4, 2015).

Cover, R. (1986). Violence in the World. *Yale Law Journal*, 95(8) (July): 1601–1629. Available at: http://digitalcommons.law.yale.edu/cgi/viewcontent.cgi?article=3687&context=fss_papers (accessed on September 4, 2015).

Dyer, R. A. (2014). Deregulated Electricity in Texas. Texas Coalition for Affordable Power, February. Available at: http://tcaptx.com/wp-content/uploads/2014/02/TCP-793-Deregulation2014-A-1.7.pdf (accessed on September 10, 2015).

Ford, J. C. (1944). The Morality of Obliteration Bombing. *Theological Studies*, 5: 261–309.

Foreign and Military Intelligence (1976). Final Report of the Select Committee to Study Governmental Operations with Respect to Intelligence Activities (94th Congress, 2nd Session, April 26, S. Rept. 755) [resource document]. Available at: https://ia600400.us.archive.org/18/items/finalreportofsel01unit/finalreportofse-l01unit.pdf (accessed on September 4, 2015).

Foucault, M. (1997). The Ethics of the Concern for Self as a Practice of Freedom. In P. Rabinow (ed.), *Ethics: Subjectivity and Truth*, 281–302. London: Allen Lane.

Friedman, U. (2012). Targeted Killings: A Short History: How America Came to Embrace Assassination. *Foreign Policy*, August 13 [resource document]. Available at: www.foreignpolicy.com/articles/2012/08/13/targeted_killings (accessed on November 16, 2013).

Giroux, H. (2005). The Terror of Neoliberalism: Rethinking the Significance of Cultural Politics. *College Literature*, 32(1) (Winter): 1–19.

Hörnqvist, M. (2010). *Risk, Power and State*. Abingdon, Oxon: Routledge.

Hutton, D. (2013). Canada's Crackdown on Government Whistleblowers. The Star, December 20. Available at: www.thestar.com/opinion/commentary/2013/12/20/canadas_crackdown_on_government_whistleblowers.html (accessed on September 5, 2015).

Jochnick, C., and Normand, R. (1994). The Legitimation of Violence: A Critical history of the Laws of War. *Harvard International Law Journal*, 35(1): 49–91.

Keeva, S. (1991). Lawyers in the War Room. *ABA Journal*, December: 52–59.

Kennedy, D. (2009). *Modern War and Modern Law: Presentation*. The Suffolk Transnational Law Review Distinguished Speaker Series. Boston, MA: Suffolk Law School.

Kramer, R. (2009). Resisting the Bombing of Civilians: Challenges From a Public Criminology of State Crime. *Social Justice*, 36(3): 78–97.

Lotrionte, C. (2003). When to Target Leaders. *The Washington Quarterly*, 26(3): 73–86.

Makwana, R. (2009). Can Economic Growth Stop Climate Change? Sharing.org, May 26. Available at: www.sharing.org/information-centre/articles/can-economic-growth-stop-climate-change (accessed on December 14, 2015).

Mayer, J. (1991). Personalizing the Impersonal: Corporations and the Bill of Rights. *Hastings Law Journal*, 41(3): 1. Available at: http://reclaimdemocracy.org/mayer_personalizing/ (accessed on September 11, 2015).

Obama, Barack (2013a). Notice: Continuation of National Emergency. The White House Office of the Press Secretary, September 10. Available at: www.whitehouse.gov/the-press-office/2013/09/10/notice-continuation-national-emergency-notice (accessed on December 14, 2015).

Obama, Barack (2013b). Statement by the President on H.R. 4310. The White House Office of the Press Secretary, January 3. Available at: www.whitehouse.gov/the-press-office/2013/01/03/statement-president-hr-4310 (accessed on December 14, 2015).

O'Grady, Lynne (2015). Weakening TUPE Law Will Put Hundreds of Thousands of Workers at Risk, warns TUC. Available at: www.tuc.org.uk/workplace-issues/basic-rights-work/employment-rights/your-rights-work/weakening-tupe-law-will-put (accessed on September 4, 2015).

Raskin, J. (2014). The Citizens United Era: How the Supreme Court Continues to Put Business First. PFAW. Available at: www.pfaw.org/media-center/publications/citizens-united-era-how-supreme-court-continues-put-business-first (accessed on September 4, 2015).

Slocum, T. (2001). Electric Utility Deregulation and the Myths of the Energy Crisis. December 14. "Energy Controversy" issue of *Bulletin of Science, Technology & Society*, 21(6). Edited by Steven M. Hoffman. Available at: www.citizen.org/documents/MYTHS_Report.pdf (accessed on December 22, 2015).

Smith, T. W. (2002). The New Law of War: Legitimizing Hi-Tech and Infrastructural Violence. *International Studies Quarterly*, 46(3): 355–374.

The Special Rapporteur (2013). Promotion and Protection of Human Rights and Fundamental Freedoms While Countering Terrorism. United Nations General Assembly. September 18. Available at: www.justsecurity.org/wp-content/uploads/2013/10/2013EmmersonSpecialRapporteurReportDrones.pdf (accessed on September 4, 2015).

Tabb, W. (2003). Race to the Bottom?. In Stanley Aronowitz and H. Gautney (eds.), *Implicating Empire: Globalization and Resistance in the 21st Century World Order*, 151–158. New York: Basic Books.

von Fallersleben, H. (1798–1874). German National Anthem. Available at: www.fallersleben-bildungswerk.de/hoffmann.html (accessed on September 4, 2015).

Watt, D. (1979). Restraints on War in the Air Before 1945. In M. Howard (ed.), *Restraints on War: Studies in the Limitation of Armed Conflict*, 57–77. Oxford: Oxford University Press.

The White House (2013a). Fact Sheet: U.S. Policy Standards and Procedures for the Use of Force in Counterterrorism Operations Outside the United States and Areas of Active Hostilities. The White House Office of the Press Secretary, May 23 [resource document]. Available at: www.whitehouse.gov/the-press-office/2013/05/23/fact-sheet-us-policy-standards-and-procedures-use-force-counterterrorism (accessed on November 18, 2013).

Official laws and documents resources bibliography

Protocols I Additional to the Geneva Convention (1977).

Protocol Additional to the Geneva Conventions of August 12, 1949, and relating to the Protection of Victims of International Armed Conflicts (Protocol I), June 8, 1977.

Protocols II Additional to the Geneva Convention (1977). Protocol Additional to the Geneva Conventions of August 12, 1949, and relating to the Protection of Victims of Non-International Armed Conflicts (Protocol II), June 8, 1977. The ICRC Resource Center. Resource document available at: www.icrc.org/applic/ihl/ihl.nsf/Treaty.xsp?documentId=AA0C5BCBAB5C4A85C12563CD002D6D09&action=openDocument (accessed on November 11, 2013).

Protocols III additional to the Geneva Convention (2005). Protocol Additional to the Geneva Conventions of August 12, 1949, and Relating to the Adoption of an Additional Distinctive Emblem (Protocol III), December 8, 2005. The ICRC Resource Center. Resource document available at: www.icrc.org/applic/ihl/ihl.nsf/Treaty.xsp?documentId=8BC1504B556D2F80C125710F002F4B28&action=openDocument (accessed on November 11, 2013).

The Geneva Conventions (1949). Conventions I, II, III, IV. ICRC Treaty Database. Resource document available at: www.icrc.org/ihl.nsf/WebNORM?OpenView (accessed on October 7, 2013).

The Hague Conventions (1899). Convention (II) with Respect to the Laws and Customs of War on Land and its Annex: Regulations Concerning the Laws and Customs of War on Land. The Hague, July 29, 1899. Resource document available at: www.icrc.org/applic/ihl/ihl.nsf/Treaty.xsp?documentId=CD0F6C83F96FB459 C12563CD002D66A1&action=openDocument (accessed on November 28, 2013).

The Hague Conventions (1907). Convention (IV) Respecting the Laws and Customs of War on Land and its Annex: Regulations Concerning the Laws and Customs of War on Land. The Hague, October 18, 1907. Resource document available at: www. icrc.org/applic/ihl/ihl.nsf/Treaty.xsp?documentId=4D47F92DF3966A7EC12563C D002D6788&action=openDocument (accessed November 28, 2013).

The Hague Conventions (1907). Convention (IX) Concerning Bombardment by Naval Forces in Time of War. The Hague, October 18, 1907. Resource document available at: www.icrc.org/applic/ihl/ihl.nsf/Treaty.xsp?documentId=F13F9FFC628FC33BC 12563CD002D6819&action=openDocument (accessed on November 29, 2013).

The Hague Conventions (1907). Convention (VIII) Relative to the Laying of Automatic Submarine Contact Mines. The Hague, October 18, 1907. Resource document available at: www.icrc.org/applic/ihl/ihl.nsf/Treaty.xsp?documentId=7D389CA23 C22337BC12563CD002D67FF&action=openDocument (accessed November 28, 2013).

The Hague Conventions (1972). Convention on the Prohibition of the Development, Production and Stockpiling of Bacteriological (Biological) and Toxin Weapons and on their Destruction. Opened for Signature at London, Moscow, and Washington. April 10, 1972. Resource document available at: www.icrc.org/applic/ihl/ihl.nsf/ Treaty.xsp?documentId=BACF97285A9CB2A2C12563CD002D6C88&action=op enDocument (accessed on November 29, 2013).

The Hague Conventions (1995). Protocol on Blinding Laser Weapons (Protocol IV to the 1980 Convention, October 13, 1995). Resource document available at: www. icrc.org/applic/ihl/ihl.nsf/Treaty.xsp?documentId=70D9427BB965B7CEC12563FB 0061CFB2&action=openDocument (accessed on November 28, 2013).

The Hague Declarations (1899–1925). Methods and Means of Warfare. Resource document available at: www.icrc.org/applic/ihl/ihl.nsf/ (accessed on November 28, 2013).

The ICRC Resource Center. Resource document available at: www.icrc.org/applic/ihl/ ihl.nsf/Treaty.xsp?documentId=D9E6B6264D7723C3C12563CD002D6CE4&actio n=openDocument (accessed on November 11, 2013).

The Intelligence Reform and Terrorism Prevention Act (2004). Public Law 108–458, 108th Congress. December 17, 2004. Available at: www.nctc.gov/docs/irtpa.pdf (accessed 26 January, 2016).

The Patriot Act (2001). Uniting and Strengthening American by Providing Appropriate Tools Required to Intercept and Obstruct Terrorism (USA Patriot Act) Act of 2001. Resource document available at: www.gpo.gov/fdsys/pkg/PLAW-107publ56/pdf/ PLAW-107publ56.pdf (accessed on November 18, 2013).

The Patriot Act (2005). USA PATRIOT Improvement and Reauthorization Act of 2005. www.GovTrack.us. Resource document available at: www.govtrack.us/ congress/bills/109/hr3199 (accessed on November 29, 2013).

The Rome Statute (1998). The Rome Statute of the International Criminal Court. Resource document available at: www.icc-cpi.int/nr/rdonlyres/ea9aeff7-5752-4f84-be94-0a655eb30e16/0/rome_statute_english.pdf (accessed on November 19, 2013).

The Terrorist Elimination Act (2001). Terrorist Elimination Act of 2001. www.GovTrack.us. Resource document available at: www.govtrack.us/congress/bills/107/hr19 (accessed on November 29, 2013).

The United Nations Charter (1945). Charter of the United Nations. Resource document available at: www.un.org/en/documents/charter/ (accessed on November 18, 2013).

The United Nations Charter (1998). Charter of the United Nations. Resource document available at: www.un.org/en/documents/charter/ (accessed on November 19, 2013).

United Nations General Assembly (2013). Promotion and Protection of Human Rights and Fundamental Freedoms While Countering Terrorism: Document number A/68/389. The United Nations, September 18. Resource document available at: www.un.org/ga/search/view_doc.asp?symbol=A%2F68%2F389&Submit=Search&Lang=E (accessed on November 21, 2013).

United Nations Security Council (2001). Resolution 1368 (2001) Adopted by the Security Council at its 4370th Meeting, on 12 September 2001: Document number S/RES/1368 (2001). Resource document available at: www.un.org/en/ga/search/view_doc.asp?symbol=S/RES/1368(2001) (accessed on November 12, 2013).

United Nations Security Council (2001). Resolution 1373 (2001) Adopted by the Security Council at its 4385th Meeting, on 28 September 2001: Document number S/RES/1373 (2001). Resource document available at: www.un.org/en/ga/search/view_doc.asp?symbol=S/RES/1373(2001) (accessed on November 13, 2013).

United States Foreign Intelligence Activities (1976). Executive Order 11905 (2–305). Weekly Compilation of Presidential Documents. Resource document available at: www.fas.org/irp/offdocs/eo11905.htm (accessed on November 25, 2013).

United States Foreign Intelligence Activities (1978). Executive Orders 12036. Weekly Compilation of Presidential Documents. Resource document available at: www.fas.org/irp/offdocs/eo/eo-12036.htm (accessed on November 25, 2013).

United States Foreign Intelligence Activities (1981). Executive Order 12333. Weekly Compilation of Presidential Documents. Resource document available at: www.archives.gov/federal-register/codification/executive-order/12333.html (accessed on November 25, 2013).

Chapter 14

Conclusion

The limitations of crimes of the powerful

This text has attempted to provide some insight into the crimes of the powerful and to try to disabuse the commonly held belief that these crimes are not as systematic, costly, violent, or harmful as those we hear about with every local and national newscast focusing on the dangerous street criminal or the "others." After all, they are far more than a "business mistake" or "bad apple" or "negligence." Beginning with the overall discussion of crimes of the powerful, we then attempted to illustrate various types of crimes and harms along with highlighting the problematic nature of typologies, given the symbiotic nature of crimes of the powerful combined with the specific cultural, historical, political, and economic conditions. Further, we have attempted to create dialogue on the problematic nature of these divisions within divisions (corporate crime, political crime, occupational crime, state-corporate crime, state crime, crimes of globalization, supranational crime, etc.), as there is a truism in the old adage "divided we fall." In other words, these abstract academic divisions inadvertently serve not only to muddy the waters of research and understanding, but as a blockade to synthesis. We have also attempted to show you the importance that neoliberalism plays in facilitating these crimes. However, as the title *Crimes of the Powerful* suggests, at the root of all of these crimes is power.

Having provided you with the basic tools for understanding the role the media plays in the concealment of crimes of the powerful and theoretical frameworks to help guide our understanding, we hope many of you will continue to explore, research and expose these harms and crimes. Moreover, we hope this text and the discussions and cases of crimes of the powerful has impassioned and outraged you.

Whether you believe in or accept that these types of crimes can be addressed "with the master's tools" or not, the chapters dedicated to examining the potential and the downfall of the current systems of control including law have hopefully given you enough information to critically examine the responses to crimes of the powerful beyond what is fed to us in hegemonic popular discourse.

Perhaps most importantly, we hope that after reading this chapter you will be cognizant of your role and complicity in the facilitation of the crimes of the powerful. This is not partaking in blaming the victims. On the contrary, it is about awareness, as awareness is the first step to any change. As such, we encourage you to continue to be engaged with current events, unveiling or unpeeling the layers of hype, discourse, and social construction: to question why, how, and why not.

The commodification and pacification of crimes of the powerful through our everyday lives

The final section of this text, Chapters 12 and 13, discussed the potentials, or lack thereof, of controls, the problems of using "the master's tools" including law—as it is too a system of violence—and forms of resistance; as such, it seems necessary to us to include a discussion on the role we all play in the ongoing perpetuation of neoliberal economics, consumption, and crimes of the powerful. After all, there is little recognition by most scholars and students of the relationship between the harms and violence of the powerful and our own consumption, pacification, tacit support, and facilitation of these crimes. Mark Neocleous (2012: 189) calls this a "training in resilience" that hardens the public to the spectacle of violent crime, where such violence and harms perpetrated by the powerful are digested and seen as a small price for the greater good of our comforts and mediatized lives. As the novel by Susan Greenfield, *2121*, suggests,

> Then, as the generations became more homogenized into a simple, a single state of continuous, monotonous adulthood, and as the body and the brain were open for all to see, with precision timing, did the screen technologies transform into mobile ones and on to invasive embedded interfacing. All the old compartments were vanishing at once ... between the internal body and the external environment, and between fantasy and reality ... There was so much more to do, so many exciting new experiences to have and technologies to enjoy.
>
> (Greenfield 2013: 225)

This is not to say that we have done so wittingly, rather, it occurs and is reaffirmed in our everyday lives and our consumption of education, propaganda of fear, hegemonic discourse of security, our technofetishism for the latest consumer good, and a host of actions we take every day without thinking of how we are complicit in the perpetual cycle of crimes of the powerful. Have a look at Image 14.1.

Image 14.1 Pacification through education (Image © Clay Butler)

In a similar vein, Omar Khayyam states, "So as to speak clearly and without parables ... We are the pieces of the game that plays the sky; We amuse ourselves with ourselves on the chessboard of Being ... and then we are returned, one by one, to the box of Nothingness" (quoted in Debord 1988).

Many of you may not recall the specifics that occurred in the United States immediately after September 11, 2001, when then President George W. Bush, masking the realities of the upcoming onslaught of state violence, urged citizens to "carry on," "Get down to Disney World in Florida ... Take your families and enjoy life, the way we want it to be enjoyed ... I ask your continued participation and confidence in the American economy" (Bush 2001b). Three months later, he commended citizens for ignoring the onset of state violence as they were pacified in their own daily lives: "People are going about their daily lives, working and shopping and playing, worshiping at churches and synagogues and mosques, going to movies and to baseball games" (Bush 2001a).

We partake in our own oppression, supporting the system that perpetuates crimes of the powerful, the neoliberal capitalistic agenda, the state, the corporations, the elite in general. Consider the common reaction when many of us first heard about the National Security Agency (NSA) "sweeping" data collections from emails, text messages, phone records, search engines, social media outlets, all in the name of surveillance for security. This was followed by revelations that the United States was not alone in this project; countries including New Zealand, Australia, the United Kingdom, to mention a few, had been actively collecting such data in the name of national security. Shortly after these revelations, we were told about the massive numbers of fusion centers bridging corporate interests with state surveillance, primarily located in the United States. We were outraged when we learned that governments, in the United States and abroad, had databases of their citizens' personal information, while simultaneously logging in to our Facebook, Twitter, or Instagram accounts to express our outrage or just posting our latest daily deed. We google the latest products available for consumption, purchase our spot in the "Cloud," join OnStar, use our Google locater app or friends' "hangout" apps, as well as use our car and phone GPS. This is all to say that we are linked in to the very things that control us under the promise of liberation and freedom.

We willingly join supermarket and grocery store loyalty card programs that trade our personal information and surveillance of shopping habits for a minimal discount on groceries. We carry our charge cards, using them to play in the land of consumerism. We jump on the bandwagon to use fingerprint identification or iris identification to shorten lines at airports or on our cell phones for "security." We think nothing of the cameras in the store that monitor our every move; rather, we are outraged if a "crime" occurs and the store cameras were not turned on. We run out to purchase our own "toy" drones, legitimating their use, thus in return validating the government's use of them for our own surveillance. We purchase home security systems that are wired in to our cell phones to monitor any activities, regulate our heat, or turn off the lights. And the list goes on for how we, as citizens, willingly accept surveillance and being monitored in our lives, actively participating and facilitating technological advances that are believed to make our lives "better." These products and "security" features we endure every day have come to be seen as a "fact of life" that "nicely captures the dominant social meaning of banal goods" (Goold *et al.* 2013: 978). It is, as argued by Boghosian (2013: 26), "normalizing cultural obedience through surveillance" to which we are active participants. We have willingly bought into a culture of fear where there is an insidious ideology that lies within this marketing and consumption. As such, we need to resist the security fetish of consumer goods that feed into the programs of surveillance, for it is this that blinds us to state power, perpetuating the system of domination and oppression, and reifies the banality of surveillance (Neocleous 2007).

In a similar vein, let us consider another aspect of our role. Nearly all of our techno-gadgets require coltan and other natural minerals (see Box 14.1).

Box 14.1 Minerals and elements in a cell phone

- Arsenic amplifier, receiver
- Copper electrical circuitry
- Gallium amplifier, receiver
- Gold electrical circuitry
- Indium liquid crystal display (LCD screen)
- Magnesium
- Compounds
- Phone casing
- Palladium electrical circuitry
- Platinum electrical circuitry
- Silver electrical circuitry
- Tin liquid crystal display (LCD screen)
- Tungsten electrical circuitry

We not only purchase all of the new cell phones, latest gadgets, smart tablets, iPads, and so on, but we also do not think about our relationship to the corporate and elite harms and crimes that are associated with their manufacture (see Box 14.2 on this point). Instead, we are concerned with consumption and having the latest and the best, and/or making our lives easier.

Box 14.2 Sierra Leone and cobalt

Like Sierra Leone with its notorious "blood diamonds," the Democratic Republic of Congo that produces major quantities of tin, tungsten, about half of the world's cobalt output and about three percent of the world's copper and gold, has been blighted by "conflict minerals," where the proceeds from resources extracted from mines controlled by government or rebel forces are used to fund war, often utilizing slave labor as a means of mining. Transnational corporations buy these materials in the global trade, while states support the export of the products and international financial institutions often provide loans and support for development of additional mines.

There is an entire e-waste (electronic waste) industry that dumps illegal surplus in Global South countries, lending to harmful toxins destroying waterways, land, and people, as children and those looking for scraps to sell filter through harmful left-over products. See Image 14.2.

Image 14.2 Electronic waste in Accra, Ghana (Credit: SIPA Press/Rex Shutterstock)

Moreover, Vidal (2013) notes:

> The global volume of electronic waste is expected to grow by 33% in the
> next four years, when it will weigh the equivalent of eight of the great
> Egyptian pyramids ... Last year nearly 50m tonnes of e-waste was gener-
> ated worldwide—or about 7kg for every person on the planet. These are
> electronic goods made up of hundreds of different materials and contain-
> ing toxic substances such as lead, mercury, cadmium, arsenic and flame
> retardants ... Once in landfill, these toxic materials seep out into the
> environment, contaminating land, water and the air. In addition, devices
> are often dismantled in primitive conditions. Those who work at these
> sites suffer frequent bouts of illness. An indication of the level of e-waste
> being shipped to the developing world was revealed by Interpol last week.
> It said almost one in three containers leaving the EU that were checked
> by its agents contained illegal e-waste.
>
> (Vidal 2013: 1)

We are all an active part of this process, including us authors, as we also
have our cell phones and computers that we use daily, as do most if not all
of you. As with the technofetishism we spoke of earlier, this consumption of

the latest and best gadgets, vying for the latest apple or smaller and smarter phone, makes us complicit in the process of living in these neoliberal capitalistic consumption states. Perhaps this begins with deliberation, or rejection of the most banal everyday activities. Not only would this mean rejecting the latest electronic gadget, but a broad-base slowing down, withdrawing, indeed "unplugging," from our socially mediated lives is implied. For certain, to live an active, engaged life outside the field of electronic communication is a difficult task. So, it seems to us, the alternative is not to lose sight of the relationship between the state and its subjects, and not to obfuscate the materiality of violence and domination.

State violence is also consumed by us daily in more subtle ways, even celebrated without our considering or perhaps knowing that we are doing just that, often in the name of patriotism, nationalism, or as a spectacle/carnival of entertainment. Consider the number of military air shows across the globe where millions flock to see the "awe" of fighter jets (see Box 14.3), without ever considering the real meaning of violence and death behind them that countries and regions such as Iraq, Syria, Palestine witness daily.

Box 14.3 Some of the largest carnivals of the spectacle

- Royal International Air Tattoo, Gloucestershire, England
- Miramar Air Show, San Diego
- Abbotsford Air Show, Abbotsford, Canada
- RAF Lossiemouth Joint Warrior, Scotland

In cities across the Global North, as the military prepares for the exercise of state power and violence, citizens conusme and enjoy, much like a carnival, the awe of the jets as they fly overhead, taking pictures, buying military products, and souvenirs.

On the other hand, we are outraged, if only momentarily, when we hear of tainted products by corporations, of the use of slave labor, and of unpaid wages to workers, at least for a moment. Yet we continue to shop at stores or buy corporate products from known habitual offenders. Consider the following mini case studies in Boxes 14.4–14.7.

For everyday lifestyle products we willingly consume, facilitating corporate crime, consider the following "worst" corporation list of 2011:

- Baked goods and baking supplies: **Kraft:** Multinational Monitor (MM) "worst corporation list" for the last five years, currently the target of two major boycotts, Greenwash award for public deception, named global climate change laggard *Nestle, Nabisco, Carnation, Banquet.*

Box 14.4 Wal-Mart

Wal-Mart is the biggest corporation in the world. It owns 5,100 stores world-wide and employs 1.3 million workers in the United States and 400,000 abroad, as well as millions more in the factories of its suppliers. Many people have heard of the way that Wal-Mart steamrolls its way into every possible town, destroying local supermarkets and countless small businesses. We have also heard about Wal-Mart's long track record of worker abuse, from forced overtime to sex discrimination to illegal child labor to relentless union busting. Wal-Mart also notoriously fails to provide health insurance to over half of its employees, who are then left to rely on themselves or taxpayers, who provide for a portion of their health-care needs through government Medicaid. Less well known is the fact that Wal-Mart maintains its low price level by allowing substandard labor conditions at the overseas factories producing most of its goods. The company continually demands lower prices from its suppliers, who, in turn, make more outrageous demands on their workers in order to meet Wal-Mart's requirements.

Box 14.5 Chevron

"The petrochemical company Chevron is guilty of some of the worst environmental and human rights abuses in the world. From 1964 to 1992, Texaco (which transferred operations to Chevron after being bought out in 2001) unleashed a toxic 'Rainforest Chernobyl' in Ecuador by leaving over 600 unlined oil pits in pristine northern Amazon rainforest and dumping 18 billion gallons of toxic production water into rivers used for bathing water. Local communities have suffered severe health effects, including cancer, skin lesions, birth defects, and spontaneous abortions" (Alternet 2015). Chevron is also responsible for the violence against peaceful opposition to oil extraction; the company has vested interests including in Nigeria, where Chevron hired a private military firm who opened fire on protesters that opposed oil extraction in the Niger Delta. Additionally, Chevron is responsible for widespread health problems in Richmond, California, where one of Chevron's largest refineries is located that produces oil flares and toxic waste. As a result, locals suffer from high rates of disease related to the corporate activities including lupus, skin rashes, rheumatic fever, liver problems, kidney problems, tumors, cancer, asthma, and eye problems. "The Unocal Corporation, which recently became a subsidiary of Chevron, is an oil and gas company based in California with operations around the world. In December 2004, the company settled a lawsuit filed by 15 Burmese villagers, in which the villagers alleged Unocal's complicity in a range of human rights violations in Burma, including rape, summary execution, torture, forced labor and forced migration" (Alternet 2015 see also International Labor Forum 2014.)

Box 14.6 Coca-Cola

Coca-Cola Company also leads in the rankings of those corporations that have a history of abuse of workers' rights, assassinations, water privatization, and discrimination. "Between 1989 and 2002, eight union leaders from Coca-Cola bottling plants in Colombia were killed after protesting the company's labor practices"; hundreds of local workers that either joined or considered joining the "Colombian union SINALTRAINAL have been kidnapped, tortured, and detained by paramilitaries who are hired to intimidate workers to prevent them from unionizing" (Global Exchange 2015). In India, Coca-Cola has been accused of destroying local agriculture through privatizing the country's water resources, reselling the water under the names of Dasani and BonAqua. Because of this the groundwater was depleted, affecting thousands of communities. The remaining water was contaminated with high chloride and bacteria levels (Red Thread 2011).

Box 14.7 Nestlé USA

Illegal and forced child labor is well known when it comes to the chocolate industry. Save the Children Canada, a non-governmental organization, stated that roughly 15,000 children between the ages of nine and twelve, had "been tricked or sold into slavery on West African cocoa farms, many for just $30 each" (Alternet 2015). Nestlé, is the third largest buyer of cocoa from Côte d'Ivoire and is aware of the ongoing slavery and forced labor. In 2005, Italian police seized more than "two million liters of Nestle infant formula that was contaminated with the chemical isopropylthioxanthone (ITX)" (Alternet 2015).

- Beer: **Miller:** Part of #2 worst company on the planet, MM's "worst corporation" list for the last five years, currently target of two major boycotts, spent over $100 million on lobbyists *PBR, Milwaukee's Best, Foster's, Guinness, Red Stripe.*
- Body care: **Lubriderm (Pfizer):** #17 in "Top 100 Corporate Criminals," worst environmental record in the industry, continues animal testing *Chapstick, Coppertone, Bananaboat, Jergens, Mitchum.*
- Butter/margarine: **Parkay:** "climate change laggard," MM's "worst corporation list" for two years, #50 in "Top 100 corporate criminals" list *Blue Bonnet, Fleischmann's, Country Crock, Promise, Imperial, I Can't Believe It's Not Butter, Land O' Lakes.*
- Candy: **M&Ms/Mars:** MM's "10 worst corporations" list, suppliers use child slave labor, target of the fair trade campaign *Wonka, Nestle, After*

Eight, Kraft, Trolli, Twix, Starburst, Skittles, Snickers, Milky Way, Three Musketeers, Life Savers.

- Canned beans and chili: **Hormel:** supports inhumane factory farming, refuses disclosure to consumers *Libby's, Ortega, Taco Bell, Rosarita's, Van Camp's, Stagg, Dinty Moore.*
- Canned fruit and vegetables: **Libby's:** Greenwash Award for public deception, named global climate change laggard, undermines overseas health standards *DelMonte, Contadina.*
- Cars: **General Motors:** named #1 polluter in auto industry, leader in fighting clean air legislation, EPA designated plant as a superfund site, paid $50 million to Washington lobbyists *Buick, Cadillac, Saturn, Chevrolet, Saab, Hummer, Pontiac, Mitsubishi, Mercedes, Chrysler, Infinit, Nissan, Jeep, Dodge, Ford, Isuzu, Jaguar, Volvo, Land Rover, Lincoln, Mercury.*
- Cereal: **Post:** Part of #2 worst company on the planet, MM's "worst corporation" list for part five years, currently target of two major boycotts, named global climate change laggard *Kraft, Nabisco, Weight Watchers.*
- Chips: **Nabisco:** Greenwash Award for public deception, refuses to disclose data on diversity, spent over $100 million on diversity, continues to do business in Burma, named global climate change laggard.
- Chocolate: **Nestle:** "most irresponsible" corporation award, aggressive takeovers of family farms, involved in child slavery lawsuit, baby formula human rights boycott *Toblerone, Swiss Miss, Dove.*
- Cleaning products: **Clorox:** MM's "10 worst corporations" list, continues animal testing, refuses disclosure to consumers, major producer of chlorine-dioxin (super chemical, look it up, it's bad news) *PineSol, Tilex, Glad, Liguid Plumr, Chore Boy, Wizard, Sara Lee, Arm & Hammer, WD40, Hefty.*
- Clothing: **Dillard:** No code of conduct for sweatshops, refuses disclosure on business, named "Sweatshop laggard" by CEP *Wal-Mart, TK Maxx, Kohl's, Marshall's, Polo, Ralph Lauren, Calvin Klein, LA Gear, Guess, Kmart, Fruit of the Loom, Land's End.*
- Cosmetics: **Maybelline:** continues animal testing, ingredients include known carcinogens, target of two major boycotts *Revlon, Almay, L'Oreal, Sally Hanson, Nivea, Cutex, La Cross.*
- Dairy Products: **Kraft:** [MM's] "worst corporation list" for the last five years, currently the target of two major boycotts, Greenwash award for public deception, named global climate change laggard *jell-O, Nestle, Hunt's, Reddi-Whip.*
- Eggs: **Egg Beaters (ConAgra):** involved in major accounting scandal, 2nd largest E. Coli meat recall in history, many worker safety and health violations *Lucerne, Eggland's Best.*
- Electronics: **GE:** Major weapons producer (including land mines), creator of five superfund sites, target of environmental boycott *Mitsubishi, Daewoo, Energizer, Samsung, Goldstar/LG, Microsoft.*

- Energy bars: **Balance:** part of #2 worst company on earth, named global climate change laggard, undermines overseas health standards, #1 contributor to Washington lobbyists *Powerbar, Slimfast, Kudos.*
- Energy drinks: **Full Throttle (Coke):** MM's "10 worst corporations" list for the last three years, hinders clean water access abroad, target of major human rights boycott *Country Time, Kool-Aid, Powerade.*
- Frozen dinners: **Stouffer's (Nestle):** Aggressive takeover of family farms, baby formula human rights boycott, "most irresponsible" corporation award, involved in union busting outside US *Boca, Hot Pockets, Healthy Choice, Marie Callendar's, Banquet, Boston Market, Uncle Ben's.*
- Gasoline: **Exxon-Mobil:** #1 worst corporation on planet, renowned human rights violator, #5 in "top 100 corporate criminals."
- Meat products: **Tyson foods:** MM's "worst corporation" list for last two years, CEP "F" for Overall Social Responsibility, guilty of 20+ violations of Clean Air Act *Oscar Mayer, Slim Jim, Butterball, Libby's, Banquet, Hormel, Jenny-O's, Farmer John, SPAM.*
- Pasta and sauce: **Kraft:** [MM's] "worst corporation list" for the last five years, currently the target of two major boycotts, Greenwash award for public deception, named global climate change laggard, part of #2 worst company on earth *Buitoni, Chef Boyardee, Hunt's, Contadina, Classico, Ragu, Bertolli, Knorr, Lawry's.*
- Retail stores: **Wal-Mart:** #3 worst company on the planet, CEP "F" for Overall Social Responsibility, sex-discrimination class-action lawsuit, documented exploitation of child labor *Rite-Aid, Kmart, Maytag, Costco, Sears, JC Penney, Wal-greens, Best Buy.*
- Soda products: **Coca-Cola:** MM's "worst corporations" list for three years, hinders clean water access abroad, target of major human rights boycott *Barq's, Fanta, Sprite, Minute Maid.*

(Taken from Red Thread 2011; the asterisk denotes brands that made the top 100 list with similar products.)

These are but a few examples of how, in our everyday lives as citizens and consumers, we support crimes of the powerful: from states to corporations, to the organized crime syndicate, to the elite of regions that have a hold over some of the richest mineral deposits in the world.

Summary

Few humans in the developed world are not a part of the crimes of the powerful, if only because they consume products that are likely somehow linked to human suffering or exploitation. To be connected in a modern society is often to be connected with corporations which exist only to make a profit, not to satisfy real human needs. Resisting complicity in crimes of the powerful on a daily basis is probably impossible for most people, as completely tuning out of society would be required. Crimes of the powerful go along with the general activities of the powerful, and, as such, being aware of the worst offenders is one practical way to try and minimize complicity. In addressing state crimes, this means being a more active and knowledgeable citizen and developing a genuine curiosity about state activities. For corporate crimes, learning about the worst offenders and boycotting their products is a reasonably feasible form of resisting complicity. After all, there are limitations to exposing and stopping crimes of the powerful, primarily owing to their complexity, as the system that undergirds these harms and crimes masks, facilitates, and reproduces the conditions for them. Of course, as with any conclusion or end, students generally want to know where we go from here. The following brief section offers some thoughts on this.

So, where do we go from here?

> We never see beyond the choices we don't make.
>
> (The Oracle in the film *The Matrix*, 1999)

There are no fast answers or one right way to address these massive harms and crimes. As we previously noted, if these harms and crimes could be tackled, we would need to first look at and reformulate the system that facilitates them as well as how to approach the issue of power within this globalplex of inequalities and priorities that embrace profit, consumption, commodification, property, and power above humanity as a whole. As the opening quote states, this can be a challenge or criticized as utopic, given that we have a tendency to not be able to see beyond the choices we do not make.

Perhaps some alternative lifestyle options can guide us toward a more humanistic and environmentally friendly system of relations and living. Consider that back in 1888 Edward Bellamy wrote the novel *Looking Backward*, which has since been translated into more than 20 languages, advancing a vision of the future that featured many products of today, including radio, television, motion pictures, credit cards, and indoor malls. It is based around the story of a time traveler who is put into a deep sleep in the 1800s to awaken in 2000, where he finds a utopic society where war, violence, crime, abuse of power, and inequalities no longer exist. Novels and films have long tried to provide an alternative vision of our societies, though generally being met with cynicism or labeled, as was Bellamy's novel, as "utopic fantasy."

On the other hand, there are real life experiments that try to address the overarching inequalities, damage, and harm to the environment with alternative livable communities. As noted by the well-known architect, Paolo Soleri (2015: 1),

> We put solar panels on a single family home but can't change the impact of inefficient construction ... We buy hybrid cars but drive in the gridlocks

of daily commutes. We buy "green washed" products but continue the same hyper consumption ... These improvements produce a "better kind of wrongness."

In an effort to address these issues (for example, pollution, energy and natural resource depletion, food scarcity, and quality of life), Soleri began an urban laboratory in 1970, a community that provides an alternative based on arcology—architecture and ecology as one integral process. The community is envisioned to hold 5,000 individuals as it continues to grow and, to date, has been successful. Soleri continues to teach architects and environmentalists from across the globe on how alternative societies could better function and provide a better lifestyle and level of happiness.

Yet, even with these alternatives, without a reworking of our collective consciousness where humanism takes center stage above profit, power, individual interests, and states' policies—first disabusing the mentality that these are all necessary—we remain skeptical on the overall impact of crimes of the powerful. In other words, if we return to Hegel's "Lordship and Bondage" master–slave dialectic piece or Karl Marx's notion of alienation and false consciousness to change this oppressive system that favors the powerful over all others, we and they must see ourselves as both subject and object and then this dialectic of master–slave, oppressed–oppressor, you and me, them and us can cease. Being a part of the solution to crimes of the powerful is not about law and criminal justice, as we have pointed out several times in this book. It is about people of good faith respecting one another and putting human needs before profit, ego, and self. Capitalism is not consistent with any of these.

To conclude, we draw from a wonderful classic novel by Leo Tolstoy, *Strider: The Story of a Horse*:

> I was quite in the dark as to what they meant by the words "his colt" ...
> I could not understand what they meant by speaking of *me* as being a
> man's property. The words "*my horse*" applied to me, a live horse, seemed
> to me as strange as to say "my land," "my air," or "my water"... those
> words had an enormous effect on me ... at last I understand the meaning
> they attach to these strange words, which indicate that men are guided in
> life not by deeds but by words ... Such words, considered very import-
> ant among them, are *my* and *mine*, which they apply to various things,
> creatures, or objects: even to land, people, and horses. They have agreed
> that of any given thing only one person may use that conventional word
> about the greatest number of things is considered the happiest. Why this
> is so I do not know, but it is so ... the whole relationship of the owners
> to the owned is that they do them harm ... And men strive in life not to
> do what they think right, but to call as many things as possible *their own*.
> (Tolstoy 1885: 59–61)

Activities and discussion questions

1. Look at the list of corporate offenders presented earlier in this chapter. From which ones do you buy products? Would you consider boycotting the corporations after hearing about their crimes?
2. To what extent do you worry about your privacy when using your smart phone? Do you think the state has too much knowledge of your personal information?
3. Research the legal issues surrounding Wal-Mart's treatment of its workers. Do you think that if more people knew of its record people would force the company to change by not giving it their business?

Resources

Child labor: www.ibtimes.com/samsung-child-labor-ask-apple-wal-mart-corporate-hu man-rights-violations-are-nothing-new-1625870.
Film: *The Vision of Paolo Soleri: Prophet in the Desert* (2012): https://arcosanti.org/.
Interactive map showing illegal dumping and e-waste dumping: www.pbs.org/front-lineworld/stories/ghana804/map/map.html.
Slave labor and corporations: www.businesspundit.com/5-giant-companies-who-use-s lave-labor/?img=42010.
Television: *South Park* episode 809 "South Wal-Mart This Way Comes": http://south-park.cc.com/clips/154597/find-the-heart.
http://southpark.wikia.com/wiki/Something_Wall-Mart_This_Way_Comes.

References

Alternet (2015). The 14 Worst Corporate Evildoers: On Issues Like War Crimes, Torture, Toxic Dumping and Stifling Freedom of Speech, Corporations like Coca Cola, Chevron and Philip Morris Are Way Out Ahead of the Rest. Available at: www.alternet.org/story/29337/the_14_worst_corporate_evildoers (accessed on September 10, 2015).
Bellamy, E. (1888). *Looking Backward.* Reprinted 2008. Biblio Bazaar.
Boghosian, H. (2013). *Spying on Democracy: Government Surveillance, Corporate Power and Public Resistance.* San Francisco, CA: City Lights Books.
Bush, G.W. (2001a). President Bush's Address in Atlanta, GA, on Homeland Security and the Ongoing War on Terrorism. November 8. Transcript available at: www.washingtonpost.com/wp-srv/nation/specials/attacked/transcripts/bushtext_110801.html (accessed on December 14, 2015).
Bush, G. W. (2001b). Remarks to Airline Employees, O'Hare International Airport, Chicago, IL. The White House Office of the Press Secretary, September 27. Available at: http://georgewbush-whitehouse.archives.gov/news/releases/2001/09/20010927-1.html (accessed on December 14, 2015).
Debord, G. (1988). Not Bored: The Society of the Spectacle. Available at: www.not-bored.org/commentaires.html (accessed on September 4, 2015).
Global Exchange (2015). Top Ten Corporate Criminals Alumni. Available at: www.globalexchange.org/corporateHRviolators/alums (accessed on December 14, 2015).

Goold, B., Loader, I., and Thumala, A. (2013). The Banality of Security: The Curious Case of Surveillance Cameras. *British Journal of Criminology*, 53(6): 977–996.

Greenfield, S. (2013). *2121: A Tale from the Next Century*. London: Head of Zeus.

International Labor Rights Forum (2014). 14 Worst Corporate Evildoers. December 12. Available at: www.laborrights.org/in-the-news/14-worst-corporate-evildoers (accessed on September 10, 2015).

Neocleous, M. (2007). Security, Commodity, Fetishism. *Critique*, 35(3): 339–355.

Neocleous, M. (2012). "Don't Be Scared, Be Prepared": Trauma-Anxiety-Resilience. *Alternatives: Global, Local, Political*, 37 (August): 188–198. First published online on June 13: doi:10.1177/0304375412449789.

Red Thread (2011). The Best and Worst Corporations. Available at: http://aleta-lane.wordpress.com/2011/05/15/the-best-and-worst-corporations/ (accessed on September 4, 2015).

Soleri, P. (2015). Introduction to Arcology. Available at: http://arcosanti.org/arcology/ (accessed on September 4, 2015).

Tolstoy, L. (1885). *Strider: The Story of a Horse*. Reprinted by Borderland Books. New York University Press.

Vidal, J. (2013). Toxic "E-Waste" Dumped in Poor Nations, Says United Nations. *The Guardian*, December 14. Available at: www.theguardian.com/global-development/2013/dec/14/toxic-ewaste-illegal-dumping-developing-countries (accessed on September 4, 2015).

Index

 # Taylor & Francis eBooks

---

Helping you to choose the right eBooks for your Library

Add Routledge titles to your library's digital collection today. Taylor and Francis ebooks contains over 50,000 titles in the Humanities, Social Sciences, Behavioural Sciences, Built Environment and Law.

Choose from a range of subject packages or create your own!

Benefits for you

>> Free MARC records
>> COUNTER-compliant usage statistics
>> Flexible purchase and pricing options
>> All titles DRM-free.

 Free Trials Available
We offer free trials to qualifying academic, corporate and government customers.

Benefits for your user

>> Off-site, anytime access via Athens or referring URL
>> Print or copy pages or chapters
>> Full content search
>> Bookmark, highlight and annotate text
>> Access to thousands of pages of quality research at the click of a button.

eCollections – Choose from over 30 subject eCollections, including:

Archaeology	Language Learning
Architecture	Law
Asian Studies	Literature
Business & Management	Media & Communication
Classical Studies	Middle East Studies
Construction	Music
Creative & Media Arts	Philosophy
Criminology & Criminal Justice	Planning
Economics	Politics
Education	Psychology & Mental Health
Energy	Religion
Engineering	Security
English Language & Linguistics	Social Work
Environment & Sustainability	Sociology
Geography	Sport
Health Studies	Theatre & Performance
History	Tourism, Hospitality & Events

For more information, pricing enquiries or to order a free trial, please contact your local sales team:
www.tandfebooks.com/page/sales

 Routledge
Taylor & Francis Group

The home of
Routledge books

www.tandfebooks.com